HATE CRIMES

HATE CRIMES

VOLUME 4
Hate Crime Offenders

Barbara Perry, General Editor
Randy Blazak, Volume Editor

PRAEGER PERSPECTIVES

Westport, Connecticut
London

Library of Congress Cataloging-in-Publication Data

Hate crimes / Barbara Perry, general editor.
     p. cm.
   Includes bibliographical references and index.
   ISBN 978–0–275–99569–0 (set : alk. paper) — 978–0–275–99571–3
(vol. 1 : alk. paper) — 978–0–275–99573–7 (vol. 2 : alk. paper) — 978–0–275–99575–1
(vol. 3 : alk. paper) — 978–0–275–99577–5 (vol. 4 : alk. paper) — 978–0–275–99579–9
(vol. 5 : alk. paper)
  1. Offenses against the person.   2. Hate crimes.   3. Violent crimes.   4. Genocide.
I. Perry, Barbara, 1962–
  K5170.H38   2009
   364.15—dc22   2008052727

British Library Cataloguing in Publication Data is available.

Library of Congress Catalog Card Number: 2008052727
ISBN: 978–0–275–99569–0 (set)
      978–0–275–99571–3 (vol. 1)
      978–0–275–99573–7 (vol. 2)
      978–0–275–99575–1 (vol. 3)
      978–0–275–99577–5 (vol. 4)
      978–0–275–99579–9 (vol. 5)

First published in 2009

Praeger Publishers, 88 Post Road West, Westport, CT 06881
An imprint of Greenwood Publishing Group, Inc.
www.praeger.com

Printed in the United States of America

The paper used in this book complies with the
Permanent Paper Standard issued by the National
Information Standards Organization (Z39.48–1984).

10 9 8 7 6 5 4 3 2 1

CONTENTS

Set Introduction by Barbara Perry   vii

Introduction by Randy Blazak   xiii

CHAPTER 1   An Overview of the Domestic Far
Right and Its Criminal Activities   1
*Jeffrey Gruenewald, Joshua D. Freilich,
and Steven M. Chermak*

CHAPTER 2   When Odin Beats Jesus: Using Racist
Religion to "Do Gender" in Prison   23
Randy Blazak

CHAPTER 3   The Space of Racial Hate   41
Kathleen M. Blee

CHAPTER 4   Hate Rock: White Supremacy in
Popular Music Forms   51
Colin K. Gilmore

CHAPTER 5   Gender, Privilege, and the Politics of Hate   69
Abby L. Ferber

CHAPTER 6   Female-Perpetrated Hate:
A Content Analysis of Hate Incidents   85
Tammy L. Castle

CHAPTER 7   Behavior or Motivation:
Typologies of Hate-Motivated Offenders   103
Christopher Fisher and C. Gabrielle Salfati

CHAPTER 8   The Banality of Anti-Jewish "Hate Crime"   137
             Paul Iganski

CHAPTER 9   The Most Hated Man in Sweden   151
             Michael Kimmel

CHAPTER 10   Skinhead Street Violence   157
             Pete Simi

CHAPTER 11   Anti-Muslim Violence in the Post-9/11
             Era: Motive Forces   171
             Barbara Perry

CHAPTER 12   Interview with a Hate Offender   189
             Randy Blazak

About the Editor and Contributors   207
Index   211

SET INTRODUCTION

Barbara Perry
General Editor

The twentieth century appeared to close much as it had opened—with sprees of violence directed against the Other. The murder of Matthew Shepard, the lynching of James Byrd, the murderous rampage of Benjamin Smith, and post-9/11 anti-Muslim violence all stand as reminders that the bigotry that kills is much more than an unfortunate chapter in U.S. history. Racial, gender, ethnic, and religious violence persist. It is a sad commentary on the cultural and social life of the United States that a series such as this remains timely as we enter the twenty-first century. The dramatic cases cited earlier are but extreme illustrations of widespread, daily acts of aggression directed toward an array of minority communities. I use the term *communities* purposefully here since these acts are less about any one victim than about the cultural group they represent. Hate crime is, in fact, an assault against all members of stigmatized and marginalized communities.

Clearly this is not a new phenomenon, even in the United States. It is important to keep in mind that what we currently refer to as hate crime has a long historical lineage. The contemporary dynamics of hate-motivated violence have their origins in historical conditions. With respect to hate crime, at least, history does repeat itself, as similar patterns of motivation, sentiment, and victimization recur over time. Just as immigrants in the 1890s were subject to institutional and public forms of discrimination and violence, so, too, were those of the 1990s; likewise, former black slaves risked the wrath of the Ku Klux Klan (KKK) when they exercised their newfound rights in the antebellum period, just as their descendants risked violent reprisal for their efforts to win and exercise additional rights and freedoms in the civil rights era; and women who demanded the right to vote on the eve of the twentieth century suffered the same ridicule and harassment as those who demanded equal rights in the workplace later in the century. While the politics of difference that underlie these periods of animosity may lie latent for short periods of time, they nonetheless seem to remain on the simmer, ready to resurface whenever a new threat is perceived—when immigration levels increase; or when relationships between groups shift for other political, economic, or cultural reasons; or in the aftermath of attacks like those on 9/11. Consequently, hate crime remains a crucial indicator of cultural fissures in the United States and around the globe. This set, then, remains similarly relevant in the current era.

Hate Crimes offers interested readers a comprehensive collection of original chapters surveying this phenomenon we have come to know as hate crime. Interestingly, the field of hate crime studies is interdisciplinary, so the contributors here represent a variety of disciplines, including law, sociology, criminology, psychology, and even public health. Moreover, since it is also a global phenomenon, we have invited not just American scholars, but international contributors as well. This comparative/cross-cultural approach adds an important element to the set. It reminds readers that hate crime is a universal problem and that approaches taken elsewhere might be of use to North Americans.

The volumes included in this set have been divided into five distinct focal areas. Volume 1, *Understanding and Defining Hate Crime*, is edited by Brian Levin of California State University, San Bernardino. He has collected a series of chapters that lay a strong foundation for the volumes that follow. The pieces here provide an introduction to what it is we mean by the term *hate crime*. There is ongoing debate about such things as whether the term is even appropriate, what behaviors ought to be included in our understanding of hate crime, and what classes of victims should be included. The relevant chapters, then, offer diverse definitions, ranging from legal to sociological approaches.

One consequence of the varied and divergent definitions used to conceptualize bias-motivated crime is that the confusion also complicates the process of gathering data on hate crime. Berk, Boyd, and Hamner (1992) astutely observe that "much of the available data on hate motivated crime rests on unclear definitions; it is difficult to know what is being counted as hate motivated and what is not" (p. 125). As a result, while both academic and media reports make the claim that ethnoviolence represents a "rising tide," the truth is that we don't know whether in fact this is the case or not (Jacobs & Potter, 1998). Thus Levin also includes a number of chapters that attempt to address the issue of data collection and measurement of hate crime.

The limitations of definition and measurement highlighted previously help to explain the limited attempts thus far to theorize hate crime. In the absence of empirical information about bias-motivated violence, it is difficult to construct conceptual frameworks. Without the raw materials, there is no foundation for theorizing. Additionally, the relatively recent recognition of hate crime as a social problem (Jenness & Broad, 1998) also contributes to the lack of theoretical accounts. This volume, however, includes chapters that begin to offer compelling models to help us make sense of hate crime.

The second volume, *The Consequences of Hate Crime*, is a particularly valuable contribution to the literature on hate crime. Editor Paul Iganski of Lancaster University in the United Kingdom has brought together a unique collection of chapters that explore both the individual and the social impacts associated with this form of violence. Running through much of the literature—even through court decisions on hate crime—is the assumption that such offences are qualitatively different in their effects, as compared to their non-bias-motivated counterparts. Specifically, Iganski (2001) contends that there are five distinct types of consequences associated with hate crime: harm to the initial victim; harm to the victim's group; harm to the victim's group (outside the neighborhood); harm to other targeted communities; and harm to societal norms and values. The first of these has been the subject of considerable scholarly attention. Research suggests that first and foremost among the impacts on the individual is the physical harm: bias-motivated crimes are often characterized by extreme brutality (Levin & McDevitt, 1993). Violent personal crimes motivated by bias are more likely to involve extraordinary levels of violence. Additionally, the empirical findings of studies of the emotional, psychological, and behavioral impacts of hate crime are beginning to establish a solid pattern of more severe impact on bias crime victims, as compared to nonbias victims (see, e.g., Herek, Cogan, & Gillis, 2002; McDevitt et al., 2001). Several chapters in this volume explore these individual effects.

Additionally, however, this volume includes a number of chapters that begin to offer insights into other often overlooked consequences of hate crime: community effects. Many scholars point to the "fact" that hate crimes are "message crimes" that emit a distinct warning to all members of the victim's community: step out of line, cross invisible boundaries, and you, too, could be lying on the ground, beaten and bloodied (Iganski, 2001). Consequently, the individual fear noted previously is thought to be accompanied by the collective fear of the victim's cultural group, possibly even of other minority groups likely to be victims. Weinstein (as cited by Iganski, 2001) refers to this as an *in terrorem* effect: intimidation of the group by the victimization of one or a few members of that group. It is these effects that contributors such as Monique Noelle and Helen Ahn Lim address.

Barbara Perry, editor of volume 3, *The Victims of Hate Crime*, introduces this volume with the caveat that little empirical work has been done on the distinct experiences of different groups of hate crime victims. Much of the literature has more or less assumed a homogeneous group known as "victims." However, this occludes the fact that the frequency, dynamics, motives, and impacts of bias-motivated violence differ across target communities. Thus the volume draws on emerging theoretical and empirical work that explores manifestations of hate crime within diverse communities. Especially novel here is the inclusion of pieces that address hate-motivated crime directed toward women and the homeless community. Consideration of these groups, in particular, forces us to expand our traditional characterization of hate crime victims, which is often restricted to race, religion, ethnicity, or sexual orientation.

Volume 4, *Hate Crime Offenders*, brings us to a consideration of the second half of the equation: perpetrators of hate crime. Randy Blazak from Portland State University has gathered an intriguing collection of chapters. The authors here have been set the task of responding to Blazak's opening question, Who are the hate mongers? Many would respond to this question by reference to members of the KKK or a skinhead group, for example. This is a very common myth. In fact, fewer than 5 percent of identifiable offenders are members of organized hate groups. Recognizing this, Blazak has asked his contributors to explore both individual perpetrators and those involved in hate groups. Thus this is an engaging and diverse collection of chapters, which explore issues ranging from women's involvement in hate crime, to typologies of hate crime offenders, to white power music. He even includes an interview with a hate offender.

Frederick Lawrence, editor of volume 5, *Responding to Hate Crime*, has solicited work from his contributors that gives us food for thought with respect to how we might respond to hate crime. Clearly there are diverse approaches available: legislation, social policy, community organizing, or education, to name just a few. In the extant scholarship, there have been relatively few concentrated analyses of such efforts to respond to or prevent bias-motivated crimes. In large part, such recommendations come by way of a conclusion and are thus not fully developed. Hence the chapters in Lawrence's volume explicitly present interventions intended to ameliorate the incidence or impact of hate crime. While the emphasis is on criminal justice responses (legislation, policing, prosecution), Lawrence also includes chapters that explore preventative measures, restorative justice initiatives, and the role of organizations like the Southern Poverty Law Center.

I speak for all of the editors when I say that we are very pleased to have been asked to develop this collection of hate crime literature. It was a unique opportunity to share emerging perspectives and analyses with a diverse audience. It is hoped that what we offer here will provide the insights that readers are seeking, but also inspiration for further explorations and interventions into this disturbing class of violence.

REFERENCES

Berk, R., Boyd, E., & Hamner, K. (1992). Thinking more clearly about hate-motivated crimes. In G. Herek & K. Berrill (Eds.), *Hate crimes: Confronting violence against lesbians and gay men* (pp. 123–143). Newbury Park, CA: Sage.

Herek, G., Cogan, J., & Gillis, R. (2002). Victim experiences in hate crimes based on sexual orientation. *Journal of Social Issues, 58,* 319–339.

Iganski, P. (2001). Hate crimes hurt more. *American Behavioral Scientist, 45,* 626–638.

Jacobs, J., & Potter, K. (1998). *Hate crimes: Criminal law and identity politics.* New York: Oxford University Press.

Jenness, V., & Broad, K. (1998). *Hate crimes: New social movements and the politics of violence.* New York: Aldine de Gruyter.

Levin, J., & McDevitt, J. (1993). *Hate crimes: The rising tide of bigotry and bloodshed.* New York: Plenum.

McDevitt, J., Balboni, J., Garcia, L., and Gu, J.,. (2001). Consequences for victims: A comparison of bias- and non-bias motivated assaults. *American Behavioral Scientist, 45,* 697–713.

Introduction

Randy Blazak

On August 5, 2007, a Sikh man named Ranjit Singh was at a truck-stop con-venience store in Oakland, Oregon, when he was attacked by three men who ripped his turban from his head. The three men were arrested, but in March 2008 a grand jury declined to charge the men with a hate crime. Amard-eep Singh, executive director of the Sikh Coalition, said afterward, "Burn-ing a cross on an African American's lawn is not a mere act of vandalism, and stealing a Sikh's turban is not a misdemeanor theft"(The Sikh Coalition, 2008). Why did the grand jury not view this as a hate crime? Was it because the men were not skinheads?

Who are the hate mongers in our society? We are routinely reminded of the statistic from Jack Levin and Jack McDevitt's 1993 text on hate crimes that members of hate groups account for only 5 percent of recorded hate crime offenders. Who are the other 95 percent? Are they unidentified mem-bers of hate groups? Are they "normal" individuals acting on mainstream bigotries? Or are they individuals who have been influenced by the violent rhetoric of hate groups?

These questions raise another for researchers: do we spend too much time focusing on members of organized hate, when the vast majority of individu-als responsible for the day-to-day terror of hate crimes have nothing to do with groups like the Ku Klux Klan and the National Socialist Movement? Perhaps membership in hate groups reduces hate crimes by giving bigots a forum to express their hatred instead of on the streets, allowing any violence to manifest within the group instead of against the objects of the hate.

This volume works on many levels to provoke as many questions as it might answer. It contributes research on hate group members who have committed grievous crimes as well as those who just sing about doing so. It also takes a close look at the reality of bias-motivated crimes and how they may or may not fit the expected profile. The body of work presented serves to provide a better understanding of those who have committed the crimes or may dream of committing such acts. This volume also serves as a challenge to social scientists to explore some of the less traveled paths of hate crime research and employ more rigorous methodologies. Ranging from case studies to meta-analysis, the scholarship in the book represents the work of some of the leading scholars in the field as well as some younger researchers, all of whom add significantly to the body of knowledge about extremist criminality.

From my early ethnographic studies on skinheads through my current research on hate criminals transitioning out of prisons, the salience of gender has always been a theme in my work. I'm proud that this theme is well represented in this book. From scholars long associated with exploring gender, like Kathy Blee, Abby Ferber, and Michael Kimmel, to Tammy Castle's pioneering work on female hate offenders, the gendered nature of hate is kept on the front burner.

This volume also lets hate criminals and members of organized hate groups speak for themselves. Researchers had unprecedented access to hate murderers, cemetery desecraters, violent street skinheads, members of the notorious racist gang known as The Order, and the stars of the hate rock scene.

Hate is also located not only in the extremist enclave but in the mainstream. Paul Iganski's chapter on anti-Semitic violence and Barbara Perry's chapter on anti-Muslim violence, as well as other contributions, demonstrate that hate is not solely the domain of the hate monger, but of the typical citizen who has been subject to misinformation, stereotypes, and the permission to hate. The violent skinhead may be the most visible representation of bigotry in our society, but the reality is much closer to home.

A BRIEF DESCRIPTION OF THE CHAPTERS

We begin this volume with a "state of the literature" report from Jeffrey Gruenewald, Joshua D. Freilich, and Steven M. Chermak. Their meta-analysis of research on hate crimes and right-wing terrorism should serve as a call to social scientists to employ more rigorous research methods to the field. They find that nearly 40 percent of social science publications on the subject rely on either one external source of information or no external sources (taking the form of editorials or opinion pieces). Research typically relies on data from watchdog groups or interviews with small groups of subjects. The authors acknowledge the subject matter does not lend itself to quantitative research; however, there needs to be an effort to collect original data that reflect uniform definitions of this always fascinating topic.

In 1991, at a Lynyrd Skynyrd concert in Alabama, I was talking to a Klan recruiter who was trying to explain to me that Mary, mother of Jesus, was born in England. He reflected the challenges anti-Semitic racists face in bending Christianity to fit their beliefs. My research was inspired by the unexpected appearance of Norse mythology among skinheads in the Pacific Northwest in the 1990s. Long the center of Christian Identity beliefs, via the Aryan Nations compound in Idaho, the region's skinheads began to embrace Scandinavian paganism. Further research revealed that much of this ideological switch was supported by incarcerated white supremacists, known as Aryan Prisoners of War. The words of the inmates themselves support a feminist analysis of the appeal of a more violent religious preference.

Kathleen Blee is well respected for her research on women in the organized racist subculture. Here, drawing on her research and the research of others, she explores how hate groups "imagine" the use of physical space. While rooted in local spaces, hate groups, like Volksfront International, increasingly see themselves as global entities. Blee points out that the thread that now links these groups across space is the centrality of anti-Semitism. Most interesting is that the "hot" areas of hate tend to be those that are racially homogeneous. You may have heard a white person say, "Where we grew up, we couldn't be racist because there were only white people." *That's* where you go to find racists.

Ian Stuart, the singer of the pioneering racist skinhead band Skrewdriver, was sentenced to a year in prison in 1985 for assaulting an immigrant on the streets of London, England. Members of prominent North American hate rock bands such as Rahowa, the Midtown Bootboys, and the Bully Boys have also served time for assaults related to their racist beliefs. Colin K. Gilmore began his expansive study of the hate rock movement while a graduate student at Portland State University. He managed to land extensive interviews with former and current stars of the hate rock world by drawing on his own background as a punk rock musician. Gilmore also compiled a massive data set of hate rock lyrics by transcribing hundreds of songs (including many that were not in English). This chapter demonstrates how hate rock musicians see their music as a way of recruiting youth into their movement and how the lyrics themselves reinforce hate-motivated violence.

We often think of hate groups as harboring ideologies based in racial, ethnic, and religious bigotry, but they can be sexist as well. Abby Ferber's research has done much to uncode the gendered nature of hate group beliefs. As reflected in my own research, she found that much of the more obvious bigotry is more an expression of a sense of threatened masculinity. In this chapter, she takes the important step of extending that argument to a larger political context. Hate group ideologies are all connected to an unarticulated belief in straight, white male privilege and the corresponding belief that that privilege is in crisis. This is an important discussion that links extremists to our own mainstream biases.

Criminologists and sociologists, in attempting to explain the typical case, are often guilty of ignoring the atypical case. According to the National Incident Based Reporting system, 17 percent of hate offenders are female (the National Crime Victimization Survey reveals an even higher rate). While the majority of hate criminals are males (who may or may not be acting out their masculinity issues), this large number of female offenders should not be ignored. Tammy Castle begins this research endeavor by analyzing a sample of hate crimes committed by females with regard to the type of offense and motivation as compared to males. We hope this will inspire other researchers to study the much-overlooked female hate offender.

In the early 2000s, I was on a hate crime panel at a criminology conference with Jack McDevitt. McDevitt, along with Jack Levin, created a typology of hate criminals that has been widely used in criminology and delinquency textbooks. McDevitt mentioned in passing that the typology had never really been put to a methodological test. The chapter here by Chris Fisher and C. Gabrielle Salfati does just that. By analyzing 91 hate-motivated homicides between 1991 and 2002, the researchers find that the established typologies hold many problems, including a large amount of overlap of varying criminal motivations. This important research should lead to a new discussion about the role criminal typologies play in the analysis of offenders.

As I write this, several swastika banners attached to helium balloons have been found floating over my city of Portland, Oregon. Were they the act of an organized neo-Nazi group? Could it be the act of an angry Muslim youth making a statement? Perhaps it was a lone individual venting a personal bias against a Jew who caused some offense? In this case, a Nazi group claimed credit for the act, but Paul Iganski's analysis of anti-Semitic attacks in London undermines the common assumption that such attacks are the work of extremists or disaffected Muslim youth. Iganski finds that an underlying "common sense" anti-Semitism held by more than just extremists can serve as a trigger for such hate crimes.

Michael Kimmel's research on issues of masculinity has been widely read in books like 2005's *The Gender of Desire: Essays on Male Sexuality*. He has also explored the issue of hate, including his work with Abby Ferber on the role of masculinity in patriot militias. Here, his research takes him to Scandinavia and a case study of a unique hate monger. Kimmel traveled to the most secure prison in Sweden to interview a man known as that country's Charles Manson. What his interview revealed was not only the complexity of racism, but also the need for programs to help hate criminals leave their hatred behind.

I first met Pete Simi when he was a graduate student. His research was similar to mine—an ethnographic study of skinheads. The difference was that Simi was spending time with some of the most violent racist skinheads in the nation. His chapter provides a useful background of the skinhead subculture and does an excellent job of letting the skinheads describe in their own words the importance of violence in their world. The chapter should also allow the reader to make comparisons between skinheads and traditional street gangs.

The Uniform Crime Report reveals a fairly consistent pattern of hate crime motivations. Antiblack crimes are most common, followed by anti-Jewish and antigay attacks. However, after the 9/11 attacks, there was a significant increase in attacks against Arabs, Muslims, or anyone looking like they might be from that part of the world, including Sikhs. (In Portland, an Italian man was attacked by a gang of youths who shouted, "This is for 9/11!") Barbara Perry has been tracking this trend and included it in her 2003 book, *Hate and Bias Crime*. In this chapter, she links the phenomenon to the level of ignorance Western hate mongers have about the Arab world. This ignorance is fueled by media representations of Arabs and Muslims as a singular group driven by a desire to "destroy us." This rhetoric comes from the usual places, as well as from a president who uses terms like "evil" to describe whole nations.

I thought it would be interesting to end this volume with the words of an individual hate offender. In the 20 years I have been researching skinheads and hate group members, I have felt it counterproductive to dehumanize hate mongers. Not only are they human, but they may be more like us than we care to admit. I know bigotry is woven into my psyche even though I oppose bigotry. In this spirit I have forged relationships with many hate mongers even though I work against their cause. Sean is one of those cases. I make punk rock CDs for him and he lends me *Family Guy* DVDs. This relationship has helped me to understand the complexity of organized hate while providing hate mongers with an exit route should they decide my diverse world is more beneficial than their homogeneous one. It is my hope that the reader will find elements of the previous 11 chapters in this conversation.

REFERENCES

Kimmel, M. (2005). *The gender of desire: Essays on male sexuality.* Albany, NY: State University of New York Press.

Levin, J., & McDevitt, J. (1993). *Hate crimes: The rising tide of bigotry and bloodshed.* New York: Plenum Press.

Perry, B. (2003). Anti-Muslim retaliatory violence following the 9/11 terrorist attacks. In B. Perry (Ed.), *Hate and bias crime: A reader.* New York: Routledge, pp. 183–201.

The Sikh Coalition. (2008, March 20). Oregon grand jury fails to indict turban attackers with a hate crime. Retrieved July 18, 2008, from http://www.sikhcoalition.org/

CHAPTER 1

AN OVERVIEW OF THE DOMESTIC FAR RIGHT AND ITS CRIMINAL ACTIVITIES

Jeffrey Gruenewald, Joshua D. Freilich, and Steven M. Chermak

This chapter explores issues related to the study of terrorism, hate crime,[1] and far-right[2] criminal activities. We focus on these areas for three reasons. First, all are politicized topics, and scholars have contributed to the evolving political debates surrounding these issues. Second, research on these topics has grown dramatically and thus provides an opportunity to compare and contrast the production of scholarly knowledge. Third, and importantly, depending on the definitions used, it is possible that the same incident could be included for studies on all three topics. For example, a racist skinhead bombing of a Jewish synagogue could be defined as a hate crime, an act of terrorism, and far-right extremism. Thus, our exploration of the overlapping boundaries among these subject areas will engage the problems of conducting research on politicized social problems as well as suggest how such definitional dilemmas could be addressed by scholars.

Complete coverage of all the theoretical, definitional, and methodological issues highlighted in these literatures is beyond the scope of this work. We therefore concentrate on the most significant topics. In the first section of the chapter we discuss some of the obstacles scholars confront when studying these issues. Next, we provide preliminary results from our ongoing systematic review of the extant literature on far-right studies to illustrate the overlap in these subject areas. In the final section, we compare hate crimes to the types of crimes committed by supporters of the far-right crime. Our goal is to show how the study of these topics can move forward in addressing key issues and result in more consistent production of explanatory knowledge about these topics (Silke, 2001).

DEFINITIONAL AND CONCEPTUAL ISSUES

Currently all three topics engender considerable scholarly interest. But, during the last 25 years, there have been periods of intense and renewed scholarly interest in each of these topics because a policy window of opportunity such as a celebrated case or high-profile policy debate occurred (Kingdon, 1984). Scholars who write about moral panics highlight how such attention has broad cultural, political, and social impacts. Importantly, there appears to be a concomitant increase in scholarly attention as well. For instance, the September 11 attacks affected society in dramatic ways and led to a growing scholarly interest in terrorism-related research. Similarly, paramilitary survivalists and militias were generally ignored by scholars until such groups were introduced to the populace because of the Oklahoma City bombing and Timothy McVeigh's connections to various far-right extremist groups. Interestingly, academic interest has waned, as these groups are now rarely presented in the news. Finally, a rash of incidents involving skinheads initially (Hamm, 1998), and numerous other cases such as the Matthew Shepard and James Byrd murders, brought attention to the issue of hate crime and, we hypothesize, also affected scholarship in this area.

The academic literature on the production of scholarship illustrates the complexity of the attention to various issue areas. Heightened attention in one sector of society (e.g., government funding agencies) affects other sectors (e.g., academic interest in a topic). Raush and LaFree (2007, p. 1) recently discussed how the availability of funding to criminologists from the Department of Homeland Security, the National Institute of Justice, the National Science Foundation, and other agencies has increased scholarly interest in terrorism. The dynamic nature of the production of knowledge highlights a common thread in this and other topic areas: academic literature is often reactive, and many papers are produced on a topic simultaneously. Journals produce special issues related to a topic (or introduce a new journal in the subject area) because of the interest. Publishers attempt to capitalize on a "hot topic" to generate books that might be adopted for the new list of specialized academic courses in these areas. For example, the following journals are just a sample of those that have devoted or will devote a special issue on terrorism since 2001: *Analysis of Social Issues and Public Policy* (2002), *Behavioral Sciences and the Law* (2005), *Criminal Justice and Behavior* (2008), *Criminal Justice Policy Review* (2009), *European Journal of Criminology* (2008), *Harvard Journal of Law & Public Policy* (2002), *Journal of Contemporary Criminal Justice* (2007), *Journal of International Criminal Justice* (2006), and *Technological Forecasting & Social Change* (2007).

The intention of scholarship is that extant knowledge provides a foundation for future empirical work. Scholarly contributions on "new" social problems should progress from descriptive to explanatory accounts in an iterative manner (Silke, 2001). One problem is that measurement and definitional issues tend to be secondary and lag behind descriptive accounts of an issue (Freilich & Pridemore, 2005, 2006). Many important papers have explored such issues and provided conceptual frameworks to move scholarship forward. There is little agreement, however, about the appropriate parameters of study in each area (Gibbs, 1989; Hamm, 1994, 1998; Mudde, 1995; Perry, 2003; Schmid, 2004). Three hurdles have affected the iterative progress of scholarly knowledge about terrorism, hate crimes, and far-right extremism. The first is the impact of technology and the growth of publication outlets. Since the number of publication outlets continues to grow, it has been become more difficult for scholars to remain current in any area. Second, all three of these topics have been engaged by scholars from different disciplines, including sociology, criminology, psychology, political science, law, history, and anthropology. The differences in theory and methods across these disciplines have led to inconsistent approaches and understandings about the nature of these social problems. Finally, many nonacademic sectors of society also engage these topics, including politicians, law enforcement, news media, and advocacy agencies. Often these different institutional sectors adhere to contradictory definitions of these important social problems.

Consider, for example, the problems with defining terrorism. There is widespread disagreement about what elements should be included within a definition. Indeed, many believe that it may be impossible to resolve some of the conceptual discrepancies (Silke, 1996; see also Weinberg, Pedahzur, & Hirsch-Hoefler, 2004). Perry (2004, p. 459), for example, analyzed 22 different definitions and descriptions of terrorism in federal law, comparing the search for a definition to the quest for the Holy Grail by King Arthur's Round Table Knights. Scholars have complicated matters further, using a variety of contradictory definitions. One important early work, in fact, surveyed scholars about the frameworks they use to define terrorism and identified over 100 different definitions (Schmid & Jongman, 1988). Similarly, Weinberg and colleagues' (2004) examination of the specific definitions used in the leading terrorism journals documented 73 different definitions.

There are a few reasons why so many competing terrorism definitions are used in various domains. First, terrorism is a global phenomenon. One key challenge is finding common ground across countries because governments ultimately create a definition that is consistent with its needs. Such laws also usually reflect the local political and cultural context of an area. Second, although most countries define some pool of acts as terrorism, most justice agencies respond to "terrorist acts" using general crime and justice legislation. Most suspected terrorists in the United States are charged with a variety of federal or state statutes, such as racketeering, conspiracy, and homicide (LaFree & Dugan, 2004). Timothy McVeigh, for example, was charged with federal conspiracy and homicide crimes. Most far-right extremists are charged locally, however, under state crime legislation and are not investigated as terrorism cases per se (Freilich & Chermak, 2007; Simone, Freilich, & Chermak, 2008). Third, terrorism carries powerful connotative meaning. The news media, for example, form a critical platform through which the public comes to develop an understanding about terrorism. Many terrorists see great value in achieving media coverage of their ideology through coverage of their terrorist acts in the news, and it is also a strategically useful topic for policy makers (Nacos, 2003). The news media do present as important news stories crimes that governments have defined as terrorism. However, the media do so selectively and actually ignore most acts (Chermak & Gruenewald, 2006). In addition, the frequent reliance on political and advocacy watch-group sources for information provides opportunities for these sources to shape public discourse about who is a terrorist and what is terrorism. Fourth, what types of behaviors are defined as terrorism changes frequently across time and place, contributing to the problems of comparative analysis (Weinberg et al., 2004).

It is more than a coincidence that scholars who study hate crime and far-right extremism also struggle greatly with definitional issues. Hamm (1998, p. 68) concludes that there is no consensus among social scientists about the definition of hate crime. There is wide variation across states about what is hate, and the problems are even more complicated when the issues are examined globally. He argues that many crimes that might be called hate or bias-related crime in the United States would be defined as right-wing violence and extremism in other countries. Perry (2003, p. 7) argues that scholars attempting to define hate crime are confronted with many dilemmas. It is difficult to develop a universal definition of the term because many definitional problems are tied to historical and cultural contexts. Similarly, Mudde (1995) discusses a wide variety of definitions used to define far-right extremism. He finds that "most of the authors involved define right-wing extremism as an ideology composed of a combination of several different, and intrinsically complex features," (p. 203) and "to the extent that a consensus of opinion among the scientists concerned with this field, it is confined to the view that right-wing extremism is an ideology that people are free to fill in as they see fit" (p. 205).

The pursuit of scholarly understanding of these issues is thus inevitably intertwined with processes of social construction that contribute and shape how terrorism, hate crime, and far-right extremism are defined. Spector and Kituse (1977) wrote the seminal theoretical piece in this area, stating that the "central task of a theory of social problems and deviance is to describe and explain the definitional process in which morally objectionable conditions or behaviors are asserted to exist and the collective activities that become organized around those assertions. Such a theory would seek to explain how those definitions and assertions are made, the processes by which they are acted upon by institutions, and how those institutional responses do or do not produce socially legitimated categories of social problems and deviance" (p. 72). Other researchers have studied serial murder, threats to children, prostitution, drugs, satanic ritual abuse, militias, and hate crimes by using a constructionist framework. Constructionists are not necessarily concerned with the objective reality of a social condition, but in the processes resulting in the concern for that social problem (Best, 1990, p. 10).

The valuable contributions by social constructionist scholars highlight a dilemma when other scholars attempt to explore the etiology of a particular social problem. Certain behaviors are defined (or excluded) as being an act of terrorism, a hate crime, or a crime of far-right extremism from a process of social construction (LaFree & Dugan, 2004; Turk, 2004). It is difficult to remain unbiased because the issues are politically and emotionally charged. The interpretation of events is linked to cultural and political processes, and institutional actors with an interest in these terms will make "conscious efforts to manipulate perceptions to promote certain interests at the expense of others" (Turk, pp. 271–272). This difficulty of interpretation is a common dilemma faced by most scholars pursuing intellectual questions, but often the social construction literature about a social problem is viewed as independent from other literature. Thus, it is important for scholars to take a step back to reflect on the general body of literature that exists in these areas and systematically describe its theoretical and methodological traditions and limitations. In the next section we begin to accomplish this as it pertains to far-right extremism.

EXISTING LITERATURE ON FAR-RIGHT CRIMINAL BEHAVIOR

In this section we systematically assess the state of the far-right extremism literature. Our assessment is based upon preliminary findings from our ongoing systematic literature review on far-right extremism. Only a select number of characteristics of the reviewed studies are addressed in the findings presented below. We use our findings to speculate on how research and theoretical practices may affect definitional, conceptual, and other theoretical issues related to far-right extremism. First, we examine who has conducted research on the far right and where their research has appeared. We capture these aspects of the far-right literature by (a) describing authorship characteristics of far-right extremism studies and (b) identifying the outlets in which far-right studies have been published (e.g., scholarly, nonscholarly, disciplines of journals). Second, we examine how extremist groups and crimes have been addressed in the literature. Finally, we examine methodological approaches used in the far-right extremism literature by describing (a) sources of information used, (b) types of observational methods used, and (c) types of data analyses used in past far-right extremism studies.

Although the far-right extremism literature overlaps with the literatures of hate crimes and terrorism, there are number of reasons why we should devote special attention to the far right. One reason is that sociologists—for example, social movement scholars—have usually studied left-wing ideologies, groups, and sensational crimes (Wright, 2007). Moreover, while there is a growing hate crimes literature, little original empirical research has been conducted specifically on far-right groups and supporters. Also, the current scholarly focus on militant Islamic terrorism in the years following the September 11 attacks has overshadowed the need for research on the current threat posed by far-right extremism. Indeed, recent research suggests that there is a significant far-right presence in most states (Riley, Treverton, Wilson, & Davis, 2005; Simone et al., 2008). Other recent studies show that domestic attacks outnumber international attacks against the United States 7:1 (LaFree, Dugan, Fogg, & Scott, 2006), and that the far-right poses a serious threat to domestic security. Hewitt (2003) found that the far right claimed over 250 lives between 1978 and 2000 and that future terrorist attacks are likely to be committed by both Islamic terrorists and far-right extremists. Freilich and Chermak (2007) have found that since 1990, far-rightists have committed 270 homicide incidents (ideologically motivated and nonideologically motivated) that involve more than 500 homicide victims and an additional 100 attempted homicide incidents involving over 200 victims. Importantly, during this period, far-rightists killed close to 30 law enforcement personnel. In fact, far-rightists murdered five law enforcement personnel in 2007, the most officers killed by domestic extremists in a single year since 1995. Freilich and Chermak also identified over 50 far-rightists who died in confrontations, committed suicide, or were executed since 1990.

Although the unique threats of far-right extremism have been established, the extant literature on far-right extremism has not devoted sufficient rigorous attention to it. After critically reviewing the terrorism literature, Silke (2004) concluded that the state of general terrorism studies is lacking in many ways. He suggested that all too often terrorism studies involve a reworking of past literature, thus retarding theoretical development and advancement of knowledge and understanding about terrorism. Silke's review assessed a number of aspects of terrorism research, including authorship, publication outlets, and other methodological characteristics of terrorism studies. In our review of the far-right literature, we borrow this approach and extend it by also considering how issues critical to the study of the far right (i.e., groups and crimes) have been addressed in the past literature.

Our literature review focuses on all scholarly and nonscholarly (e.g., journalistic accounts) books, book chapters from edited volumes, journal articles, and research reports published on far-right extremism in the United States. Again, the set of studies reviewed here does not constitute the entire universe of studies, as our literature review is ongoing. Our assessment of the literature is based upon the 218 studies we have reviewed thus far. In addition, some types of studies were intentionally not included in our review. First, studies focusing primarily on hate or bias crime were omitted. That is, if the focus on the article was not obviously on some aspect of the far-right movement or far-right extremist groups, the study was not included (e.g. Levin & McDevitt, 1993; Perry, 2003). Second, studies that focused primarily on the general issues of terrorism, rather than far-right crime and terrorism specifically, were excluded. Third, we did not include doctoral dissertations or master's degree theses but restricted our review to published works. Finally, studies that addressed far-right extremism in nations other than the United States (e.g., xenophobia in Germany; see Hagan, Merken, & Boegke, 1995) were not included.

A template was developed and systematically applied to all studies included in the review. A database was created based on the fields from the summaries, and was used here to describe the state of the far-right extremism literature. In this review, we were first interested in who has authored studies on far-right extremism. Reviewing terrorism studies, Silke (2004) concluded that terrorism research has relied on the effort of too few researchers who usually work alone on small-scale projects. We were interested in whether this assessment also applied to the far-right extremism literature.

As shown in Table 1.1, it appears that in three of the major outlets for far-right extremism studies, over 70 percent of the studies reviewed were single-author works. Similar to Silke's (2004) findings for general terrorism studies, those researching far-right extremism tend to work alone on their research projects. One could speculate that lone researchers also tend to work on smaller-scale projects, and by extension, that lone authorship and small-scale studies hinder theoretical development and advancement of knowledge about this topic.

Despite these findings, there were a number of authors who pursued active research agendas on far-right extremism. For instance, Michael Barkun, Mark Hamm, Jeffrey Kaplan, and Leonard Weinberg authored multiple scholarly studies on the far right. In addition, Mark Pitcavage, employed by the Anti-Defamation League, also authored multiple articles and reports

Table 1.1   Multiple- and Single-Authored Far-Right Publications ($N = 189$)

	Scholarly journal ($N = 136$)	Book chapters ($N = 33$)	Books ($N = 20$)
Single author	98 (72.1%)	25 (75.8%)	16 (80.0%)
Multiple authors	38 (27.9%)	8 (24.2%)	4 (20.0%)

Note: The table shows the extent that far-right extremism studies were authored by single and multiple authors. The table does not present authorship data for nonscholarly publications.

related to the far right. While there were a few other scholars with more than a single publication, the more important finding is that most scholars had only a single publication that focused on far-right extremism. As is the case with terrorism research (Schmid & Jongman, 1988; Silke, 2004), the findings suggest that far-right extremism studies are authored by those with primary research interests outside of terrorism.

We were also interested in discovering what types of outlets far-right extremism studies have appeared in. Based on the studies considered, we found that studies tended to be peer-reviewed articles. Thus, it appears that most of the far-right extremism literature is coming from the academic community (see Table 1.2). Book chapters from edited volumes were the second-most popular type of outlet. Both books and book chapters from edited volumes were most often published by nonuniversity publishers. One explanation for this finding is that many of these publications were authored by nonacademics. In fact, some of the most important works on the far-right have been authored by journalists and law enforcement with inside knowledge of the far right.

Moreover, from table 1.2, it is clear that most scholarly articles have been published in terrorism journals. In particular, *Terrorism and Political Violence* was the most salient outlet for scholarly articles on far-right extremism,

Table 1.2   Far-Right Publication Outlets ($N = 218$)

Scholarly Articles ($N = 136$)	Book Chapters ($N = 33$)	Books ($N = 20$)	Other ($N = 29$)
Terrorism (n = 53, 39.0%)	University press (n = 11, 33.3%)	University press (n = 8, 40.0%)	Government report (n = 11, 38.0%)
Sociology (n = 36, 26.5%)	Other press (n = 22, 66.7%)	Other press (n = 12, 60.0%)	Watchdog (n = 8, 27.6%)
Polit. Science (n = 21, 15.4%)			Magazine (n = 8, 27.6%)
Criminology (n = 14, 10.3%)			Conference paper (n = 1, 3.4%)
Religion (n = 7, 5.1%)			Thesis or dissertation (n = 1, 3.4%)
Race/Ethnicity (n = 4, 2.9%)			
Anthropology (n = 1, 0.7%)			

Note: The categories listed under scholarly articles represent the various disciplines of the academic journals in the reviewed studies. Books and book chapters are disaggregated by university and other publishing outlets. The "other" category consists of government reports, watch or advocacy group reports (e.g., Southern Poverty Law Center, Anti-Defamation League), various magazine articles, conference papers, and academic theses and dissertations.

while *Studies in Conflict and Terrorism* came in a distant second place. Most of the scholarly journals represented in the studies reviewed had one or two articles related to the far right. After the two primary terrorism journals, select sociology journals were most salient. What is also interesting is the lack of scholarly attention to far-right extremism from criminology journals (for exceptions, see Freilich, Pichardo-Almanzar, & Rivera, 1999; Freilich & Pridemore, 2006); it is interesting because of the relevance of many far-right activities to criminology. For instance, members of the far right are often involved in criminal gangs (e.g., neo-Nazi skinheads) and commit crimes that are both ideologically and nonideologically motivated. Therefore, there is a need for criminologists to focus research activities on these topics.

Research on the nature of far-right groups and their activities is important because it is one way to conceptually distinguish between far-right and other bias-motivated activities. Moreover, focusing research on far-right groups could allow scholars and others to examine the effects that group association has on individual criminal behavior. In our review, we identified the number of studies that examined general and specific groups, and noted the three groups that were most prominent in the study. This method seemed adequate, as the majority of studies did not mention more than three groups, and those that did mention more than three groups did not study more than three far-right groups in-depth.

Table 1.3 shows that the vast majority of studies addressed at least one general far-right group. Most studies addressed the general topic of white-supremacist groups or militia groups. That is, studies more often than not included a general overview of different types of far-right wing groups, while only approximately 50 percent of the studies reviewed mentioned or focused on a specific far-right extremist group. Of the studies that mentioned specific groups, the vast majority discussed the Ku Klux Klan, and the Aryan Nations was the second-most discussed group. Most of these far-right group descriptions involved the reworking of old material, and little new information was provided about the groups. Although the Klan and Aryan Nation were often discussed, many other groups were mentioned only a single time. Keeping

Table 1.3   Far-Right Studies that Mentioned Groups ($N = 218$)

	n	Percentage
No groups mentioned	29	13.3
Only general group types	85	39.0
General and specific groups mentioned	104	47.7

Note: For all reviewed far-right extremist studies, this table shows the extent that specific groups (e.g., Ku Klux Klan) and general groups (e.g., Skinhead) were mentioned or discussed.

in mind that we noted only the three most prominent groups for each study, we found that 41 groups were mentioned only once in the literature in the reviewed studies. Thus, it appears that many groups, such as specific militia groups and dangerous white-supremacist groups that currently pose a threat to public security, have been understudied in the past from all disciplines.

There are also many reasons to study crimes committed by those associated with the far right. Far-right perpetrators, for instance, are more likely to be charged with traditional criminal charges than terrorism charges in the United States (Freilich & Chermak, 2007; Simone et al., 2008). Many far-right perpetrators are also involved in other sorts of traditional criminal activities, whether crimes are committed as preparatory crime for terrorist acts or in other instances not related to acts of domestic terrorism. We identified the first three most prominent types of crimes mentioned in each study.

It is clear from Table 1.4, however, that 60 percent of far-right extremism studies did not focus on any crimes committed by the far right. In addition, when crimes were discussed in studies, the focus was frequently on the same specific high-profile incidents, often particular homicides or bombings, thus resulting in little new information or insights about the criminal activities of the far right. While some far-right scholars have noted the prevalence of tax-related and other financial crimes common to the far right, there was little mention of these and other less serious or violent crimes in the far-right extremism literature. It is clear from our review that research needs to also examine other types of crimes, such as attempted homicides, thwarted terrorist acts, and other financial crime that may serve as preparatory crimes for more serious ideologically motivated attacks. Focusing on the crimes can also allow scholars to address a number of theoretical questions related to the far right—for instance, whether or not far-right perpetrators tend to specialize by committing only ideologically motivated crimes (Hirschi & Gottfredson, 2001) or are more versatile offenders (Blazak, 2001; Hamm, 1998).

Shifting now to a review of methodological approaches used in the far-right extremism literature, we identify the types of informational sources that authors relied upon. It is clear from Table 1.5 that scholars tended to draw from multiple sources of information.

Table 1.4   Percentage of Studies Mentioning Crime ($N = 218$)

	n	Percentage
No crimes mentioned	123	56.4
Single crime	19	8.7
Multiple crimes	76	34.9

Note: For each far-right study reviewed, the first three types of crimes mentioned in the study were noted. This table captures the extent that studies mentioned different types of crimes.

Table 1.5   Information Sources Used in Studies ($N = 218$)

	n	Percentage
No data	31	14.2
Single	49	22.5
Multiple	138	63.3

Note: All sources of information relied on were noted for each far-right extremist study reviewed. This table captures the extent that studies relied on no sources of outside information, a single source, or multiple sources of information.

Nonetheless, almost 40 percent of studies relied upon either no external source of information (e.g., editorial style article or opinion piece) or relied upon a single source of information. Furthermore, many far-right studies relied upon other academic research as a source of information, resulting in the reworking of old material. Table 1.6 shows that of the studies reviewed, over 40 percent relied on either academic studies or media sources as primary sources of information on the far right.

The findings presented here support the findings of scholars who have reviewed general terrorism studies. Schmid and Jongman (1988) also found a heavy reliance on data produced by others, thus possibly hindering the creation of new knowledge and theory development. Scholars have suggested that typical sources used to conduct crime-related research are seldom used to study terrorism (Hamm, 2005; LaFree & Dugan, 2004; Leiken & Brooke, 2006; Ross, 1993; Silke, 2001). Consequently, most theoretical work and hypothesis testing occurs with questionable or insufficient data (Hamm, 2005; Ross, 1993).

Based on our review, the conclusions regarding general terrorism studies can be applied to far-right extremism research. The issues of data reliability and validity that occur when researchers rely only on open-source or secondary data sources for information on terrorism-related activities also apply to the far-right extremism literature (see LaFree et al., 2006; Silke, 2004). In short, media sources are problematic as they are often inaccurate, biased, and intended for particular audiences. Future far-right extremism research needs to focus on integrating other sources of information and on triangulating data sources when possible.

Overwhelmingly, the most common methodological approach used in far-right studies involved variations of nonsystematic reviews of various sources of information. The majority of studies utilized what can be referred to as an archival approach, relying on the perusal of select far-right group Web sites and writings, watch-group publications (e.g., Anti-Defamation League, Southern Poverty Law Center), and media coverage of far-right activities. The second-most common method used was nonsystematic interviews, often

Table 1.6   All Sources of Information ($N = 460$)

	n	Percentage
Academic	99	21.5
Media	95	20.7
Watch groups	69	15.0
Far-right extremist groups	62	13.5
Far-right individual	55	12.0
Police/government	62	13.5
Researcher observation	7	1.5
Nongovernmental documents	6	1.3
Population survey	5	1.1

Note: All sources of information for each study were noted for each far-right extremist study reviewed, equaling 460 sources of information for 218 studies. Academic sources refer to various sources of information, such as journal articles and books. Media sources refer to all types of media (e.g., print news, television). Watch-group reports mostly refer to publications of advocacy groups (e.g., Southern Poverty Law Center, Anti-Defamation League) that serve as watchdog organizations for extremist crimes. Far-right extremist groups may include militia groups, the Ku Klux Klan, and many other such organizations. Far-right individuals were leaders, members, or other affiliates of these organizations. Police/governments sources of information were often police investigation files or case reports, interviews with criminal justice agencies, and specific court documents. Researcher observation as a source of information often entailed the research observing a far-right event or other happening related to the far-right movement. Nongovernment documents were organizational documents often used to learn about the activities of far-right organizations. Finally, population surveys were used as information to often gauge public attitudes, sympathy, or other perceptions of issues related to far-right extremism.

conducted with far-right group members or supporters. These interviews usually occurred on an ad hoc basis and were not systematic. Thus, while interviews may have led to specific insights in some studies, drawing any generalizations about the far right from these interviews would be challenging.

There are a number of reasons why secondary data analysis and nonsystematic interviews are popular in the far-right extremism literature. Far-right groups and supporters are a difficult population to study and present a number of practical obstacles to research. Nonetheless, some scholars have been able to incorporate in-depth observation, systematic interviews, and ethnographic methods into their research on far-right groups (e.g., Dobratz & Shanks-Meile, 1997; Hamm, 1993). In addition to future systematic field work of far-right groups, research can take advantage of other sources of information commonly used in far-right research, integrating them with official sources of data commonly used in criminological research (e.g., court documents), thus triangulating sources of information to increase reliability and validity of data.

The final aspect of the literature to be discussed is the analysis of data in far-right studies. In our review we noted whether studies utilized multivariate, descriptive, or no form of quantitative analysis. Again, the most common method of studying the far-right was a nonsystematic, archival approach, so it is not surprising that Table 1.7 shows that over 80 percent of studies reviewed did not use any statistical analyses.

This finding is also true of the general terrorism studies, as statistical analyses are seldom used in this literature (Leiken & Brooke, 2006; Merari, 1991; Schmid & Jongman, 1988). In fact, scholars have found that only 3 percent of articles in terrorism journals used inferential analysis (Lum, Kennedy, & Sherley, 2006; Silke, 2001). While studies that rely on archival approaches are useful in exploring various aspects of far-right extremism, it is clear that there is a need to collect original data and systematically analyze quantitative data on the far right. Doing so will allow scholars to better describe, make inferences, and advance knowledge about the nature of far-right extremism in the United States.

In sum, the state of the far-right extremism literature is in poor condition. Our ongoing literature review has identified a number of research practices and methodological issues that may be hindering the advancement of knowledge about far-right extremism in the United States. Researchers tend to work alone on far-right studies, and few scholars publish more than a single study on the topic. We also found that criminology journals rarely publish studies on the far right. This is likely related to our other finding that key issues of far-right group dynamics and criminal activities are understudied topics of research. In addition, the overuse of nonsystematic, archival approaches utilized in far-right studies has led to quantitative and statistical analyses being rarities, thus hindering far-right researchers' abilities to move beyond exploratory research and overview studies. Although we are able to draw tentative conclusions about the state of far-right research based on our review, we have yet to directly address the issue of defining far-right groups and activities as conceptually distinct from other ideologically motivated behaviors. It is to this task that we now turn.

Table 1.7   Type of Statistics Used by Study ($N = 218$)

	n	Percentage
None	181	83.0
Descriptive	23	10.6
Multivariate	14	6.4

Note: For each far-right extremist study, what type of (descriptive or multivariate) statistical analyses that were conducted and whether they were conducted was noted.

COMPARING FAR-RIGHT CRIMES TO
HATE CRIMES

In this section, we compare hate crimes to the types of crimes committed by supporters of the far right. On one hand, these two categories overlap, as some far-right groups—for example, racist organizations and skinhead gangs—encourage such crimes. For example, to many people a cross burning in North Carolina may generate images of perpetrators who are KKK members dressed in hoods. There is a long list of high-profile deadly hate crimes that were, in fact, perpetrated by supporters of racist groups like the World Church of the Creator (e.g., Benjamin Smith's 1999 shooting rampage), Aryan Nations (e.g., Bufford Furrow's 1999 shooting attack), and the White Aryan Resistance (WAR; e.g., the 1988 murder of an African immigrant in Portland by skinhead supporters of WAR). On the other hand, empirical studies on these crimes yield two other important findings: first, most crimes committed by far-rightists are either non-ideological/routine crimes (e.g., profit-motivated drug dealing) or ideologically motivated—but not hate-inspired—crimes (e.g., tax refusal or motor vehicle violations); and, second, most hate crimes are committed for the thrill or the excitement. Similarly, the vast majority of hate crime perpetrators are young males who are *not* members of organized hate groups (Levin & McDevitt, 1993; Levin, McDevitt, & Bennett, 2003). We discuss each of these points in more detail below.

Our ongoing systematic literature review on all studies examining far-right extremism demonstrates that far-right extremists have been investigated by federal and state authorities and that they are involved in a variety of criminal acts, violent and nonviolent, as well as ideological and non-ideological/routine crimes. Significantly, only a minority of these illegal acts are hate crimes. Crimes committed by far-rightists that are not hate crimes and that the literature discusses include (1) tax refusal; (2) gun charges; (3) land-use violations; (4) violations of regulations requiring license plates and driving licenses, and other similar regulations; (5) false liens and financial schemes; (6) abortion-related crimes; (7) antipornography attacks; (8) antigovernment strikes; (9) antiglobal attacks; (10) attacks against leftists and other ideological enemies; (11) attacks against opponents within the movement (i.e., crimes committed due to intramovement strife); (12) possession and planned use of chemical, nuclear, radiological, and biological weapons; (13) preparatory crimes (such as bank robberies, counterfeiting, credit card theft, weapons procurement and the manufacture of illegal firearms, drug dealing, cyber-crime and identity theft); (14) other crimes that further the movement's survival or ideology; and (15) nonideological "routine" crimes. These crimes have been perpetrated by lone wolves, multiple perpetrators, and organized groups.

Importantly, Freilich and Chermak's (2007) ongoing DHS and National Consortium for the Studies of Terrorism and Responses to Terrorism (START) funded project that is building a database on all crimes committed by supporters of the far right in the United States since 1990 supports our literature review findings. Thus far, this study has found that far-rightists have committed over 4,000 criminal events that involved over 4,600 perpetrators and over 3,800 victims. The majority of these incidents were tax-refusal cases, gun/weapons crimes, antigovernment plots, and antiabortion incidents. Only a minority of incidents were, in fact, hate crimes. For example, their analysis of the more than 250 homicide incidents found that less than 30 percent were hate crimes.

Similarly, Simone et al.'s (2008) survey of the 50 state-police agencies also documented that far-rightists commit a variety of crimes, most of which are not hate crimes. For instance, more than 30 percent of the responding agencies reported that supporters of the far right in a typical year commit more than six false liens/financial crimes (40%), motor vehicle violations (38%), nonideological routine crimes (32%), and tax-refusal crimes (30%). In addition, 27 percent of the agencies reported that in a typical year far-rightists committed more than six gun crimes in their state. However, only 29 percent of responding agencies reported that far-rightists commit more than six hate crimes in their state in a typical year. Further, at least a quarter of the responding agencies reported that supporters of the far right commit more than 31 motor-vehicle violations (30%) or routine nonideological crimes (24%) in their state in a typical year. Certain agencies also reported that supporters of the far right commit more than 31 false liens and financial crimes (14% of states), tax-refusal crimes (8%), gun crimes (8%), or land use and environmental crimes/violations (8%) in their state in a typical year. Conversely, only 5 percent of agencies reported that supporters of the far right commit more than 31 hate crimes in a typical year.

Meanwhile, the hate crimes literature consistently finds that most hate crime perpetrators are not far-rightists. Scholars have empirically investigated the characteristics of hate crime incidents, the perpetrators and victims of such crimes, the motivation for such attacks, and the spatial distribution of these events. Many microlevel studies on hate crime perpetrators support the typology created by Levin, McDevitt, and Bennett (2003). This typology groups hate crimes into four categories: (1) crimes motivated by the thrill and excitement of committing such a forbidden act, (2) crimes committed as revenge in response to perceived attacks on one's group, (3) crimes committed to defend one's neighborhood, and (4) "mission" crimes committed to fulfill one's ideological worldview that certain groups must be destroyed. Most studies find that thrill-seeking crimes constitute the overwhelming majority of hate crimes (Byers & Crider, 2002; Byers, Crider, & Biggers, 1999; Franklin, 2000; Levin, McDevitt, & Bennett, 2003). Indeed, Levin et al. argue that because most hate crime perpetrators are not ideologically motivated, the most effective criminal justice responses would stress rehabilitation as opposed to more punitive policies. Similarly, a number of macrolevel studies conducted by Green and colleagues (Green, Glaser, & Rich, 1998; Green, Strolovitch, & Wong, 1998) found that hate crimes were more likely in areas that were demographically changing as greater numbers of minorities moved in. Green and colleagues concluded that these crimes were committed to protect the neighborhood from perceived invaders. These conclusions are also bolstered by ethnographic accounts with young males from these neighborhoods who explained that they committed hate crimes to defend their neighborhood (Green, Strolovitch, & Wong, 1998).

Although most crimes committed by far-rightists are not hate crimes and most hate crime perpetrators are not members of organized hate groups, some horrific violent hate crimes have been perpetrated by far-rightists. Levin, McDevitt, and Bennett (2003) speculate that though most perpetrators are not committed members of the movement, they may have been influenced by the ideological climate created by far-right racist groups. Green and Rich's (1998) examination of cross burnings in North Carolina support this possibility. Green and Rich found that cross burnings were more common following rallies held by white supremacists. The authors state that because none of the suspected cross burners were associated with racist organizations, it is possible that the racist rallies encouraged others to conduct cross burnings. Green and Rich also note, however, that it is possible that racist organizations intentionally organize rallies in locations where they have the most support. In any case, the most important finding from these studies is that only a minuscule minority of hate crime perpetrators are ideologically committed far-rightists acting on behalf of a racist organization.

One reason why most crimes committed by far-rightists are not hate crimes is that some segments of the far right are not racist or anti-Semitic. Although all far-rightists share certain beliefs, it is important to remember that there are also strong disagreements within movements over fundamental issues such as racism, anti-Semitism, the role of religion, the use of violence, and the openness of the political system (Chermak, Freilich, & Shemtob, in press; Dobratz, 2001; Durham, 2003). For example, the John Birch Society, despite its endorsement of a variety of conspiracy theories, for years has rejected violence, racism, and anti-Semitism. A more contemporary example is the far-right tax-refusal movement that has attracted support across many sectors of American society, including minorities and Jews. For instance, African American actor Wesley Snipes recently attracted much publicity when he was tried for nonpayment of taxes along with prominent white far-right tax refusal activists. In fact, the far-right tax-refusal movement shares ideas, publications, and ideological pronouncements with extremist black nationalist groups (e.g., the Moors) who share their antigovernment and antitax beliefs. Further, the notorious racist white supremacist prison gang the Aryan Brotherhood has at times supported alliances with Hispanic gangs in opposition to African American gangs behind bars. Additionally, other white-supremacist gangs (e.g., Public Enemy Number One) occasionally place a greater premium on routine criminal goals as opposed to their ideological goals. In short, scholars and others should avoid making generalizations about the far right and instead pay close attention to the nuances that characterize the movement. This is especially important when the issue is the relationship between the far right and hate crimes.

CONCLUSION

This chapter has reviewed significant issues associated with the study of terrorism, hate crime, and far-right criminal activities. Our investigation of these important topics reviewed both the overlapping boundaries among these areas as well as points where these scholarly areas have diverged. We discussed the difficulties of conducting research on such politicized social problems and set forth suggestions about how scholars could effectively address some of the definitional dilemmas they face. Specifically, we first outlined the major hurdles academics face when engaging these issues; these issues primarily deal with definitional and conceptual concerns. Second, we presented some initial findings from our ongoing systematic literature review on studies that focused on the far right. Importantly, the findings reveal a number of weaknesses with the extant literature on far-right extremism. Similar to the terrorism literature, there is a need for scholars to collect original data, conduct explanatory—in addition to descriptive—studies, collaborate with others, and work on long-range research projects. The chapter concluded with a comparison of hate crimes to crimes commonly committed by far-rightists. This comparison indicates that the study of these topics could result in more consistent production of explanatory knowledge if scholars paid careful attention to the nuances that characterize far-right extremism, hate crimes, and terrorism.

NOTES

1. We rely on Perry's (2001) definition that hate crimes "involve acts of violence and intimidation, usually directed toward already stigmatized and marginalized groups. As such it is a mechanism of power and oppression, intended to reaffirm the precarious hierarchies that characterize a given social order. It attempts to recreate simultaneously the threatened (real or imagined) hegemony of the perpetrator's group and the 'appropriate' subordinate identity of the victim's group. It is a means of marking both the Self and the Other in such a way as to reestablish their 'proper' relative positions, as given and reproduced by broader ideologies and patterns of social and political inequality" (p. 10).

2.   Defining the domestic far right is not easy because there is no universally accepted definition and prior research has not sufficiently addressed this issue. Drawing
upon our systematic review of studies published on far-right extremism in general and
its association with political crimes in particular—including important works that offered typologies, definitions, and descriptions (see, for example, Barkun, 1989; Berlet &
Lyons, 2000; Coates, 1987; Duffy & Brantley, 1998, Durham, 2003; Kaplan, 1993, 1995;
Mullins, 1988; Smith, 1994; Sprinzak, 1995; see also Dobratz & Shanks-Meile, 1997;
Weinberg, 1993)—we rely upon the following description. The domestic far right is
composed of individuals or groups that subscribe to aspects of the following ideals:
they are fiercely nationalistic (as opposed to universal and international in orientation), anti-global, suspicious of centralized federal authority, and reverent of individual
liberty (especially their right to own guns and be free of taxes); they also believe in
conspiracy theories that involve a grave threat to national sovereignty and/or personal
liberty and a belief that one's personal and/or national "way of life" is under attack
and is either already lost or being imminently threatened (sometimes such beliefs are
amorphous and vague, but for some the threat is from a specific ethnic, racial, or religious group), as well as a belief in the need to be prepared for an attack by participating in paramilitary preparations and training and survivalism. It is important to note
that mainstream conservative movements and the mainstream Christian right are not
included.

REFERENCES

Barkun, M. (1989). Millenarian aspects of white supremacist movements. *Terrorism
    and Political Violence, 1*, 409–434.
Berlet, C., & Lyons, M. N. (2000). *Right-wing populism in America: Too close for comfort.*
    New York: The Guilford Press.
Best, J. (1990). *Threatened children: Rhetoric and concern about child victims.* Chicago:
    The University of Chicago Press.
Blazak, R. (2001). White boys to white men: Target recruitment of Nazi skinheads.
    American Behavioral Scientist, 44, 982–1000.
Byers, D. B., & Crider, B. W. (2002). Hate crimes against the Amish: A qualitative
    analysis of bias motivation using routine activities theory. *Deviant Behavior, 23*,
    115–148.
Byers, D. B., Crider, B. W., & Biggers, G. K. (1999). Bias crime motivation: A study of
    hate crime and offender neutralization techniques used against the Amish. *Journal
    of Contemporary Criminal Justice, 15*, 78–96.
Chermak, S. M., Freilich, J. D., & Shemtob, Z. (in press). Law enforcement training
    and the domestic far-right. *Criminal Justice and Behavior.*
Chermak, S. M., & Gruenewald, J. A. (2006). Domestic terrorism and the media. *Jus-
    tice Quarterly, 23*(4), 428–461.
Coates, J. (1987). *Armed and dangerous: The rise of the survivalist right.* New York: Hill
    and Wang.
Dobratz, B. A. (2001). The role of religion in the collective identity of the white
    racialist movement. *Journal for the Scientific Study of Religion, 40*, 287–301.
Dobratz, B. A., & Shanks-Meile, S. L. (1997). *White power, white pride! The white sepa-
    ratist movement in the United States.* New York: Twayne.

Duffy, J. E., & Brantley, A. C. (1997). Militias: Initiating contact. Federal Bureau of Investigation. Retrieved November 18, 1998, from http://?www.fbi.gov/library/leb/1997/July975.htm

Durham, M. (2003). The American far right and 9/11. *Terrorism and Political Violence, 15*, 96–111.

Franklin, K. (2000). Antigay behaviors among young adults: Prevalence, patterns, and motivators in a non-criminal population. *Journal of Interpersonal Violence, 15*, 339–362.

Freilich, J. D., & Chermak, S. M. (2007). *Final DHS Summer Faculty and Student Research Team Grant Report: Creation of a database of U.S. extremist crime, 1995–2005.* Washington, DC: Department of Homeland Security, Science and Technology Directorate.

Freilich, J. D., Pichardo-Almanzar, N., & Rivera, C. J. (1999). How social movement organizations explicitly and implicitly promote deviant behavior: The case of the militia movement. *Justice Quarterly, 16*(3), 655–683.

Freilich, J. D., & Pridemore, W. A. (2005). A reassessment of state-level covariates of militia groups. *Behavioral Sciences and the Law, 23*(4), 527–546.

Freilich, J. D., & Pridemore, W. A. (2006). Mismeasuring militias: Limitations of advocacy group data and of state-level studies of paramilitary groups. *Justice Quarterly, 23*, 147–162.

Gibbs, J. P. (1989). Conceptualizations of terrorism. *American Sociological Review, 54*, 329–340.

Green, D. P., Glaser, J., & Rich, A. (1998). From lynching to gay bashing: The elusive connection between economic conditions and hate crime. *Journal of Personality and Social Psychology, 75*(1), 82–92.

Green, D. P., & Rich, A. (1998). White supremacist activity and cross-burnings in North Carolina. *Journal of Quantitative Criminology, 14*(3), 263–282.

Green, D. P., Strolovitch, D. Z., & Wong, J. S. (1998). Defended neighborhoods, integration, and racially motivated crime. *American Journal of Sociology, 104*(2), 372–403.

Hagan, J., Merkens, H., & Boegke, K. (1995). Delinquency and disdain: Social capital and the control of right-wing extremism among East and West Berlin youth. *American Journal of Sociology, 100*(4), 1028–1052.

Hamm, M. S. (1993). *American skinheads: The criminology and control of hate crime.* Westport, CT: Praeger.

Hamm, M. S. (1994). Conceptualizing hate crime in a global context. In M. S. Hamm (Ed.), *Hate crime: International perspectives of on causes and control* (pp. 173–194). Cincinnati, OH: Anderson.

Hamm, M. S. (1998). Terrorism, hate crime, and antigovernment violence: A review of the research. In H. W. Kushner (Ed.), *The future of terrorism: Violence in the new millennium* (pp. 59–96). Thousand Oaks, CA: Sage.

Hamm, M. S. (2005). *Crimes committed by terrorist groups: Theory, research, and prevention.* Final report to the National Institute of Justice, U.S. Department of Justice, Washington, DC.

Hewitt, C. (2003). *Understanding terrorism in America: From the Klan to Al Qaeda.* New York: Routledge.

Hirschi, T., & Gottfredson, M. R. (2001). Self control theory. In R. Patternoster & R. Bachman (Eds.), *Explaining criminals and crime* (pp. 81–96). Los Angeles: Roxbury.

Kaplan, J. (1993). The context of American Millenarian revolutionary theology: The case of the "Identity Christian" church of Israel. *Terrorism and Political Violence, 5*(1), 30–82.

Kaplan, J. (1995). Right wing violence in North America. *Terrorism and Political Violence, 7*(1), 44–95.

Kingdon, J. W. (1984). *Agendas, alternatives, and public policies.* Boston: Little, Brown.

LaFree, G., & Dugan, L. (2004). How does studying terrorism compare to studying crime? *Sociology of Crime, Law and Deviance, 5,* 53–74.

LaFree, G., Dugan, L., Fogg, H., & Scott, J. (2006). *Building a global terrorism database.* Final report to the National Institute of Justice.

Leiken, R. S., & Brooke, S. (2006). The quantitative analysis of terrorism and immigration: An initial exploration. *Terrorism and Political Violence, 18,* 503–521.

Levin, J., & McDevitt, J. (1993). *Hate crimes: The rising tide of bigotry and bloodshed.* New York: Plenum Press.

Levin, J., McDevitt, J., & Bennett, S. (2003). Hate crime offenders: An expanded typology. In B. Perry (Ed.), *Hate and bias crime: A reader* (pp. 173–194). New York: Routledge.

Lum, C., Kennedy, L. W., & Sherley, A. J. (2006). *The effectiveness of counter-terrorism strategies: A Campbell systematic review.* Retrieved from http://db.c2admin.org/doc-pdf/Lum_Terrorism_Review.pdf

Merari, A. (1991). Academic research and government policy on terrorism. *Terrorism and Political Violence, 3*(1), 88–102.

Mudde, C. (1995). Right-wing extremism analyzed: A comparative analysis of the ideologies of three alleged right-wing extremist parties. *European Journal of Political Research, 27,* 203–224.

Mullins, W. C. (1988). *Terrorist organizations in the United States.* Springfield, IL: Charles C. Thomas Books.

Nacos, B. L. (2003). The terrorist calculus behind 9–11: A model for future terrorism? *Studies in Conflict and Terrorism, 26,* 1–16.

Perry, B. (2001). *In the name of hate: Understanding hate crimes.* New York: Routledge.

Perry, B. (2003). Where do we go from here? Researching hate crime. *Internet Journal of Criminology.* Retrieved November 25, 2008, from http://www.internetjournal ofcriminology.com/Where%20Do%20We%20Go%20From%20Here.%20Researc hing%20Hate%20Crime.pdf

Perry, N. J. (2004). The numerous federal legal definitions of terrorism: The problem of too many grails. *Journal of Legislation, 30,* 249–274.

Rausch, S., & LaFree, G. (2007). The growing importance of criminology in the study of terrorism. *The Criminologist,* November/December, 1–5.

Riley, K. J., Treverton, G. F., Wilson, J. M., & Davis, L. M. (2005). *State and local intelligence in the war on terrorism.* Santa Monica, CA: Rand.

Ross, J. I. (1993). Research on contemporary oppositional political terrorism in the United States: merits, drawbacks & suggestions for improvement. In K. D. Tunnel (Ed.), *Political crime in contemporary America: A critical approach* (pp. 101–116). New York: Garland.

Schmid, A. (2004). Frameworks for conceptualizing terrorism. *Terrorism and Political Violence, 16*(4), 777–794.

Schmid, A., & Jongman, A. (1988). *Political terrorism: A new guide to actors, authors, concepts, data bases, theories and literature.* Amsterdam, Holland: Transaction Books.

Silke, A. (1996). Terrorism and the blind men's elephant. *Terrorism and Political Violence, 8*(3), 12–28.

Silke, A. (2001). The devil you know: Continuing problems with research on terrorism. *Terrorism and Political Violence, 13*(4), 1–14.

Silke, A. (2004). The road less traveled: Recent trends in terrorism research. In A. Silke (Ed.), *Research on terrorism: Trends, achievements and failures* (pp. 186–213). New York: Taylor and Francis.

Simone, J., Freilich, J. D., & Chermak, S. M. (2008). *Surveying state police agencies about domestic terrorism and far-right extremists.* Research Brief published by the National Consortium for the Study of Terrorism and Responses to Terrorism (START).

Smith, B. L. (1994). *Terrorism in America: Pipe bombs and pipe dreams.* New York: State University of New York Press.

Spector, M., & Kituse, J. I. (1977). *Constructing social problems.* Menlo Park, CA: Cummings.

Sprinzak, E. (1995). Right wing terrorism in a comparative perspective: The case of split delegitimization. *Terrorism and Political Violence, 7*(1), 17–43.

Turk, A. T. (2004). Sociology of terrorism. *Annual Review of Sociology, 30,* 271–286.

Weinberg, L. (1993). The American radical right: Exit, voice, and violence. In P. Merkl & L. Weinberg (Eds.), *Encounters with the contemporary radical right* (pp. 185–203). Boulder, CO: Westview.

Weinberg, L., Pedahzur, A., & Hirsch-Hoefler, S. (2004). The challenges of conceptualizing terrorism. *Terrorism and Political Violence, 16*(4), 777–794.

Wright, S. A. (2007). *Patriots, politics, and the Oklahoma City bombing.* Cambridge, UK: Cambridge University Press.

CHAPTER 2

WHEN ODIN BEATS JESUS: USING RACIST RELIGION TO "DO GENDER" IN PRISON

Randy Blazak

I was standing on the top of Mt. Hood skiing when "Odin" came to me and told me about the struggle for existence of the white race.
—*e-mail from racist group leader, May 18, 2001*

From the Crusades through the Ku Klux Klan's modern reign of terror, Western religion has been used to validate oppression and victimization of specific groups of peoples. Among recent developments in religious trends among white supremacists has been the increasing popularity—especially in correctional facilities—of a form of Northern European paganism known as Odinism. The growth of the religion of Odinism among racist inmates has significant implications for the spread of hate crimes, domestic terrorism, racial divisiveness, and the destabilization of prison populations. Odinism has experienced a split between Germanic Neopagans, or "heathens," who engage in ancestral customs, and racist Odinists, who highlight the more tribal traditions of the faith. Racist Odinism is rooted in an ideology of domination based on race, religion, gender, and loyalty to cause. What is the appeal of Odinism among prison inmates, as well as its influences on violence, aggression, and criminal behavior outside these institutions? Odinism, a modern version of the Norse mythology of the Scandinavian Vikings, is now being recognized as a religion and is gaining in popularity in prisons across the United States. For many inmates, Odinist affiliation provides a spiritual justification that supports violence and racist activism as the means to rescue white Americans from their perceived enemies. This chapter supports James Messerschmidt's (1993) theory that male crime tends to be a response to emasculating forces that undermine popular definitions of masculinity. This research also serves as a focal point for further investigations of social change within racist prison gangs and the increased influence of Odinism in encouraging racist movements, as well as its impact on nonracist prison Odinists.

PRISON ODINISM

While many people are attracted to pre-Christian forms of paganism, like Wicca, Odinism (sometimes referred to as Ásatrú) has had a growing, captivating appeal for persons identifying themselves as part of the radical racist right. Odinism is often practiced as a means to support racist philosophies and calls to violence, both within prison culture and also in society as a whole. Of particular concern is its appeal to at-risk youth, disillusioned with mainstream religions. Of concern to the civil rights community and social science researchers interested in racist ideologies is the growth of Odinist beliefs among criminals as a means to justify violence. Odinism is now spreading widely in America's prison system. *Cooper v. Pate*, the 1964 Supreme Court decision that gave religious rights to Muslims and other religious minorities in prison, is now used to secure religious rights for Odinists. This right was upheld in 1972 in the *Cruz v. Beto* decision. What literature prison officials could previously suppress as propaganda for white prison gangs, like the Aryan Brotherhood, is now allowed as religious material. The Religious Land Use and Institutionalized Person Act (RLUIPA), signed by President Clinton in 2000, has also been used by radical religions to secure rights (Levin, 2003). However, there are still religious restrictions. In an important 2003 Supreme Court decision, *United States v. Trainer*, Robert Trainer lost his right to be involved in the racist Creativity "religion" while on parole because he had been convicted of a hate crime. However, in 2003 two Odinists won the right to have religious accommodations when the Supreme Court decided in their favor in *Cutter v. Wilkinson*. The state of First Amendment religious rights for inmates and parolees is constantly in negotiation.

Odinism has its roots in pre-Christian Scandinavian tribal culture. It is a heroic ancestral religion of elemental gods and goddesses, ruled by the father god, Odin, who resides in Valhalla. The early Viking explorers and warriors carried elements of their pagan beliefs into much of European culture, especially the Celtic settlements of the British Isles, Germany, and Iceland. Besides Celtic culture, Odinic images and themes appear in novels of J.R.R. Tolkien (*Lord of the Rings*), Mighty Thor comics, popular images of Viking warriors, the epic poem *Beowulf* (made into a popular film in 2007), and now inside correctional facilities. Contemporary Odinism venerates the battle, using the battle-ax and Thor's hammer as signifiers of loyalty to the ethnic struggle. Odinism has many followers, both racist and nonracist, among those looking for cultural traditions and spiritual beliefs tied to their European ancestry. Odinists place heightened emphasis on folk (kinship) relations, similar to tribal or clan identifications. One Odinist group states that

> Odinism is a living religion, a combination of cultural, material, ethical and spiritual realities as they relate to our folk family and our place in creation. It evolves, as we evolve, we evolve, as it evolves. (The Odinic Right, 2005, p. 1)

More traditional neopagans have had to contend with new presence of racist Odinists. Nonprison groups—including the Odinic Right, the Troth, and the Ásatrú Alliance—have had to clearly state that they do not practice or promote hate or racism on their Web sites and in their by-laws. There is strong evidence that the more violent and racist positions of Odinism are not contained by prison walls. Prisons have been described as "porous" institutions because inmates have the ability to communicate with noninmates, and most inmates will be paroled at some point. Therefore, prison issues affect issues in the area of criminal behavior outside prison, as inmates often return to communities supportive of illegal behavior. For many, the racist Odinist ideology follows inmates upon release. It also flourishes on the Internet and is taking root in the established hate movement. Greg Etter (2001), who has researched racist gangs, writes, "Unlike most people whose participation in the pseudo-paramilitary culture is mere escapist fantasy and is acted out in the viewing of movies, reading of books and participation in games: the white supremacists have elected to actually attempt to live out their fantasies in the real world" (p. 49). Etter found the pseudowarrior culture of racist religious groups increases their propensity for violence.

The rise of racist prison gangs like the Aryan Brotherhood has been well documented. According to the Anti-Defamation League (ADL), prison officials estimate that up to 10 percent of the nation's prison population is affiliated with such gangs. The ADL's 2002 report, "Dangerous Convictions: An Introduction to Extremist Activities in Prisons," outlines how racist prison gangs are responsible for violence both inside and outside of prisons, including the 1998 dragging death of James Byrd Jr. in Jasper, Texas. The attackers in that case were members of a racist prison gang called the Confederate Knights of America. It has been alleged that they were also members of another racist prison gang known as Aryan Circle, which claims some Odinist members.

The ADL and the Southern Poverty Law Center (SPLC) have both charted the rise of Odinism among these groups. In its 2000 report, "Pagans and Prison," the SPLC linked the popularity of Odinism among surviving members of a violent racist gang that led a crime spree in the 1980s, called The Order, to the growth of the faith among incarcerated racists nationwide. The Order initially followed the Christian Identity faith, but some converted to the racist version of Odinism in prison.

Many officials around the country say that Odinism/Ásatrú is the fastest growing religion behind prison walls, although most states do not keep statistics on how many inmates are involved. Of those that do, Texas apparently has the largest number, with 189 known Ásatrúers or Odinists in state penitentiaries. In Kansas, there are 120; in Colorado, 92; and in Arizona, 90—figures that some experts say probably underrepresent the real number. Officials in many other states and the federal system report a significant, if unquantified, presence.

These prisoners are often especially violent. "Many of them graduate to a higher security level than we have here," says Jack Ludlow, senior chaplain for the Arizona state prison complex in Tucson. Minnesota prison official Mary Hulverson adds that these neopagans "are monitored probably more than any others" (Southern Poverty Law Center [SPLC], 2000).

The growing presence of racist Odinists outside of prisons is evident on the Internet. An Oregon group, Volksfront, began as a skinhead group in 1996 (with roots in white prison gangs) that advocated for the establishment of an "autonomous Aryan homeland." It has evolved into an Odinist group that uses its Web site to provide lessons on Ásatrú and outreach to Odinist inmates, including members of The Order. The presence is also felt on the street. Racist skinheads now patronize pagan shops and Celtic festivals. In May 2002, a 21-year-old member of European Kindred was arrested in the murder of a black man in Portland, Oregon. European Kindred is an Odinist prison group in the Oregon penitentiary system. In July 2003, several buildings in Portland were hit with graffiti that featured "EK" inside a shield. This is the symbol of European Kindred. Local police reported that this symbol had not been seen outside the prison until this time. In April 2008, two European Kindred members were charged with attempted murder and arson in Portland for trying to silence a victim of a robbery who was preparing to testify (Bernstein, 2008).

A significant subgroup of white supremacists in prison is known as the Aryan Prisoners of War (POWs). Aryan POWs include those who are incarcerated for hate crimes and other acts believed to be actions against a government controlled by Jews (or who were just identified as racist before their incarceration). Aryan POWs have a certain celebrity status among white supremacists. Their addresses are posted on Web sites, and racists are encouraged to correspond with them. Volksfront operates a prisoner outreach program called Race Over All. Contact with Aryan POWs keeps racist inmates engaged in the white supremacists' subculture, providing them emotional support as well as support upon release.

RACISM AND RELIGION

Throughout the twentieth century, racist groups had been predominantly influenced by a racist interpretation of Christian theology. From the cross burnings of the Ku Klux Klan to the anti-Semitism practices of sects known as "Christian Identity," including the Aryan Nation, "whiteness" was embedded with sacred power. Picking up where the Ku Klux Klan left off, Christian Identity is a racial reading of the Bible that starts with the creation of the first white man, Adam, and ends with a racial holy war in Revelations. The Jews are believed to be the descendants of Satan and the embodiment of evil on Earth. Nonwhites are the "mud-races," descendants of animals, and are considered less than human.

But the Christian element brought with it inherent contradictions. Christ was a Jew. Christianity is a patriarchal religion but filled with feminine values: forgiveness, humility, charity, sacrifice, repentance, shame from sin, loving one's enemy, and compassion. Additionally, its origins were in the Middle East and only later co-opted by northern European culture.

Because of these contradictions, many of these groups began becoming disillusioned with their interpretation of Christian values. By the 1990s many young racist skinheads and radicals began turning to pre-Christian European paganism and Odinism's pantheon of Norse mythology. This allowed them to find a European spiritual tradition and cast Christ as a "crucified loser" and Christianity as a Jewish cultural product. These racists then became an influence in organized Odinist groups, emphasizing racist interpretations. They began turning Odinism into a Nazi-type religion (Goodrich-Clarke, 2002).

Hate group researcher Mark Hamm (1993) has written about the impact of Viking imagery in Led Zeppelin's music on the modern racist skinheads. Mattis Gardell, professor of religious history at the University of Stockholm and author of *Gods of the Blood: The Pagan Revival and White Separatism* (2003), has described these new Odinists as the generation raised on *Lord of the Rings* and the game Dungeons and Dragons. According to Gardell (SPLC, 2000), "Odinism offered them a new grand narrative. They could belong to something more important than themselves. They looked with distaste at American Society with its consumerism and materialism and its stupid TV programs. Medieval knights and Vikings and all that looked attractive" (p. 24).

The forefathers of prison Odinism are surviving members of The Order, Richard Kemp and David Lane (who died in 2007). The Order was a 1980s racist gang that robbed banks and armored cars, and assassinated a Jewish radio personality in an effort to start a racial civil war. Their heroic Odinist rhetoric is believed to appeal to white inmates in the same manner in which Islam appeals to many black inmates. It serves as a way to reject institutional prison Christianity and reinforces their oppositional social position with a language of "good and evil" forces and righteousness of battle against forces of oppression.

Odinism's Northern European focus and its heroic warrior gods stand in stark contrast to the more passive values of mainstream religions. While the scriptures of Christianity, for example, ask followers to love their enemies, racist Odinism demands that followers smite their enemies with the hammer of Thor. A popular Odinist group, the Ásatrú Folk Assembly, states its mission as "to call the sons and daughters of Europe back to their native spirituality and to the tribes which are their birthright" (Ásatrú Folk Assembly, 2003). It should be mentioned that heathens who claim the nonracist Odinist traditions typically reject violent applications of Thor's hammer and tribal identity. While a minority of Odinists are criminals or affiliated with the racist radical right, there is a growing concern regarding organizing for "Rahowa" or "racial holy war," a movement that includes several well-known Odinists.

ODINISM AND RIGHT-WING HATE GROUPS

Prison Odinism and its connection to the radical racist right is a subject that has not yet been fully researched by social scientists. It has been hinted at in the studies of skinheads by Hamm (1993) and Blazak (1998), but this research has focused tangentially on the appeal of religion for racist youths. Research on prison gangs occasionally refers to white groups like the Aryan Brotherhood, but not their religious expressions. Similarly, research on inmate religiosity has traditionally focused on Christians and Muslims, not pagans. There is a wide gap in the literature that links the religious experience of inmates to beliefs in violence and aggression. This research takes the novel approach of letting racist inmates discuss their religious faith in their own words. In the naturalistic setting of the prison, Odinists can make the case for their own religious expression.

While there is some useful research on the role of religion in prison (Zaitzow & Thomas, 2002, for example), there is no research on incarcerated Odinists. Additionally, any research on racist Odinism is primarily on the evolution of the religion and not on the appeal of the faith and the tolerance of violence, aggression, and racism by its adherents.

After the terrorist attacks on September 11, 2001, both the public and law enforcement became more aware of the need for a greater understanding of the connection between religious extremism and acts of mass violence. The June 2002 arrest of Jose Padilla (a.k.a. Abdullah al-Muhajir) for alleged plans to detonate a radiological bomb in the United States put the issue of prison conversions into the dialogue on the war on terrorism after it was revealed that Padilla became a radical Muslim while incarcerated. In 1995, after the bombing of the Federal Building in Oklahoma City, America's focus was primarily on criminal behavior among right-wing domestic groups. In the 2000s, there is another source of potential terrorists, racist prison Odinists and the popularization of the idea of Rahowa.

The desegregation of prisons in the 1960s led to the formation of racist prison gangs, most notably the Aryan Brotherhood in California's San

Quentin prison, which emerged from racist biker gangs (Smith, 2002). Racist prison gangs actively recruit white inmates who are expected to follow the radical racist agenda upon release. Wesley Dillinger, leader of the East Coast Aryan Brotherhood, said, "Prisons can be used as a training facility and should be" (Moser, 2002, p. 10).

The need for research in the areas of race, religion, and incarceration is imperative. The Order, a Christian Identity terrorist group, was responsible for a string of bank robberies, bombings, and a murder in the 1980s. Oklahoma bomber Timothy McVeigh and John King, the man who dragged James Byrd to death in Jasper, Texas, were devotees of a novel titled *The Turner Diaries*, a Rahowa guidebook rooted in a Christian Identity philosophy but popular with all racist activists. Peter Georgacarakos and Richard Scutari, two Odinist inmates in Florence, Colorado, were investigated for killing an alleged "race traitor" while incarcerated.

Many racist activists, including radical Odinist groups like Volksfront, believe in a Northwest Imperative and are actively recruiting inmates to help them with their efforts to create an "autonomous Aryan Homeland." Based on a mix of Norse Mythology, the writings of former Klansman David Duke, the racist fantasy of *The Turner Diaries*, and the crime spree of The Order in the 1980s, the Pacific Northwest was selected as this homeland. The secession of the Northwest from the United States is believed to be achievable. Although some believe this secession can be a peaceful transition, others believe it will require armed struggle, terrorism, and a form of ethnic cleansing.

THEORETICAL PERSPECTIVE

This research on the appeal of Odinism and its influences on violence and criminal behavior builds on James Messerschmidt's feminist theory of crime. Messerschmidt has researched the ways in which male criminality is a way of "doing gender" and has argued that male crime tends to be a response to emasculating forces that undermine popular definitions of masculinity. Gender is defined differently in different cultures. In America, one of the values associated with masculinity is autonomy. Messerschmidt found that boys who felt their autonomy had been taken away perceived themselves as losing masculinity. In response, criminal behavior was a way to regain autonomy and therefore their masculinity. Referred to as structured action theory, Messerschmidt's work has demonstrated that violence is a male resource that can be drawn upon so that men and boys can demonstrate to others that they are "manly" (2000, p. 12). Messerschmidt's work is widely cited in works on hate crimes (Perry, 2001) and gangs (Joe-Laidler & Hunt, 2001). This theory will also be useful in looking at the appeal of Odinism and its influence outside of prisons.

This use of Messerschmidt's (2000) theory relates to Blazak's (1998) research, "Hate in the Suburbs: The Rise of the Skinhead Subculture." In this ethnographic study of racist skinheads, subjects found the expression of race as a way to "do gender." For example, by opposing black integration, feminists, and homosexuals, skinheads were re-asserting their white masculinity above minorities, gays, and women. Violence against specific target groups (and even other skinheads) was a way of demonstrating hegemonic masculinity. These findings have been reinforced by the research of Abby Ferber (1998), who found the images in white-supremacist discourse as motivated by a desire to reclaim a sense of lost masculinity.

The value of autonomy that Messerschmidt (2000) discusses as key to the definition of hegemonic masculinity is a valued commodity in prisons where inmates' movement is restricted 24 hours a day. Activity is controlled by both the formal prison authorities and the informal power of inmate politics, including prison-gang influences. Religious privileges allow inmates a certain amount of freedom based on their rights to practice their faith; for example, Muslims are allowed time for prayer rituals and to celebrate religious holidays.

This research investigates how prison Odinism connects the need to perform masculinity to criminality and hate-motivated violence. In turn, the findings will further the understanding of causes of racial violence, both inside and outside of prisons. This understanding will result in the ability to develop strategies to ameliorate hate-motivated violence and aggression. It is guided by the theory that the social control mechanisms of the prison undermine the masculinity of inmates. In response, inmates seek out strategies to regain autonomy and masculinity. For white inmates, the legal right to practice Odinism has become an avenue for autonomous behavior. It makes sense to hypothesize that prisoners guided by racist themes of the faith will be more likely to agree with the criminality of bias-motivated violence and seek to further "Rahowa" outside of the correctional institution.

There are varying levels of Odinist activism and commitment in prison. Previous research has shown that Christianity can serve as a coping mechanism for incarcerated populations (Zaitzow & Thomas, 2002). Some prisoners see the appeal of prison Odinism as an avenue to win prison privileges such as time for religious ceremonies, as well as a way to cope with prison life and society in general. However, those recognized as "Aryan POWs" by the white-supremacist community identify with need for aggressive racist activism. The question that remains is which end of the spectrum attracts more inmates?

For this study, it was hypothesized that inmates who had a favorable view of Odinism would have a negative view of Christianity because of its feminine tendencies, but would have positive views toward Islam because of its masculine "warrior" appeal. Additionally, Odinists were expected to have negative views of the future that required dramatic action to save the white race, instead of waiting for "racial justice" to be meted out by their god or in the afterlife.

RESEARCH METHODOLOGY

This research was conducted through a mail survey funded by the Hate Crimes Research Network (HCRN) at Portland State University, Oregon. The names of 75 self-identified Aryan POWs were collected from various white-supremacist Web sites, including

Free the Order: http://www.freetheorder.com/
White Revolution: http://www.whiterevolution.com/pow.shtml
Volksfront: http://www.volksfront-usa.org/pow.shtml

During the winter of 2003, questionnaires were sent to all inmates who had been identified by themselves or by hate groups as political prisoners in a "war against the government," which is believed to be controlled by an international Jewish conspiracy. Many of these Aryan POWs claim Odinism as their faith, while others claimed Christian Identity, Creativity, or no religious identification.

The survey was mailed from the Portland State University Sociology Department and included a prestamped return envelope. A letter requesting that inmates fill out the survey was signed by a graduate student in case the research of Randy Blazak was known to the respondent. These brief open surveys asked the following questions:

1. What is your opinion of Odinism and/or Ásatrú?
2. What is your opinion of Christianity?
3. What is your opinion of the Islamic religion?
4. In your opinion is there a heaven and, if so, how do you get into it?
5. How do you describe America's future?
6. Would you be willing to do an in-person interview about Odinism?

Of the 75 surveys mailed out, 37 were completed and returned. The 49 percent return rate is considered to be adequate, considering contacted inmates may have been released, in transfer, or simply nonresponsive. Many of the returned surveys answered questions briefly but several added additional pages of commentary. The returned letters were transcribed by a graduate student and coded in terms of gendered themes in responses. Only 5 percent of the respondents did not wish to remain anonymous. The respondents skewed toward inmates who were in federal correctional facilities. Federal inmates tend to be incarcerated on more serious offenses or civil rights violations. Federal inmates are also more likely to be residing in cells instead of dormitories, making responding to surveys a more private activity.

Follow-up letters to those who expressed interest in further interviews on the subject allowed the researcher to ask clarifying questions. In addition, a series of informal interviews was conducted with a local racist Odinist who publishes an Aryan inmate newsletter to aid in the interpretation of the findings.

FINDINGS

The data from the letters reveal some interesting patterns. Thirty-five of the 37 respondents (all those whose replies were not anonymous) agreed to participate in an in-person interview about Odinism, even if they did not feel knowledgeable on the topic. Those replying to the mail survey included four members of The Order. Respondents were coded as Odinist, Christian, or Other, based on their response to the question, "In your opinion is there a heaven and, if so, how do you get into it?" Those who answered with responses involving "halls of heroes" or Vahalla or other Norse images were coded as Odinist. For example, one subject replied,

> Well, I can only speak for my Odinist beliefs. In my opinion, heaven is reached by passing on the life force that is the blood of the race, so that our future generations will survive. By doing this, the person is, in essence, living forever, through his descendants.
>
> Odinist's are also taught through the Sagas that in death from battle, they are rewarded by living forever in the feasting halls of Valhalla, with other brave comrades and the Gods, celebrating daily the honor found through their bravery.

Those who replied with expressly Christian visions of heaven were coded as Christian (primarily Christian Identity). "Others" were those who either did not believe in heaven or gave a response that was not clearly related to one specific faith.

Description of Inmate Sample

Odinists	25	(68%)
Christians	5	(14%)
Other	7	(19%)
Total	37	(100%*)

Percentages are rounded.

While this represents a relatively small sample it is fairly representative of Aryan Prisoners of War. Subjects were both high-profile hate criminals and inmates who claimed Aryan POW status through the racial nature of their offenses. The sample is less representative of racist prison group members (known in prisons as Security Threat Groups) because there were no known members of more traditional skinhead gangs, like Nazi Low Riders or Public Enemy Number 1, in the sample. The sample was also not representative of white supremacists as a whole because of the absence of neonazis. As discussed earlier, this sample does not represent Odinists because of the exclusion of traditional nonracist heathens from the survey. However, this sample does offer a window into the belief system of a number of highly committed racist inmates that can provide questions for future research.

Views of Odinism

Not surprisingly, all those coded as Odinists had favorable views of Odinism. Christians were split on Odinism, two having favorable views, two feeling they did not fully understand it, and one having a negative view. All those who coded as "Other" had favorable views of Odinism except for one anonymous respondent who wrote:

I think Odinism is an interesting belief. I don't believe in it, it seems more like fairy tale, it reminds me a lot of "Homer's Odyssey." I do think that Odinism is a lot better and believable than religions of today because its stories can apply more to realistic situations than others. From what I know, the people I've met that follow the religion have much pride in their faith and that is what matters.

The views of Odinists about their faith were overwhelmingly framed in masculine terms. Prison Odinists see the belief as a way of acquiring a "true" ethnic identity and claiming the mantel of manhood. Comments include

I believe Odinism to be a "religion" of great value and meaning to the Nordic man. Having been authored by Nordic man in the simplest, noblest and proudest time of history, I feel it by far best reflects all that is great about the pagan spirit within us, being our primal self conscious, and it best reflects the binding thought, the eternal thought that is inherent at birth.

My experience with Odinism is limited to the prison Odinist community. I'm of the subset of that community that do not believe in literal Vikings in the sky, but do think the values embodied in the Odinist "God-Sense" are especially pertinent for imprisoned Caucasians. Most prisoners are victims of religious intolerance; they're convicted of "offenses against (an idea) the United States." Blasphemy. Odinism is a sanctuary from the twisted doctrine and intolerant tyranny of the state religion, of which they are the minority. Non-believers. Prisons is the Police State Utopia of the State religion; where it can enforce its dogmas to the extreme. A fundamental dogma of that religion is "all men are created equal," a self-evidently ridiculous assertion. Odinism, with its idealizing of Folk, and Culture, and its values in opposition to the religion of meekness and subservience is an antidote.

I believe that Odinism is an altered form of true Christianity which came about when Christians became passive and unwarrior-like. There are several areas that demonstrate parallels between Odinism and Christianity. For example, Odin is the All Father (above the other gods) and Yahweh is the All Mighty God (above all angels, Jesus, and Lucifer and the Legions of Demons.

Respondents regularly referred to blood and honor in their descriptions of Odinism, describing the belief as a "religion of the blood," where Odinists "live and die for honor."

Views on Christianity

No Odinists had a positive view of Christianity. They used feminizing terms to describe a religion that had failed to defend ethnic whites and been subverted by Jewish conspiracies. Reponses included

I feel Christianity was authored by people who at the time, were on the path to extinction and they used it as a tool to give their otherwise honorless, cowardly people, a crutch to stand on, on which to fight and uprise to save themselves. I feel it is a religion full of contradiction that when applied to conventional thought and even uneducated debate can be seen for the farce that it is.

A religion of lies, contradictions and one all can embrace, it robs people of their culture and heritage, and goes against the laws of nature.

It is a foreign religion created by a foreign people who were not my ancestors. It is considered a "slave religion," requiring its adherents to bend knee and neck. It coddles the weak and the lame.

It is my opinion that Christianity is a mental affliction that is retarding our folk. Millions of our folk have been murdering each other under the Christian banner. I believe it is a religion for weak people.

While expressing negative views toward Christianity, Odinists were careful to not alienate their Christian Identity comrades. Repeatedly Odinists described the force that feminized Christianity as a result of Jewish agency. One subject articulated it this way:

I believe we can safely conclude that after 2003 years of Christianity, it has been of no help whatsoever to the white race. It did however plunge the white race into a thousand years of the dismal dark ages and has been a major enemy of the white race ever since. It has aided and abetted the Jews and put the skids under the White race at every opportunity. After 2003 years of Christianity and spooks in the sky insanity is the white race in a better or worse position relative to the prevent flood of mud races that threaten to engulf own planet? Christ-insanity is a demeaning, self destructive slave philosophy. "Delenda Est Judica."

Views of Islam

Contrary to expectations, Odinists did not have a favorable view of Islam. It was initially thought that the Muslim idea of jihad, or holy war, would be appealing to Odinists as a masculine call to arms justified by faith. Slightly less than a third (29%) had favorable comments about Islam, such as

Well, I haven't given the Islamic religion a lot of thought, as its belief system seems to be foreign to those teachings I have learned.

However, I realize they are a major force in the world today, and the true Islamics of the Middle East appear very devout to their religious beliefs, to the point that many of them are willing to fight to the death for what they believe, which to me is an admirable and honorable virtue, perhaps a virtue that may one day be required for our people for their preservation.

Though referencing, in its roots, the same texts as Christianity, Islam is much less hypocritical in doing so. Islam does much more of "practicing what it preaches" A Nation, in its proper definition, is a people with common ethnicity, culture, and values. Law is the generalization of moral values. Government is the power (force) that is delineates and enforces law. All power comes from faith. Faith means sufficient belief to cause action. Belief, insufficient to cause action, is meaningless. Belief in one thing, while actions empower something different is hypocrisy. And cowardice. "Government" and "Religion" are interchangeable terms. "Believing" in one religion/government, while serving and obeying (empowering) another is "separation of church and state." Another term for it is "mental illness." I would be as unhappy under an Islamic theocratic tyranny as I am under the democratic (man's rule/man's god) [theocratic] tyranny. But I admire their consistency and courage in living their faith.

Half of the Odinists expressed an unfavorable view of Islam, identifying it with minority populations of Muslims, but not terrorists. Comments included

Islam is just one more simple perversion of the Old testament Hebrew text. Whether its Jesus and Yahweh, or Mohammed and Allah, its all in bed with Zionism and demands that all free men around the world be subservient to some omnipotent spooks in the sky. It seems to help keep a few Negroes from selling crack, so what the hell, let them have their fun.

The religion of Islam is definitely Anti-white in its foundations. I believe that Islamic practices grew from the descendents of Esau (which sold and later despised his birthright), and is an eternal struggle between the white race and the defiled descendents of Esau. (Jacob's bloodline was kept pure while Esau no longer preserved the same bloodline, therefore defiling it as race mixing always will).

The remaining 20 percent had no particular view of Islam.

Views of the Future

Prison Odinists hold very negative views of the future of race relations in America. Only one respondent expressed any optimism for his racial situation, saying, "I think that the white race, that is the Northern European stock, will eventually wake up to the fact that there is a serious racial problem in America." The remaining 24 Odinists expressed beliefs that the white race would continue to be emasculated by the social forces lined up against it. Nearly all the Odinists discussed a violent or militaristic solution to the problem requiring "warriors" and "battle." Many expressed the idea of "the Northwest Imperative," a belief that an "Aryan Homeland" (like Serbia) should be established within the continental United States. Responses include

I believe America will become balkanized, it's already happening. You have the mestizos, the niggers, and the slopes all wanting their own communities for years now and it's only getting worse. Do I feel there will be a war? Maybe. I feel if the white man is pushed far enough into a corner he will defend himself violently.

The "Melting Pot" experiment was doomed from the start. How can people with differing ethnicity, culture, and values (the source of law)—with different laws in their hearts—live in peace under one law? There is no amount of force that a state can possess (even the world's only superpower!) to maintain this illusion. Civil war, bloodshed, balkanization is a certainty. It's just a matter of when.

I do not live to sit around and blame others for my or our problems. The white race is in this dilemma because it has become too weak to properly defend itself. Our Achilles' heel has been discovered and will be used against us until we either fight back, draw back, or become extinct.

We seem to let every other race come over to the country and we support them while they rob, rape, and murder the white race. How many blacks rape white women compared to whites who rape black. We need to go ahead and set up a white part of the U.S. and keep all others out.

I think that the racial future for America is dim and very oppressive unless we "turn our plowshares into swords" and destroy those dark forces and mongrel hordes (all Jews and non-whites must be killed, men, women, and children). It is a sin to kill another white person. The Ten Commandments were meant for the white people (called Israelites). "Thou shalt not kill," an Israelite cannot kill an Israelite but is required to kill strange or alien races of mankind.

CONCLUSION

The racist Odinist inmates in this study shared a negative view of Christianity. This negative value was based on the perception of Christianity as a feminizing religion. Follow-up interviews reinforced this point, with one Odinist simply responding, "Why would I subscribe to a religion that tells me to love my enemy?" Another response put it more clearly: "All I know is that Odin could kick Jesus' ass." Similarly, Odinists had a negative view of the future, clearly articulating forces that are believed to undermine straight, white male hegemony. These forces included minority reproduction rates, black rapists, Jewish conspiracies, homosexuality, and feminism. One follow up letter was signed, "Endangered white man."

Contrary to expectations, there was no consistent opinion on Islam. The local racist Odinist shed some light on this finding. While racial separatists who desire to create an "Aryan homeland" have some admiration of radical Islamic separatists, like the Palestine Liberation Orgainization, who have created ethnically defined spaces through violent struggle, the world of the prison is much different. According to the contact (and implied in the letters), inside the prison, Islam more closely resembles the black nationalist organization know as the Nation of Islam (NOI), associated with Minister Louis Farrakhan and Malcolm X. NOI followers believe that whites were created by an evil scientist. Prison Odinists often interact with black Muslims who are using their religion to justify status over whites (ironically, just as racist Odinists do).

Prison Odinists belong to a subculture that sees a world in crisis. White men are undermined by black rapists, Jewish media influences, and "multicultural Muslims." Christianity, the traditional faith of white supremacists, is seen as a feminized faith that has allowed the enemies of the white race to advance while Christians made "claims of peace-love-harmony" and turned the other cheek. This articulation of white emasculation is consistent with the findings of Ferber (1998). Her analysis of white-supremacist discourse found recurring themes of surrendered masculinity and a need to violently reclaim the gendered status of white men.

The Odinists in this study portray an eroded culture where white men are being bred out of existence. Several subjects repeated the belief that only 8 percent of the world's population is white, only 2 percent are white women of child bearing age. They put their faith in a racial awakening and a violent battle for a white-only homeland where the honored warriors are rewarded the entry into the Hall of Heroes in Valhalla. These inmates, by virtue of being listed as Aryan POWs, are in regular contact with rank-and-file members of the white-supremacist movement. Some, like Order members Richard Kemp and the late David Lane, both of whom participated in this study, have been involved in Odinist outreach outside of the prison. Lane's Odinist writings often appear on Web sites like www.mourningtheancient.com and www.pyramidprophecy.net. Their religious justification for racial separation has become more normative in traditional hate groups, like Volksfront, that now promote themselves as a "heritage" group instead of a skinhead group.

Hate groups can be a disruptive force in a society that values diversity and tolerance. While some of these groups are merely exercising their constitutional rights, many others have been listed as terrorist groups by the Federal Bureau of Investigation and law enforcement. As mentioned, some of these terrorists have claimed to be Odinists. Academic researchers should lead the way in understanding the genesis of Odinism in America's prison and how that influences the activity of hate groups in the general population.

This research serves as a starting point for other criminologists and sociologists to understand the causes and manifestations of an ideology of domination and the role that prison Odinism has in the larger racist movement as well as how legal authorities make decisions with respect to inmates' religious liberties. Additionally, the results of this research will allow criminal justice workers to make more informed decisions regarding the management and monitoring of Odinist inmates and parolees.

Odinism is still an enigma to many sociologists who study violence and aggression, and to people who work with inmates and ex-inmates. For example, Odinists often use an ancient runic alphabet that can also serve as a secret prison or gang code. Acts of violence may be committed to honor Norse icons or commemorate events important in Odinism, like Leif Erickson Day (October 9). The desire to respect unique religious choices may lead investigators not to research how faith can also reinforce violence.

After this research was completed, the founder of European Kindred agreed to be interviewed. Recently paroled in 2007 and living in a halfway house, he was looking for work and a way to get his life back on track with the prison gang world behind him. He still clung to his Odinist beliefs. When asked about his clearly visible swastika tattoo, he replied that it was merely a reflection of his German ancestry. He was struggling with reconciling his race-based religion with the demands of living in a diverse society, saying,

> When we (racists) come out, we really have nowhere to go. We're thrown in with all the nonwhites. All competing for the same shitty jobs. Some of us have gotten welding jobs down at (a shipping yard) but even that is pretty diverse. I've gotta work with these people and I'm not really used to it.

The following year he was back in police custody after he and his girlfriend were arrested for selling a handgun to another individual (Bernstein, 2008).

In September 2008 I spent an evening in one of the largest prisons in Texas interviewing 16 self-identified Odinists. Most of these men expressed concern that their faith had been perverted by violent racists and wished to clear the name of an ancient and noble belief. But the three Odinists I interviewed in the Administrative Segregation Unit of the prison clung to the belief that Odinism reinforced the supremacy of their European ancestry. Prisons will increasingly be confronted with the conflict between legitimate neopagans and racists who are looking for a cover for their beliefs. As prison Odinists are paroled along with millions of other incarcerated Americans, their impact on the community as well as on the white-supremacist subculture will need to be studied.

Future research can have practical applications. Knowledge of prison Odinism would allow parole boards to assess plans for continued Odinist activities upon inmates' release. This research can provide correctional facilities' staffs with information to help them understand and deal with the growing role that Odinism plays in correctional facilities. Finally, such information can provide law enforcement and probation/parole officers with knowledge to assist them in managing released Odinists. It is the belief that this research will be useful in understanding a new trend in intolerance and will be useful in the amelioration of social conflict.

REFERENCES

Ásatrú Folk Assembly. (2003). Retrieved October 9, 2005, from http://runestone.org/

Anti-Defamation League. (2002). *Dangerous convictions: An introduction to extremist activities in prison.* New York: Author.

Bernstein, M. (2008, April 1). Tape nails firebomb suspects. *The Oregonian*, p. B1.

Blazak, R. (1998). Hate in the suburbs: The rise of the skinhead subculture. In L. McIntyre (Ed.), *The Practical Skeptic: Readings in Sociology* (pp. 49–57). Mountain View, CA: Mayfield.

Etter, G. W. (2001). Totemism and symbolism in the white supremacist movements: Images of an urban tribal warrior culture. *Journal of Gang Research, 8*(2), 49–75.

Ferber, A. L. (1998). *White man falling: Race, gender, and white supremacy.* Lantham, MD: Rowman & Littlefield.

Gardell, M. (2003). *Gods of the blood: The pagan revival and white separatism.* Durham, NC: Duke University Press.

Goodrick-Clarke, N. (2002). *Black sun: Aryan cults, esoteric Nazism and the politics of identity.* New York: New York University Press.

Hamm, M. S. (1993). *American skinheads: The criminology and control of hate crimes.* Westport, CT: Praeger.

Joe-Laidler, K., & Hunt, G. (2001). Accomplishing femininity among girls in the gang. *The British Journal of Criminology, 41*, 656–678.

Levin, B. (2003). Radical religion in prison. *Intelligence Report, 3*, 61–64.

Messerschmidt, J. (1993). *Masculinities and crime: Critique and reconceptualization of theory.* Lanham, MD: Rowman & Littlefield.

Messerschmidt, J. (2000). *Nine lives: Adolescent masculinities, the body, and violence.* Boulder, CO: Westview Press.

Moser, B. (2002). From the belly of the beast: A white supremacist plot hits the streets—with an unusual ëaryaní at the helm. *The Intelligence Report,* Winter 2002, No. 108, pp. 8–17. Montgomery, AL: Southern Poverty Law Center.

Odinic Right. (2005). *What is Odinism.* Retrieved October 9, 2005, from http://www.odinic-rite.org/

Perry, B. (2001). *In the name of hate: Understanding hate crimes.* New York: Routledge.

Smith, R. C., Sr. (2002). Dangerous motorcycle gangs: A facet of organized crime in the Mid-Atlantic region. *Journal of Gang Research, 9*(4), 33–44.

Southern Poverty Law Center (SPLC). (2000). Pagans and Prison. *The Intelligence Report,* Spring 2000, No. 98, Author.

Zaitzow, B. H., & Thomas, J. (2002, April). *Praise the Lord and get me the hell outta here: The role of religion on prison coping.* Paper presented at the 2002 Southern Sociological Society Meeting, Baltimore, MD.

CHAPTER 3

THE SPACE OF RACIAL HATE

Kathleen M. Blee

The spatial dimensions of racist groups are revealing, yet often overlooked. Paradoxically, modern organized racial hate is both emplaced and nonplaced. That is, racial hate groups are simultaneously rooted in specific geographic settings and oddly placeless. Reflecting their spatial contexts, locations, and geographic scales (Flint, 2003a), racist groups both inhabit local, material places and exist in abstract, immaterial space (Gieryn, 2000). The peculiar entanglement of emplaced and nonplaced concerns in modern U.S. racist groups provides a way to understand new dimensions of organized racial hate and violence.

Organized racism in the contemporary United States encompasses a variety of groups scattered across the country with differing ideologies, agendas, tactics, and viability. Here, I focus primarily on groups that express overt racist and anti-Semitic ideas, the Ku Klux Klan, neo-Nazis, and Christian Identity groups. Perhaps the most widely recognized racist group is the Ku Klux Klan, a movement that traces its identity back to the rural white Southerners who terrorized African Americans and their white supporters in the years following the Civil War. Today there are a handful of fairly small Ku Klux Klan groups, generally in the South or Midwest, with a scattering of chapters in other regions. Most Klans have experienced considerable decline in recent decades, despite efforts by various Klan leaders to revitalize the movement either by moving in a more politically mainstream direction, toward an image of the "business suit Klan," or by allying with more extreme and overtly violent groups.

Generally more vibrant than the Klan are the numerous neo-Nazi groups that operate under different names in various locales. These range from small groups that emulate World War II–era German Nazism or work to create a modern U.S. version of a Nazi state, like the National Socialist Movement, Aryan Nations, or National Alliance, to groups of young white-power skinheads operating under names like Volksfront, White Wolves, and Northern Hammerskins. One key to the vitality of neo-Nazis is the success that some have had in attracting younger members through white-power music concerts and festivals. Neo-Nazi groups are found across the country, although most cluster on the East and West Coasts. They operate with a loose, ganglike structure that promotes a culture of violence against racial enemies as well as against friends and racial comrades.

A third and more complicated sector of the racist movement is based on a philosophy known as Christian Identity. Depicting Jews as the literal descendants of Satan and African Americans and other peoples of color as nonhuman, Christian Identity preaches eternal warfare against Jews, nonwhites, and those they regard as the allies of Jews. Christian Identity has penetrated into traditional racist groups, so a number of Klan and neo-Nazi leaders now identify themselves as Christian Identity ministers. It also exists in explicitly Christian Identity communities that operate under names like Church of the True Israel, Yahweh's Truth, and Scriptures for America.

In this chapter, data are drawn from extensive ethnographic observations of racist-group events, analysis of racist-movement documents and Internet postings, and semistructured interviews with Ku Klux Klan, neo-Nazi, and white-power advocates from around the country.[1] Using recent theories of spatiality in social life, three aspects of contemporary organized racial hate are explored: its simultaneous localized and globalized character, its strength in racially homogenous places, and the increasing centrality of anti-Semitism in racist groups. Understanding its spatial dimensions can reveal much about the complex and dangerous world of the racist right.

LOCAL AND GLOBAL

The first issue is the emplaced and nonplaced nature of U.S. organized racism. In the terminology of geographic theorists, the question is do modern racist groups dwell in *places*—that is, in finite and bounded locations that have physical form that is made by human work (what Thomas Gieryn (2000, p. 465) characterizes as "stuff") and invested with meaning, history, and value? Or are today's organized racist groups detached from boundaries, territories, and meaningful interpretive locations, existing in a placeless *space* (Gieryn, 2000)? To put the question in more familiar terms, is organized racial hate best understood as a form of reactionary localism that can be traced to the social conditions and tensions of particular nations, regions, or locales—that is, an outgrowth of the narrow, specific, and immediate concerns of its advocates, like machine-wrecking in early industrial societies or anti-immigrant English-only movements today? Or are racist movements yet another disturbing underside of political globalization, a result of a clash of cultures that transcends the concerns of particular places? The answer is not straightforward.

On the one hand, it is clear that modern organized racial hate is intensely but narrowly emplaced. Racist groups are found in many places (Southern Poverty Law Center, 2007),[2] but there are pronounced concentrations in a small range of places—largely in the South and on the East and West Coasts. Moreover, even within these geographic locations, racist groups operate in a very constricted range of places. They meet, publish flyers and newsletters, and post their messages to the Internet largely from the homes of their members. They burn crosses in the fields of friendly landowners. They socialize with each other and recruit new members at white-power concert venues in out-of-the-way places like marginal music clubs and abandoned warehouses. And their headquarters—for the few groups that maintain these—are generally bedraggled clusters of old trailers or ramshackle buildings.

Racist activists envision a future for themselves in an even narrower geographic territory. Over the past decades, many hoped to move to isolated parts of the Pacific Northwest—an area they characterize as environmentally and racially pure—and then collectively secede from the rest of what they regard as a racially and environmentally polluted United States. A few did so, living in racist compounds far from public sight. Their efforts to establish a racist homeland in the Pacific Northwest shaped a widespread sense that the region is a uniquely racist place. But such a conclusion assumes that racist activists operate in the locations they come from, ignoring the deliberate migration of racists across locations. In fact, it is not that a place like Idaho produces a disproportionate share of racists. Rather, racist enclaves have been created in Idaho and elsewhere through the deliberate settlement of racists who come from other places.

One interesting characteristic of the racist spaces created in the Pacific Northwest, and to a lesser extent in other regions, is that they are prefigurative. They provide a framework in which groups can model the social relationships that they advocate for society as a whole. Generally, scholars have termed as prefigurative those spaces associated with progressive or leftist social movements, such as feminist bookstores, communal living spaces, and activist groups that practice the traits they are seeking to create in the larger society like egalitarianism, shared leadership, or internal cooperation (Breines, 1989; Polletta, 1999). Racist-group spaces, in contrast, prefigure very different values, such as racial separation, antiegalitarianism, and internal hierarchy.

It is not only a desire to retreat into isolated areas that makes racist groups operate in ever more restricted spatial locations. They also are engaged in spatial retrenchment because they fear detection and prosecution by authorities. Such concerns have made many racist groups increasingly wary about interacting with strangers and unwilling to recruit those who lack personal ties to current members. Accelerating this trend has been the recent shift in the racist movement to what its leaders term "leaderless resistance," which replaced earlier racist structures of linked organizations and networks with an isolated small-cell structure that is more difficult for authorities to penetrate. The Internet and other forms of telecommunication have made some social movements that lack place and location both possible and successful (Adams, 1996)—witness the efforts of MoveOn.org to mobilize against U.S. involvement in Iraq. Yet, even as some racist groups have access to high-tech equipment and know-how, they recruit and form networks in ever more locally restricted fashions, a point that Scarpaci and Frazier (1993) make about other forms of modern protest.

It is misleading, however, to regard racist groups as simply emplaced, or as hopelessly bound to the local. Organized racists also operate in immaterial space. While their organizations are bounded and territorial, the ideas that drive racist localism are surprisingly broad. Indeed, and ironically, it is precisely because U.S. racist groups are developing nonlocal strategies, networks, and ties that they see a need to operate in a more constricted space.

Until recently, most U.S. racist groups operated as national groups. They had few networks with racists outside the U.S., and their agendas reflected nationalism and xenophobia, with an emphasis on "America first" and "100 percent Americanism." Nationalism and xenophobia still flourish in some areas of the racist movement, but these ideas are declining. Instead, U.S. racist groups are increasingly embracing ideas of internationalist pan-Aryanism, creating ideological and sometime actual links to racist and anti-Semitic networks around the world. Such internationalism makes allegiance to any particular nation meaningless or antithetical to a racist agenda. At the same time, fear of an apocalyptic worldwide Jewish conspiracy pushes racist groups toward envisioning, if not enacting, ever more spectacular acts of violence and terrorism. This increases their desire to avoid detection by the authorities and furthers the trend away from structured and linked racist groups toward loose networks of small racist cells.

In their move toward internationalism and a diffuse cell structure, racist groups are creating new and differently bordered *places* that reflect their adoption of the deliberately *unplaced* (spatial) ideas of pan-Aryanism. Thinking about organized racism this way, as operating within the tensions of space and place, helps avoid common errors of understanding about modern U.S. racist groups. For example, by considering the broad spatial aspirations of organized racism, we are reminded that these groups are not simply reactionary. In fact, few racist groups simply glorify the past as reactionary movements do, since racist groups depict past times as having been sullied by racial contention and intermixing. Too, recognizing the broad spatial sweep of organized racism undermines too-easy characterizations of racism as a classical fascist movement since, unlike fascist groups, many organized racists disdain the U.S. government, regarding it as irrevocably tied to Jewish interests or what they term a "Zionist Occupation Government" (ZOG). Rather, the allegiances of modern racist groups are to the ideals of racial unity and racial purity; the borders of race may—but often do not—coincide with national boundaries. Moreover, a spatial understanding of modern racism prevents misleading depictions of racist groups as either simply swept on the tide of political globalization or as laggards guarding the parochial interests of their advocates. To the contrary, organized racism in the United States is neither simply globally expansive nor narrowly national or local. U.S. racist groups have become more emplaced—in the sense that they retreat to confined spatial arenas—but their retreat has come about at the same time—and because—the ideas that motivate them are increasingly placeless or global. Thinking spatially thus allows us to understand the ways in which the localism and the globalism of racial hatred are complementary. As telecommunications links far-flung racists together, Aryan supremacy outweighs earlier xenophobic, national racial agendas, encouraging the constriction of movement and membership that reduces their vulnerability to detection. A particularly striking example of how the U.S. racist right straddles space and place is their admiration for violent Middle Eastern Islamic fundamentalists (with whom they share a disdain for Jews) even as their anti-Semitic beliefs make stable alliances with Islamic groups impossible.

There is a further spatial paradox here, related to the geographic concept of scales. The localized racial spaces and organizing structures of U.S. racist groups that are created in response to globalizing ideologies of pan-Aryanism both enable certain kinds of challenges, seen in the increasing aspirations of many groups toward violent terrorism, while they foreclose other possible challenges, particularly efforts to target enemies outside the United States. Just as geographic theorists have criticized what they term "state-centric social science" (Flint, 2003b, p. 98) for failing to appreciate how social life is moving toward a global geographic scale, so too are U.S. racist groups trapped in a problem of scale. Increasingly, their strategic visions are global. But their organization, and thus the targets that are effectively accessible for them to attack, are national or local. The odd result is that racist groups bomb tiny land offices in Nevada in an effort to combat international Jewry. U.S. racist groups can be violent and their ambitions are even more so, but their inability to operate across geographic scales limits their strategic effectiveness, especially compared to more globalized networks of terrorism. Place and space operate, in this case, with intertwined but inverse dynamics.

ANTI-SEMITISM

A second issue about the spatial nature of modern organized racism is the recent centrality of anti-Semitism in the movement, against the general secular trend of declining anti-Semitism in the general population of the United States. Although hatred of Jews has been an element of racist ideology throughout U.S. history, it is only in the past few decades that it has assumed a particularly important place in virtually all U.S. racist groups. In part, the widespread infusion of anti-Semitism occurred as racist groups adopted the doctrines of Christian Identity, which spread from Britain through Canada to the United States. In the doctrine of Christian Identity, Jews are literally agents of Satan who, to divert attention from their nefarious works, foment racial antagonism among other groups. Thus, according to Christian Identity adherents, Jews are responsible for the prolonged historical tension between blacks and (Aryan) whites in the United States. In the doctrine of Christian Identity, Jews, even more than people of color, have interests that are antithetical to those of Aryan whites.

The belief that the primary racial antagonism is between Jews and Aryans differs considerably from traditional U.S. racist notions that the major division in society is between blacks and whites. Indeed, adding anti-Semitic ideas into the traditional black vs. white framework of racist thought has produced complications for organized racists. Why this is so is best understood by thinking about the sociogeographic concept of scale, especially if we think of scales as "not simply an external fact awaiting discovery but a way of framing conceptions of reality" (Delaney & Leitner, 1997, cited in Marston, 2000, p. 221). The issue of scale arises because U.S. racists have long believed that racial groups are identifiable by their skin color. Yet Christian Identity argues that Jews are not a physically identifiable social group. Rather, they view Jews as a highly abstracted, conspiratorial force that rules in an unseen and unknowable fashion, controlling all aspects of life from international finance to the minutiae of personal fate. Such abstraction makes Jews difficult to attack, as compared to traditional enemies of racist groups like African Americans, Hispanics, Catholics, and nonwhite immigrants who can be contained through enforcement of racial borders, privileges, spatial separation, and expulsion. But, if they are placeless, Jews cannot be stopped by these means. The notion of a worldwide Jewish conspiracy that is the basis of modern racist-group anti-Semitism is the belief that Jewish communists, bankers, academics, doctors, and UN officials are everywhere and thus nowhere. The Jewish conspiracy is frightful because it cannot be emplaced and thereby combated. A 2007 posting titled "What is Next from the Jews" on the Nazi Web site "Stormfront, White Pride, World Wide" is illustrative, describing how Jews

> caused the Great Depression with their Federal Reserve and manipulation of the markets. In the midst of the turmoil and despair, FDR swooped in and defeated on the Constitution as he grabbed more and more power

for the federal government to be used against our race later on in the "Civil Rights Movement." During this usurpation of White control and identity, they laid the foundations for today's "multicultural" America of affirmative action, bussing, hate speech, and every imaginable flavor of political correctness. Only recently, we have experienced another power grab in the aftermath of 911 under the auspices of the "Patriot Act" and the Military Commissions Act . . . [But] the winds of change are beginning to blow . . . What does he do then? Cause a massive global economic collapse to attempt one more power grab that will end any chance at peaceful resistance? Back off for a while and let things cool off so that he doesn't appear so overt in his machinations (We know from history that the jew can't stop himself and always over does it, becoming the cause of his own ill fate)? Continue to push for unpopular wars in the Middle East while stepping up the "terrorist" rhetoric? (Stormfront, 2007, para. 14)

In the anti-Semitic worldview of modern organized racism, the very invisibility and amorphousness of Jewish power are markers of its dangerous strength. To racist groups, Jews are the ultimate expression of immateriality, as they are spatial rather than emplaced.

Finally, racist activists see themselves as fighting for the rightful place of Aryans across the globe. They envision—or in Benedict Anderson's (1991) term "imagine"—the possibility of a global Aryan community. Yet the notion of global Aryanism is highly problematic. Just as studies have shown that whiteness is invisible to its possessors because those who have privilege find it difficult to see their privilege (Frankenberg, 1993), so too is Aryanness invisible to the population that organized racists regard as the Aryan race. Thus, racist activists must "imagine" into existence an Aryan community when they are among the few who even identify themselves as Aryan. They try to do so by naming themselves as Aryan, inventing a lineage of Aryan culture, and creating an Aryan history (Goldberg, 1993). Yet these efforts are difficult to sustain. For example, attempts to create a glorious Aryan history by celebrating Hitler's ascension to power in Germany might bolster a sense of Aryan pride, but in the context of the United States it also risks incurring the ire of those who regard Hitler's Germany as an enemy. Similarly, suggesting a glorious Aryan lineage that can be traced back to ancient Nordic gods risks celebrating a religion that is antithetical to many in the U.S. racist movement (Blee, 2003). The competing scales of race and nation are thereby entangled in current racist ideologies.

SOCIAL HOMOGENEITY

The final issue concerns the existence of organized racism in racially homogenous places. The common assumption is that multiracial spaces are most likely to experience racial antagonism due to intergroup conflict and competition. Yet there are many counterexamples that suggest this assumption might not be true. Anti-immigrant sentiment is high in the fairly racially homogenous country of Sweden. Anti-Semitism persists in modern Poland, despite its tiny Jewish population. In the United States, the massive Ku Klux Klan of the 1920s was fueled by anti-Catholicism in robustly Protestant communities. Today's racist groups recruit youth from suburban schools with few racial minorities (Blee, 1991; Pred, 2000). How is it that social sameness can be the cradle of racism?

One way to understand the strength of racism in racially homogenous places is to use a central observation of social geography: places are made, they don't just appear (see Miller, 2000). Racialized spaces are thus the effect (as well as perhaps the cause) of racial actions and ideas in the past (Kobayashi & Peake, 2000; Sullivan, 2001). Sweden's whiteness, or Indiana's Protestantism, or Poland's Christianity, or suburban U.S. whiteness are not sui generis; they are not historical accidents. Rather, the respective racial compositions of the places are legacies of prior racial actions in which immigrants were barred, non-Protestants prevented from settling, Jews killed or expelled, or nonwhites unable to enter. Thus, what we observe when we see Sweden or Indiana or Poland or suburban U.S. communities today are slices of geohistory that are the culmination of sequences of prior actions and events (Pred, 1981). The racial geography of places, perhaps better termed the "accomplishment of racial place" (Molotch, Freudenburg, & Paulsen, 2000), reflects the effects of actions that configure spaces differently. Their racial homogeneity is the sedimentation of racial practices of inclusion or exclusion, possibilities or their foreclosure, that occurred in the past and continue into the present.

In a geographic sense, racism is about matching territories to races, assessing who belongs and who does not belong in certain spaces, and expelling those who do not belong (Perry & Blazak, 2007). This is why homogenous spaces can sustain racist groups. Racist groups do not require spaces of overt racial antagonism or racial competition. They just need social contexts in which race is a clear marker of borders. Racist groups flourish when communities recognize racial distinction and racial hierarchies, either by their presence or by their absence.

CONCLUSION

In conclusion, where do we find the space of racial hate? It is found in tightly bound dynamics of localism and spatiality; in struggles over poorly integrated scales of Aryanism, whiteness, and nationality; and in shifting definitions of inclusion and exclusion. It is too easy to dismiss today's racist groups as hopelessly confused, strategically unreflexive, and tied to flash points of racial and political turmoil. Using a spatial lens, however, helps us see modern racist groups differently, as entities that struggle with competing dynamics of space and place, interacting scales of ideology and organization, and contexts that are both restricting and enabling. Perhaps the greatest contribution of the spatial lens in this area is to underscore the weaknesses and to warn of the possible strengths of organized racism in the United States and elsewhere.

NOTES

1. Details of the methodology of this study are found in Blee (2002).
2. The Southern Poverty Law Center lists racist groups by location, with all groups represented equally, regardless of their size. This can create a misleading impression of geographic spread since many racist groups are very small. The distribution of larger racist groups is more geographically concentrated.

REFERENCES

Adams, P. C. (1996). Protest and the scale politics of communications. *Political Geography, 15*(5), 419–441.

Anderson, B. (1991). *Imagined communities: Reflections on the origin and spread of nationalism* (Rev. ed.). London and New York: Verso.

Blee, K. M. (1991). *Women of the Klan: Racism and gender in the 1920s.* Berkeley: University of California Press.

Blee, K. M. (2002). *Inside organized racism: Women in the hate movement.* Berkeley: University of California Press.

Blee, K. M. (2003). The geography of racial activism: Defining whiteness in multiple scales. In C. Flint (Ed.), *Spaces of hate: Geographies of hate and intolerance in the U.S.* New York: Routledge, pp. 49–68.

Breines, W. (1989). *Community and organization in the new left, 1962–1968: The great refusal.* Piscataway, NJ: Rutgers University Press.

Flint, C. (2003a). Introduction. In C. Flint (Ed.), *Spaces of hate: Geographies of hate and intolerance in the U.S.* New York: Routledge Press, pp. 1–20.

Flint, C. (2003b). Political geography II: Terrorism, modernity, governance and governmentality. *Progress in Human Geography, 27*(1), 97–106.

Frankenberg, R. (1993). *White women, race matters: The social construction of whiteness.* Minneapolis: University of Minnesota Press.

Gieryn, T. F. (2000). A space for place in sociology. *Annual Review of Sociology, 26,* 463–496.

Goldberg, D. T. (1993). *Racist culture: Philosophy and the politics of meaning.* Malden, MA: Blackwell.

Kobayashi, A., & Peake, L. (2000). Racism out of place: Thoughts on whiteness and an antiracist geography in the new millennium. *Annals of the Association of American Geographers, 90*(2), 392–403.

Marston, S. A. (2000). The social construction of scale. *Progress in Human Geography 24*(2), 219–242.

Miller, B. A. (2000). *Geography and social movements: Comparing antinuclear activism in the Boston area.* Minneapolis: University of Minnesota Press.

Molotch, H., Freudenburg, W., & Paulsen, K. E. (2000). History repeats itself, but how? City character, urban tradition, and the accomplishment of place. *American Sociological Review, 65*, 791–823.

Perry, B., & Blazak, R. (2007). *Places for races*: The white supremacist movement's organization of U.S. geography." Presented at the 2006 Annual Meeting of the American Society of Criminology, Los Angeles, CA, November 1–4.

Polletta, F. (2006). "Free spaces" in collective action. *Theory and Society, 28*(1), 1–38.

Pred, A. (1981). Production, family, and free-time projects: A time-geographic perspective on the individual and societal change in nineteenth-century U.S. cities. *Journal of Historical Geography, 7*, 3–36.

Pred, A. (2000). Even in Sweden: Racisms, racialized spaces, and the popular geographical imagination. Berkeley: University of California Press.

Scarpaci, J. L., & Frazier, L. J. (1993). State terror: Ideology, protest and the gendering of landscapes. *Progress in Human Geography, 17*(1), 1–21.

Southern Poverty Law Center. (2007). *Hate groups active in the United States, 2006.* Retrieved October 6, 2007, from www.splcenter.org

Stormfront. (2007). *What is next from the Jews?* Retrieved October 6, 2007, from http://www.stormfront.org/forum/showthread.php/next-jews-413695.html

Sullivan, S. (2001). The racialization of space: Toward a phenomenological account of raced and antiracist spatiality. In S. Martinot & J. James (Eds.), *The problems of resistance* (pp. 86–104). Amherst, NY: Humanity Books.

CHAPTER 4

HATE ROCK: WHITE SUPREMACY
IN POPULAR MUSIC FORMS

Colin K. Gilmore

The contemporary white-supremacist movement includes a number of youth subcultural factions that are largely organized around the promotion and distribution of racist rock music. Human rights organizations dedicated to monitoring the activities of the racist right in the United States, such as the Southern Poverty Law Center (SPLC) and the Anti-Defamation League of the B'nai B'rith (ADL), have tracked the growth of this "white-power" music industry for many years. Antiracist activists argue that sales of this material help to sustain the white-supremacist movement financially while disseminating a message that may inspire unaffiliated youths to join the ranks of neo-Nazi organizations or skinhead groups (ADL, 1995, 2006; SPLC, 2001).

These concerns are well founded, as an extensive selection of music promoting white-supremacist beliefs remains available for sale or free download online. Currently, over a dozen distributors of white-power music are operating from within the United States alone. More disturbingly, recruitment campaigns involving music have been attempted by a number of white-power record labels in recent years. In 2004, an American record label launched a campaign titled "Project Schoolyard," designed to distribute free compact disc samplers of racist music to students in public schools.

While it would be a mistake to suggest a causal connection exists between any form of music and criminality, it is not uncommon for those involved in the creation of white-power music to act on their beliefs. To date, a considerable number of prominent white-power musicians have been prosecuted and incarcerated for violent criminal offenses. In addition, the profits generated from the sales of this material have previously been utilized to fund other forms of violent and criminal activity by organized white-supremacist groups (Hamm, 2004; Lowles & Silver, 1998; SPLC, 2001).

In the United States, expressions of racial intolerance are constitutionally protected forms of free speech, which gives relatively small American white-power music distributors considerable influence among racist skinheads internationally. The demand for white-power music is said to be especially high in Eastern Europe, where the largest numbers of active racist skinheads are believed to reside (SPLC, 2001). However, the performance or sale of white-power music is forbidden by law in many European countries, where symbols and rhetoric associated with the Third Reich remain heavily policed by government agencies. The German government in particular has been especially aggressive in its legal campaigns, sentencing members of white-power bands to prison for the promotion of racial hatred (Barber-Kersovan, 2003).

A number of sociologists have previously sought to explain the significance of music in shaping the identity of participants in subcultural groups. It is often argued that music helps frame reality for the individuals involved, communicating prevailing norms and values of the larger group to the listener (Hebdige, 1979; Laing, 1985; Wood, 2006). White-power musicians occupy a unique position in their respective music-based subcultures; they are cultural creators who serve to inform other participants of the group's ideological positions and normative behaviors. White-power music also shares a common frame of reference with many of the organized racist groups that collectively comprise the contemporary white-supremacist movement. Prior research suggests that people tend to become involved in the movement because of perceived status threats or feelings of anxiety they experience as a result of rapid social change. Participants may be inspired by a wide range of phenomena: changes occurring in societal gender roles, an increased sense of downward economic mobility, or the perception that demographic changes are eroding traditional status hierarchies (Blazak, 1998, 2001; Daniels, 1997; Ferber, 1998; Kimmel, 2003). The present study seeks to explore ways in which these frustrations find expression in one of the movement's primary forms of propaganda.

The following analysis is based on research that was conducted over the span of one year, utilizing a multiple-method approach to data collection. A series of interviews was completed with a purposefully chosen sample of 17 individuals currently or formerly involved in the creation or dissemination of white-power music. Participants included members of popular racist skinhead bands, the heads of two of the largest neo-Nazi organizations in the United States, several high-profile music distributors, and musicians involved in the production of various subgenres of contemporary white-supremacist music. In addition, a rigorous content analysis of popular white-power songs was conducted by studying a purposefully chosen sample of lyrical texts for thematic concentrations. The researcher also obtained and studied numerous subcultural artifacts related to white-power music, including compact discs, fanzines, newsletters, DVDs, and videotapes featuring white-supremacist musical content.

A BRIEF HISTORY OF WHITE-POWER MUSIC

White-power rock music can be likened to modern folk songs for the white-supremacist movement. Lyrics often include narratives describing prior battles or revisionist accounts of historical events in order to convey a message of racial superiority. Some white-power songs present stories of heroic figures for contemporary white supremacists, celebrating their deeds through song. Narratives such as these help define the salient issues for those committed to the white-supremacist cause and allow these ideas to be passed along to successive generations of subcultural participants. It is perhaps unsurprising that many of the dominant lyrical themes in contemporary white-power music can also be located in earlier examples of racist musical material.

Organized racist groups in the United States began utilizing music as a platform to promote their views very early in the history of recorded music. During the 1920s, a number of artists published sheet music and 78 rpm records extolling the virtues of the Ku Klux Klan. One Indiana-based label, KKK Records, released songs based on traditional religious hymns with titles like "The Bright Fiery Cross" and "Why I'm a Klansman," and lyrics focusing on anti-Catholic and anti-immigration themes (Tosches, 1977, p. 226). The founder of the American Nazi Party, George Lincoln Rockwell, also utilized music as part of his promotional and recruiting efforts. Several 45 rpm records were released by Rockwell on his own Hatennany Records label in the mid-1960s, including a release credited to "G. L. Rockwell and the Coon Hunters" (Schmaltz, 2000).

A number of small independent record labels began releasing records promoting segregationist politics and racial hatred during the civil rights era. Between the years 1966 and 1972, a songwriter and producer named Jay D. Miller ran a small independent record label devoted to racist country music called Reb Rebel Records out of his Crowley, Louisiana–based music store (Tosches, 1977). In total, the label released 21 singles and one long-playing compilation album titled "The Segregationist Hit Parade," featuring performers with names like Johnny Rebel and James Crow.

During the 1970s, music-based youth subcultures began to be viewed as potential resources for recruitment by organized racist groups in England. By 1983, the British National Front, a small right-wing political party, had launched a record label called White Noise Records in hopes of using racist music to attract larger numbers of young skinheads and punk rockers to their ranks. Among the label's first releases was a 45 rpm single titled "White Power" by a neo-Nazi skinhead band called Skrewdriver (Pearce, 1987).

Inspired by the music of Skrewdriver, other white-power skinhead bands formed throughout Britain during the 1980s. In 1987, following a dispute with National Front leadership over the use of music-generated revenue, a number of these bands joined together to create a promotional organization called Blood and Honour. This organization has since established itself internationally, with charter groups appearing in North America and numerous countries throughout Europe (Lowles & Silver, 1998). Over the last several decades, Blood and Honour charter groups have helped organize white-power concerts and attempted to establish an international network for producing and distributing neo-Nazi music (Brown, 2004).

Many of the first organized skinhead groups in North America were formed as a direct result of their participants coming into contact with the music of English white-power bands such as Skrewdriver (Hamm, 1993). A flyer distributed by one such group during the late 1980s describes, with considerable hyperbole, the formation of a new American white-power band:

> A new breed of heroes have sprung from the Midwestern soil, brave skinhead patriots ready to fight for race and nation! These talented musicians and courageous warriors have put together white power lyrics with an energetic beat to produce the best in American skinhead anthems. (Chicago Area Skinheads, flyer circa late 1980s)

White-power skinhead bands began forming during the late 1980s and early 1990s in larger American cities, utilizing provocative-sounding names like the Midtown Bootboys, the Bully Boys, Bound for Glory, Aggravated Assault, or Max Resist (Center for New Community [CNC], 1999; Lowles & Silver, 1998). These bands were formed within various localized punk scenes, performing music heavily derivative of the styles popular within the larger punk subculture at the time. Bands were typically formed by loosely organized groups of friends, who would host their own concerts in the basements of private residences or rented halls.

The North American white-power music scene received a substantial boost during the 1990s when a record label called Resistance Records launched its own professionally printed music magazine and began distributing this material through an online distribution service (CNC, 1999). In its first three years of operation, Resistance sold an estimated 60,000 to 100,000 compact discs and cassette tapes annually (SPLC, 2001). In 1999, the label was acquired by the National Alliance, a West Virginia–based organization founded by former physics professor Dr. William Pierce. Although Pierce died in 2002, the National Alliance continues to sporadically release compact discs and publish new issues of its promotional music magazine.

Although the majority of white-power music produced to date is the product of neo-Nazi skinheads, artists performing acoustic folk-styled music or various subgenres of heavy metal have become increasingly common (CNC, 1999; Moynihan & Søderlind, 1998). There is some overlap in terms of the individuals involved in the creation of these various forms of music, as well as common distribution networks for their products. Concert events are often sponsored by skinhead "crews" or white-power organizations and range from small regional gatherings to larger destination events for individuals to gather. In the United States, larger concerts are held infrequently and serve as networking opportunities for various factions within the subculture. These events often feature speakers representing neo-Nazi political organizations interspersed between performances by white-power bands.

HOW THOSE INVOLVED IN WHITE-POWER MUSIC VIEW THEIR WORK

White-power rock-and-roll music first emerged during a time when massive structural changes were occurring in the global economy, as deindustrialization contributed to a heightened sense of downward economic mobility among the white working class in the United States and abroad. Among organized white supremacists, these perceptions are often exacerbated by a sense that one's national or ethnic identity is being threatened with extinction. Hypermasculine youth subcultures, such as the white-power music scene, offer an appealing fantasy world for young men who view their previously dominant statuses to be eroding. For many, white-power music serves as their initial attraction and primary connection to the larger white-supremacist movement.

> I know that the majority of young people that are involved in any kind of pro-white activism in North America anyway, it's because of music, you know? I mean, people in jail might get [Christian] Identity literature from Aryan Nations or stuff like that. But, if it wasn't for the music, the vast majority of young people may not have ever been attracted to just pamphlets and thoughts and ideas and historical opinions, you know? That goes for myself as well, the music kind of drew me in, and you meet like-minded people and you end up talking about stuff, but the music is kind of the central point around which everything else revolves. (White-power music distributor, interview, October 7, 2006)

Live musical events provide a structure for collective activity within the white-power movement by bringing people together to communicate and form common bonds in a group setting. Concerts are more than just musical performances; they provide a context for social networking that helps keep the core of the subculture together.

> Music moves people's souls and it also brings people together of common interests, Music established a scene for the pro-white movement. Shows

are more than just concerts . . . minds gather, literature is spread, people rally. That's how the German National Socialist party began in a way, in the beer halls. So on a huge level, music has made the pro-white scene in the past two decades. (White-power musician, personal communication, November 5, 2006)

Many bands perform in front of live audiences only a handful of times, or not at all, before dissolving. While a handful of musicians have remained active long enough to perform several hundred concerts over the course of their musical career, this level of success is fairly uncommon. Live musical performances for white-power bands are inherently difficult to arrange and tend to be infrequently organized (Futrell, Simi, & Gottschalk, 2006). These events have historically attracted unwanted attention from police and anti-racist protesters, often escalating into confrontations around the venues in which they are held.

I've worked with musicians who have had families and union jobs, and to have our pictures in the newspaper, or at a venue or event that is protested by the anarchists or the Anti-Defamation League or whatever, you know, it's difficult when you try to get to a club and there's protestors there, throwing rocks and then you have the media trying to film it and stuff. It's hard for people to say, "Hey, you know, I got a day job. I don't want my boss to find out that I'm doing this." (Skinhead singer, interview, January 4, 2007)

For some of the individuals involved in white-power music, part of the appeal of the music is its inherent shock value. For many white-power musicians, it is simply appealing to be able to provoke others and be viewed as "extreme." To sing about taboo subjects openly, despite widespread condemnation of such ideas within the larger society, is also perceived to lend authenticity to the music and its creators. For some, participation in criminal activities is an additional way in which white-power musicians can demonstrate their "legitimacy" to other members of the subculture and demonstrate a commitment to group values.

When I discovered punk rock, it was an alternative and the music was edgy and raw and provoking. It made me interested in it and it's really what got me motivated to be in a band, a band like Skrewdriver, that came across so strong and seemed really genuine. And the fact that they were outcasts and stuff, that there's this forbidden band that it's almost impossible to get ahold of made it even more attractive. You know, what's the first thing, when you tell a little kid not to do something, what's the first thing that they're going to do? They're going to do it, right? So, I mean, I think the fact that it was forbidden and taboo made it way more interesting. (Skinhead singer, interview, January 4, 2007)

Those involved in the white-power music scene often describe their activities as a response to perceived threats to white economic survival, or to declining living standards for whites. Many attribute this to the economic changes brought about by globalization, or the loss of jobs to increasing numbers of immigrants in formerly all-white communities. Anxieties associated with demographic changes are common among white-power musicians, who view their rightful homeland to be in the process of being "invaded" by immigrant populations. The process of globalization is considered equally detrimental, as it weakens the traditional social arrangements of societies based upon white, heterosexual cultural hegemony.

These individuals perceive multiculturalism to be a manipulative and Jewish-controlled plot to undermine "white culture," resulting in a loss of collective boundaries in previously all-white areas. They often express concerns that other racial groups are taking away resources from the white working class, who are forced to pay for "freeloading minorities" through their tax dollars.

> In the lower classes we deal with a lot of the problematic nonwhite minorities in a very face to face fashion. This leads many of us who work hard and pay taxes to hold a grudge for supporting many lazy incompetent classes of people who generally live around us or close to our places of employment. The working class takes the poverty stricken people and welfare cases in a lot more serious of a light. Most working class people considered 'blue collar' are white folks. With that in mind, it makes it very difficult to watch those who do not attempt to speak our language, bother to get educated, or hold jobs other than selling drugs take the money we work so hard to feed ourselves and family with. It isn't the blue collar [worker] in the lower middle class or middle class, or even poverty level, committing crime. (White power guitarist, personal communication, October 13, 2006)

The identification and dehumanization of targeted groups within white-supremacist rhetoric may offer an explanation for their perceived loss of status or provide members of this subculture with a way to cope with their frustrations (Blazak, 1998, 2001). For many white-power musicians, songwriting is a means to document their feelings and express their sense of anger.

> It's just that because of my background in rock and roll and my working class history, it just seemed like a natural avenue for me to explore, was through music. I have friends that I've been associated with, that took it to a different level. I've got friends who've died in street activities. I also have some friends that are in prison, for you know, robbing banks and being revolutionary thinkers and stuff. So, everyone has a choice in deciding how they want to be involved and this was just one of the ways that worked out for me. (Skinhead singer, interview, January 4, 2007)

The anxieties of white supremacists are often exacerbated by their perception that increasing crime rates are associated with minority populations. Images in the popular media reinforce their belief that these groups pose an impending threat to the safety of themselves or other members of their communities. Some claim that these feelings stem from traumatic events that have occurred in their personal lives, including witnessing other white youths being attacked by minority gangs in school. They describe how these experiences have made them fearful of additional minority violence and served as a motivating factor for their involvement in the white-supremacist movement.

> My lyrics are a warning to what is yet to come, and an encouragement to the people to prepare for survival and to fight for freedom. Freedom has been fought for in the past and it shall be fought for once again. (White-power skinhead, personal communication, February 7, 2007)

White supremacists often describe feeling as though contemporary society is becoming increasingly totalitarian, with Jewish-run government agencies actively conspiring to suppress white citizens. The white-power musicians interviewed for the present study often discussed how they perceived the institutions of contemporary society to be controlled by Jewish influence, including all aspects of the mass media, the public school system, and major economic institutions. Participants described how the Jewish-controlled media promote music designed to corrupt the morals of white youth or to promote multiculturalism through its lyrical messages. Some participants described how they were motivated by a desire to see history presented accurately, believing the leaders and policies of the Third Reich to be unfairly vilified within other forms of media.

WHITE-POWER MUSIC AND RECRUITMENT

> As society continues to decay, as the quality of life continues to crumble, I think, more and more white youth will feel alienated, and they will be looking for answers. Right now, a lot of them feel alienated. We're trying to give them rationale for their alienation, for their anger. (White-power label owner, interview, October 3, 2006)

The potential recruitment of young people to the white-supremacist cause is one of the primary goals behind the creation and distribution of white-power music. One strategy is to target regional areas with music-based recruitment efforts, handing out large quantities of free compact discs in hopes that this material will have a contagion effect in the hands of small groups of young people. These campaigns also serve as effective publicity stunts, as the distribution of these discs tends to attract valuable media attention for the labels involved.

We're able to reach young people in a way that we were never able to reach them before. I mean, I can give a fantastic speech and I might get a hundred people listening to me. I could produce a CD and get thousands and thousands of people to hear me, so I'm able to reach a much larger audience through music. And we're really, you know, we're really trying to reach young people. Young people, I mean, we're living in the sound-bite generation, people they really don't read that much, especially young people, but they all listen to music—and when they hear the messages in the lyrics over and over again—it becomes embedded in their minds—and eventually, we hope they'll develop. (White-power label owner, interview, October 3, 2006)

Music is often used by white-power organizations to reach out to new people and "get the word out" to potential allies. The music is considered to be an effective means to spread the message of white supremacy outside of the immediate social networks of subcultural participants and to inspire others to become involved. As discussed above, members of this subculture realize that part of the appeal this music has for young people is its taboo status. This taboo helps to sell the music, as kids are attracted to the violent rhetoric and the sense that they are participating in something "forbidden."

There's a lot of frustration in America right now in general, where people are fed up with the system, they're fed up with the government taking advantage of us, opening up our borders and letting all these Third Worlders stream in here and destroy our culture and our heritage and that makes them angry, so if they can put a hard-rock CD in, whether it's a mainstream band or it's one of our bands, you know, that's another way that the message gets out to them—and we're taking full advantage of that. (White-power activist, interview, October 12, 2006)

WHITE-POWER LYRICS

What are the messages being conveyed through white-power music? Opponents and proponents of this music both argue that it plays a significant role in sustaining the contemporary white-supremacist movement, but what does the music itself communicate to the listener? In order to answer these questions, lyrical texts of popular white-power songs were collected from various sources and transcribed so that they could be studied for thematic concentrations.

The sample of white-power songs used in this analysis was obtained by consulting back issues of *Resistance Magazine*, a white-supremacist music publication that published a total of 27 issues between the years 1994 and 2007. A regular feature in these magazines is a page filled with individual "top ten" lists, in which readers submit listings of their favorite white-power songs. These lists have been featured in 23 of the 27 issues published to date,

with a combined total of 221 lists. As a way of obtaining the most representative sample possible, the frequency with which individual songs appeared on
these lists was used as the determining factor for inclusion in the analysis.

In total, 1,429 songs appear on these "top ten" lists, performed by 463 different bands. The relative popularity of these bands and their products varies
greatly, with an obvious popularity cluster around a small number of groups
and songs. For example, the band Skrewdriver appears 197 times on the lists,
nearly twice the frequency of any other group. Half of the total songs that
appear on these charts are performed by just 24 bands, with over a third of
the songs produced by 10 extremely popular groups. Table 4.1 presents the
most popular bands among the magazine's readership.

The album covers and compact disc booklets in which these releases are
packaged typically feature artwork with a consistent set of thematic elements.
Muscular skinheads brandishing weapons or posing in menacing positions
are among the most frequently depicted images. Illustrations of Viking battle
scenes or muscular warriors engaging in acts of violence are also common. In
addition, photos or illustrations from Nazi Germany are often utilized, including images reproduced from old Third Reich propaganda posters. Several of
the songs contained in this study's sample were released on albums featuring
explicit photographic images from Nazi concentration camps on their covers.

**Table 4.1   Bands Appearing Most Frequently in 221 Reader-Submitted
"Top ten" Lists in *Resistance Magazine* (1994–2007)**

Band Name	Lists
Skrewdriver	197
Bound for Glory	118
Rahowa	104
No Remorse/ Paul Burnley	76
Brutal Attack	70
Blue Eyed Devils	47
Bully Boys	40
Nordic Thunder	40
Fortress	39
Centurion	36
Berserkr	34
Max Resist	34
Landser	33
Angry Aryans	29
Midtown Bootboys	29

Some of the most frequent lyrical themes within white-power music are those describing the degraded economic and social conditions that whites in contemporary society are perceived to be experiencing. Songs that suggest the white race is being unfairly treated or persecuted by governmental agencies are common. An example of this type of lyric is featured in a song by the popular skinhead band Bound for Glory, in which the group's vocalist describes how "through hardship and struggle we have survived through the ages, we had been murdered, we had been enslaved, we had been in cages" (Bound For Glory, 1994a, Track 10).

White-power songs often lament the loss of status for the white race. The lyrics describe the loss of white-occupied territory, or a decline in racial hegemony in a formerly white-controlled nation. The songs occasionally describe the author's perception that traditional forms of white culture are disappearing. "It's getting tougher day by day, for the white man to make his pay" sings the band Definite Hate, who describe how "there's no decent jobs for us whites [because] they're given to blacks by those fucking kikes" (Definite Hate, 2001, Track 4).

The lyrics of white-power music are often directed at adversaries or groups targeted by the subculture; those identified as ideological foes or natural enemies of members of the white race. These songs frequently describe scenarios where problems are occurring within formerly tranquil neighborhoods or where there is an increase in incidents involving criminal victimization at the hands of predatory minority populations. In one song by the white-power band Day of the Sword, the lyrics focus on how "our country holds new Aryan graves, those murdered by its former slaves" (Day of the Sword, 1996, Track 1).

Over half of the songs analyzed contain lyrics organized around racial issues, though surprisingly few contain explicit racial slurs. Songs discussing black street criminals are particularly common, with lyrics describing them as drug dealers who prey upon white children or the elderly. In a song by the band Bound for Glory, for example, the lyrics describe a scenario where "low life dirt . . . roam the streets, preying on the innocent, the helpless and the weak" (Bound for Glory, 1994b, Track 8).

Immigrants are depicted in a similar manner, regularly described as predatory criminals, who both victimize the law-abiding members of society and exploit the system for financial gain. They are often portrayed as "parasites," invaders of white territory who deprive noble whites of their collective economic resources. For example, one song by the band Skrewdriver discusses how government agencies "give them money, give them jobs [yet] ignore the British whites" and how the songwriter "won't stand and watch our land be taken without a fight" (Skrewdriver, 1984, Track 1). White-power songs often advocate the expulsion of immigrant populations from what the authors perceive to be historically white-occupied territories.

Conspiratorial thinking is common among participants in this subculture, and these ideas often find expression within the lyrics of white-power music. Frequently, these conspiracies involve some type of elaborate plot devised by Jews to take power away from members of the white race. Although Jews are the most commonly mentioned conspirators within these songs, governmental agencies and the media are also frequently cited. These groups are presumed to be working in collusion, in the interests of what white supremacists perceive to be a Jewish-controlled Zionist Occupational Government (ZOG). Jews are described within white-power lyrics as though they constitute a racially homogenous and monolithic group, capable of exercising total control over nearly every aspect of contemporary society through the powerful influence of ZOG. They are often accused of covertly controlling the economy to deprive whites of their resources or using the media to promote multiculturalism. They are frequently depicted as manipulators, spreading false information regarding the Holocaust in order to gain public sympathy.

Homosexuals are another targeted group within white-power music, described as "freaks" or hypersexual perverts and almost always on the receiving end of physical violence. The lyrics often express the belief that homosexuality is another Jewish-sponsored plot to undermine the moral fabric and traditional gender relations of white society. In their song entitled "Faggots Give Rainbows a Bad Name," the singer for the skinhead band the Angry Aryans shouts, "You advertise your lifestyle, shove it right into our face, demanding equal rights, faggot's disgrace" (Angry Aryans, 1998, Track 16).

VIOLENCE IN WHITE-POWER MUSIC

In addition to dehumanizing descriptions of targeted groups, white-power lyrics often provide a plan of action for resolving specified problems or sources of social strain. A total of 68.7 percent of the songs analyzed for this study contain lyrics that address current or potential allies. The lyrics often address the listener directly, calling upon the audience to respond or act. In a song by the Australian skinhead band Fortress, the vocalist urges the listener to "throw your radio out your window, put your boot through your TV," while reassuring them that "if you're sick of that infernal bullshit, white power rock is what you need" (Fortress, 1994, Track 2).

Violence against targeted groups tends to be described as a group endeavor within this material. Collective action against targeted groups is suggested within a majority of the material analyzed, although a significant amount describes individual acts of violence as well. There is a sense of urgency in many of these statements, as songs tend to describe situations where time is running out for the white race and immediate action is required. Nearly half of the songs analyzed contain lyrics that express a call to action or direct appeal to the listener to respond to an identified problem. For example, the lyrics of a song by the band Rahowa express the idea that "we gotta rise up now, white man, take a stand," while arguing that "if we all bond together we can take back our homeland" (Rahowa, 1993, Track 1).

Within the 150 lyrical texts analyzed, a total of 95 songs contain lyrics that describe acts of violence against perceived enemies of the white race. A song by one of North America's earliest white-power skinhead bands, the Midtown Bootboys, describes a scenario in which the songwriter imagines himself to be shooting African Americans. "Bang bang, watch them die," shouts the group's vocalist, "watch the niggers drop like flies" (Midtown Bootboys, 1994, Track 10).

Within the sample of songs analyzed, a significant number suggest some form of vigilantism to resolve the problem of street crimes perpetrated by racial minorities. This is usually portrayed as a form of "mob justice" in the lyrics, with lynching being the most commonly proposed method of corporal punishment. In one song, the singer for the white-power band Berserkr directs his lyrical message to would-be victims of this sort of violence, stating that their "judgment day is here" and they have "been sentenced to death by the people of America" (Berserkr, 1994, Track 10).

A considerable amount of white-power music contains apocalyptic themes, with lyrics describing an impending and inevitable final confrontation or war between the races. Often the struggle for white supremacy is portrayed as a life or death struggle or a "fight to the death" within the lyrics. The lyrics of a song entitled "Showdown" by the band Skrewdriver describe the sequence of events that precedes this race war dramatically. "The sky darkens, night falls, the battle's coming now, your race calls," sings the group's deceased vocalist Ian Stuart, who goes on to describe how the white race will "carry on the fight 'til the day we die, against the people that would kill us for the flags we fly" (Skrewdriver, 1990, Track 7).

Criminal violence is often neutralized within this material (Sykes & Matza, 1957). In nearly 80 percent of the songs depicting criminal acts of violence against perceived enemies, the songwriter justifies the crime by shifting the responsibility for the act away from the white perpetrator. Most often, these lyrical expressions describe the target of violent victimization as somehow deserving of their fate. Racially motivated violence is often attributed to the white perpetrator's commitment to higher loyalties—an act committed out of obligation to his or her race, religion, or nation.

Some white-power songs make reference to some aspect of the skinhead subculture itself. Skinheads are typically described as street-fighting "warriors," invariably intoxicated and eager to participate in acts of violence. For example, a song by the British skinhead band No Remorse describes how legions of "white power skins in steel-capped boots" are "picking out who to annihilate" and leaving a "trail of destruction" on the streets (No Remorse, 1994, Track 1). The image that emerges from this material is of a quasi-militaristic group, hunting targeted populations and engaging them in physical confrontations.

Other organized white-supremacist groups are discussed within the material as well. For example, there are a number of songs that celebrate the activities of the imprisoned revolutionary white-supremacist organization The Order. The group was responsible for a series of violent crimes in the 1980s that included bank robberies, several bombings, and the murder of Jewish radio talk-show host Alan Berg. Robert Mathews, the group's leader, was killed in a standoff with federal authorities in 1984 and remains a highly regarded figure among many white-power activists. White-power songs often portray Mathews as a heroic figure who stole money from Jewish-controlled banks in order to further the white-supremacist cause. In a song performed by the band Nordic Thunder, the author describes how Mathews "fought off ZOG, the best he could, for he was the Aryan Robin Hood" (Nordic Thunder, 1994, Track 11).

The celebration of martyrdom and involvement in criminal activities described above offers insight into the mind-set of those involved in the often violent racist skinhead subculture. In 1994, shortly after this song was written, the singer for Nordic Thunder became another martyr for the white-power subculture. Following a white-power musical event organized to pay tribute to the deceased singer of the band Skrewdriver, he was fatally shot in an altercation with black youths in a convenience store in Racine, Wisconsin (ADL, 1995).

The white-supremacist movement has traditionally been a male-dominated subculture, and the propaganda it produces tends to reflect this fact (Daniels, 1997; Ferber, 1998). The lyrics analyzed for this study present an overwhelmingly male-centered worldview, wherein white men tend to be described either in terms of their role in the struggle for racial supremacy or as victims of an unfair system. They are often referred to as "brothers" in white-power songs, united in a common fight against perceived enemies. The Detroit-based skinhead band Max Resist, for example, recorded a song entitled "White Man," in which the author describes how white males are "here to collect our inheritance" and states that "we will take it back or we'll take our revenge" (Max Resist, 1997, Track 10).

While almost half the songs in the sample discuss white men or their role in the subculture, there are relatively few that mention white women in any capacity. Only 11 of the 150 songs contain lyrics that discuss white females. Four of these describe these women as "racial traitors," responsible for the demise of the white race through their failure to sexually reproduce with members of their own racial group. Involvement in interracial sexual relationships is attributed to the alleged promiscuity of these women, with words like "whore" and "slut" used regularly to characterize them. In a song by the Angry Aryans, the group's vocalist addresses one such woman by stating, "your body's been tainted and the purity's no more, just another white trash nigger loving whore" before calling for her execution (Angry Aryans, 2000, Track 3).

These depictions of promiscuous race-mixing females contrast sharply with a second image of white women evident within this material. In some songs, white women are revered as objects of beauty or comrades in the struggle for white supremacy. In a song by the British skinhead band Brutal Attack, the lyrics describe a romance between an "Aryan maid of pure blood" and an "Aryan man of steel," in which the female subject is described as an integral part of the future of the white race and "a gift from the gods above" (Brutal Attack, 1994, Track 6).

White women are also described within this material as a motivation for the action of white men, as a positively valued group who are in need of defense or protection. Both women and children are portrayed as victims, or in danger of being attacked by minority groups. For example, in songs describing impending racial conflicts, white men preparing for battle are often described as though they are making a noble sacrifice for other members of their family. The lyrics of a song by the Californian skinhead band Final War, for example, contains a description of a "simple man" who proclaims his wife and children "are the reason I fight this fight." Upon his deathbed, the song's subject tells his son, "now you are the one that holds the flame, carry it forth and one day we'll win" (Final War, 2002, Track 7).

CONCLUDING THOUGHTS

White-power music appears to offer an outlet for its creators, who find in this subculture a way to resolve the frustrations they feel through the performance or consumption of music. This research suggests that involvement in white-power music serves as an "imaginary subcultural solution" or "problem solver" for participants in these activities (Blazak, 1998, 2001; Clarke, 1976; Cohen, 1955). Through interaction with like-minded others, those involved are able to experience a feeling of community or brotherhood, while collectively expressing their rejection of the dominant culture's political and social values.

The lyrical content of white-power music has remarkable thematic consistency and provides insight into the dominant focal concerns and salient issues for members of the subculture as a whole. The fantasies presented in this material describe a situation where traditional social arrangements are capable of being reestablished through collective forms of violence or revolution. The lyrics often include dehumanizing descriptions of targeted groups, portraying them as inhuman monsters or conspiring threats to white survival. These depictions can be read as an attempt to justify criminal victimization at the hands of skinheads or other organized white-supremacist groups (Perry, 2001).

The songs describe scenarios in which heterosexual white male hegemony is reasserted, as society is restored to an imagined glorious past through violent or revolutionary means. The white male protagonists of white-power lyrics are portrayed as protectors of a diminishing white civilization. Their primary role within this material is to carry out remorseless physical attacks against dehumanized target groups, or participate in an impending and inevitable war between the races. This presents an appealing fantasy for young males who perceive their relative privilege to be eroding due to rapid social change. The hypermasculine warrior-themed imagery utilized in this music, as well as the covers of records and compact discs, speaks to angry and frustrated young men who see their status being threatened in a rapidly changing and heterogeneous society.

The subculture of organized white supremacy has a long history, offering a time-tested solution to status-based problems for successive generations of frustrated and anomic young males (Blazak, 1998, 2001). However, it cannot be considered to be independent of the prevailing ideologies and social relations of the societies in which it has taken shape. Although the rhetoric contained in white-power music can easily be dismissed as pure fantasy, the white males who make up the bulk of the membership in organized groups are responding to real changes in structural and political conditions. Within their creative efforts, white-power musicians identify sources of collectively experienced social strain while suggesting a course of action for dealing with these problems. As a result, many in this subculture envision this music to be an effective vehicle for disseminating political messages and mobilizing others for collective activism.

These songs help to define the white-supremacist cause for participants in this subculture, as well as explain the goals of the movement to potentially sympathetic outsiders. While the violent lyrics may not provoke most listeners to commit acts of violence against targeted groups, the effect this music has on the proposed targets of this maliciousness is important to consider. The fantasies expressed within this material can have very real consequences for those within targeted communities, who live in fear of victimization at the hands of this subculture's participants.

REFERENCES

Angry Aryans. (1998). Faggots give rainbows a bad name. On *Racially motivated violence* [CD]. Newark, DE: Tri-State Terror Records.

Angry Aryans. (2000). Miscegenation (fade to black). On *Too white for you* [CD]. Newark, DE: Tri-State Terror Records.

Anti-Defamation League of the B'nai B'rith. (1995). *The skinhead international: A worldwide survey of neo-Nazi skinheads*. New York: Author.

Anti-Defamation League of the B'nai B'rith. (2006). *Army of hate: The resurgence of racist skinheads in America*. New York: Author.

Barber-Kersovan, A. (2003). German Nazi bands: Between provocation and repression. In M. Cloonan & R. Garofalo (Eds.), *Policing pop* (pp. 186–205). Philadelphia: Temple University Press.

Berserkr. (1994) Justice. On *The voice of our ancestors* [CD]. Detroit, MI: Resistance Records.

Blazak, R. (1998). Hate in the suburbs: The rise of the skinhead subculture. In L. McIntyre (Ed.), *The practical skeptic: Readings in sociology* (pp. 49–57). Mountain View, CA: Mayfield.

Blazak, R. (2001). White boys to terrorist men: Target recruitment of Nazi skinheads. *American Behavioral Scientist, 44*(6), 982–1000.

Bound for Glory. (1994a). The hammer falls again (Ragnarok). On *The fight goes on* [CD]. Detroit, MI: Resistance Records.

Bound for Glory. (1994b). Your worst nightmare. On *The fight goes on* [CD]. Detroit, MI: Resistance Records.

Brown, T. S. (2004). Subcultures, politics and pop music: Skinheads and pop music in England and Germany. *Journal of Social History 44*(1). 7–178.

Brutal Attack. (1994). Odin's daughter. On *Conquest* [CD]. Germany: Excalibur Records.

Center for New Community. (1999). *Soundtracks to the white revolution: White supremacist assaults on youth music subcultures.* Chicago: Author.

Chicago Area Skinheads. (n.d.) Flyer, Wilcox Collection of Contemporary Political Movements, Spencer Library, University of Kansas, Lawrence.

Clarke, J. (1976). The skinheads and the magical recovery of community. In S. Hall & T. Jefferson (Eds.), *Resistance through rituals* (pp. 99–102). New York: Routledge.

Cohen, A. K. (1955). *Delinquent boys: The culture of the gang.* Glencoe, IL: Free Press.

Daniels, J. (1997). *White lies: Race, class, gender and sexuality in white supremacist discourse.* New York: Routledge.

Day of the Sword. (1996). Casualties. On *Hail victory* [CD]. England: ISD Records.

Definite Hate. (2001). Definite hate. On *Carolina sons* [CD]. Hillsboro: WV: Resistance Records.

Ferber, A. L. (1998). *White man falling.* Lanham, MD: Rowman & Littlefield.

Final War. (2002). The nationalist. On *Glory unending* [CD]. Newport, MN: Panzerfaust Records.

Fortress. (1994). Hail rock n roll. On *Seize the day* [CD]. Australia: Victory Records.

Futrell, R., Simi, P., & Gottschalk, S. (2006). Understanding music in movements: The white power music scene. *The Sociological Quarterly, 47,* 275–304.

Hamm, M. S. (1993). *American skinheads: The criminology and control of hate crime.* Westport, CT: Praeger.

Hamm, M. S. (2004). Apocalyptic violence: The seduction of terrorist subcultures. *Theoretical Criminology, 8*(3), 323–339.

Hebdige, D. (1979). *Subculture: The meaning of style.* London: Routledge.

Kimmel, M. S. (2003). Globalization and its mal(e)contents: The gendered moral and political economy of terrorism. *International Sociology, 18*(3), 603–620.

Laing, D. (1985). *One chord wonders: Power and meaning in punk rock.* Milton Keynes, England: Open University Press.

Lowles, N., & Silver, S. (Eds.). (1998). *White noise: Inside the international Nazi music scene.* London, England: Searchlight.

Max Resist. (1997). White man. On *Second skin* [CD]. Detroit, MI: Resistance Records.

Midtown Bootboys. (1994). Bang bang. On *The Time has come* [CD]. South St. Paul, MN: White Terror Records.

Moynihan, M., & Søderlind, D. (1998). *Lords of chaos: The bloody rise of the Satanic metal underground*. Venice, CA: Feral House.

No Remorse. (1994). Under the gods. On *Under the gods* [CD]. Stockholm, Sweden: Nordland Records.

Nordic Thunder. (1994). True heroes. On *Born to hate* [CD]. Detroit, MI: Resistance Records.

Pearce, J. (1987). *Skrewdriver: The first ten years*. London: Skrewdriver Services.

Perry, B. (2001). *In the name of hate: Understanding hate crimes*. New York: Routledge.

Rahowa. (1993). White people awake. On *Declaration of war* [CD]. Detroit, MI: Resistance Records.

Schmaltz, W. H. (2000). *Hate: George Lincoln Rockwell and the American Nazi Party*. Washington, DC: Brassey's.

Skrewdriver. (1984). When the boat comes in. On *This is white noise* [7-inch vinyl EP]. England: White Noise Records.

Skrewdriver. (1990). Showdown. On *Gods of war vol. 3 and vol. 4* [CD]. Germany: Rock O Rama Records.

Southern Poverty Law Center. (2001). White pride worldwide. *Intelligence Report*, (103), 24–31.

Sykes, G., & Matza, D. (1957). Techniques of neutralization: A theory of delinquency. *American Sociological Review, 22*(6), 664–670.

Tosches, N. (1977). *Country: The biggest music in America*. New York: Stein and Day.

Wood, R. T. (2006). *Straight edge youth: Complexity and contradictions of a subculture*. Syracuse, NY: Syracuse University Press.

CHAPTER 5

GENDER, PRIVILEGE, AND THE POLITICS OF HATE

Abby L. Ferber

HATE CRIME AND GENDER

The Federal Bureau of Investigation (FBI) reported 9,000 instances of hate crime in 2005, based on race, religion, ethnicity, sexual orientation, or disability (Van Brakle, 2007, p. 3). The actual number is far higher, however, due to underreporting. The Southern Poverty Law Center (SPLC) estimates the real number to be closer to 50,000 (SPLC, 2001).

Sociologist Valerie Jenness (2004) defines *hate crime* as "a politically determined and legislatively defined subset of criminal behavior" (p. 182). As a result of the civil rights movement, discussion of hate crime in the United States began percolating in the 1970s. While bias-motivated crime has existed throughout history, it is relatively recently that societies have begun to identify these acts as a unique subset of crime. As a result of the politicization and criminalization of hate crime, we recognize the broader impact of bias-motivated violence. Lawmakers, law enforcement, and the judiciary all play a part in the process of constructing the meaning of "hate crime." According to Jenness (2004), we have

> constructed the problem of bias-motivated violence in ways that distinguish it from other forms of violent crime; state and federal politicians made legislation that defines the parameters of hate crime in ways that distinguish it from other types of violent crime; judicial decision-makers elaborated and enriched the meaning of hate crime as they determined the constitutionality of 'hate crime' as a legal concept that distinguishes types of violence based on the motivation of the perpetrator; and law enforcement

officials continue to investigate and prosecute bias-motivated incidents as a special type of crime that warrants enhanced penalties. (p. 183)

Hate crime statutes, which vary from state to state, identify specific protected statuses to be covered by the law—for example, race, religion, or disability. These status provisions define who does and does not qualify as a victim of a hate crime, and constructs specific groups as vulnerable to bias-motivated crime. Victims are usually unknown to the perpetrators and selected because of their group membership.

In addition to state law, federal legal protection covers the following protected statuses: race, color, religion, and national origin. For many years, gender was purposefully excluded from the protected status categories (McPhail, 2002). In 1994 the Violence Against Women Act was passed; however, it was not until 2001 that a crime was first prosecuted as a hate crime based on gender (Jenness, 1999). The Federal Hate Crimes Statistics Act, passed in 1990, mandates only the collection of data for hate crimes based on race, ethnicity, religion, and sexual orientation. Much of the research on hate crime policy and legislation also ignores issues of gender. Indeed, "gender is best envisioned as a 'second-class citizen' in social, political, and legal discourse in the United States that speaks directly to the larger problem of violence motivated by bigotry and manifest as discrimination (i.e., bias-motivated violence)" (Jenness, 2004, p. 182). Other scholars have found, like Barbara Perry (2001), that the "diversity and limitations of available data sources make it virtually impossible to accurately estimate the extent of violence against women" (p. 26).

Efforts have been made to expand the protected classifications covered by federal law. Senator Edward Kennedy has introduced The Local Law Enforcement Hate Crimes Prevention Act, also known as the Matthew Shepard Act, each year since 1997, yet it still has not been passed by congress.

Looking at some of the literature on hate crime, one might think that gender as a motivation is not a serious problem. To the contrary, violence against women is possibly the most prevalent form of violence in our society. If we are to examine hate crimes and gender, we cannot limit ourselves to analyses focused on the legal classifications of hate crime, which render gender-motivated violence virtually invisible. Instead, it calls for an expanded conceptualization of what constitutes bias-motivated violence.

Feminist scholarship and theorizing has much to contribute to our understanding of hate crime, reconceptualizing it as part of the larger dynamics of privilege and oppression. Works by a variety of feminist scholars argue for a perspective which sees hate crime as a politically determined category that must be understood within a broader political, social, and cultural context (Ferber, 1998; Jenness, 2004; Perry, 2001). U.S. society is characterized by pervasive inequality, based primarily upon gender, race/ethnicity, sexual orientation, class, and ability. Within this context, hate crime can be seen as falling on a continuum of inequality, power, and privilege. It is, in a majority of cases, an overt, violent means of asserting white male privilege.

Perry (2001) argues that hate crimes are a means of "doing difference" (p. 2). Perry defines hate crime as "a mechanism of power intended to sustain somewhat precarious hierarchies, through violence and threats of violence (verbal or physical). It is generally directed toward those whom our society had traditionally stigmatized and marginalized" (p. 3). This definition moves away from the problems inherent in narrow legal definitions and focuses instead on what, in essence, these actions are about—maintaining relations of power. "Bias motivated crime," she writes, "provides an arena within which white males in particular can reaffirm their place in a complex hierarchy and respond to perceived threats from challengers" (p. 2).

Both my work on the white-supremacist movement and Perry's (2001) work on hate crime, emphasize that these phenomena are not about a fringe group, or the acts of extremist psychopaths, but instead must be seen as part of the larger fabric of white supremacy and patriarchy. They are strategies that members of privileged groups turn to in order to demonstrate, protect, or extend their privilege and power.

This chapter examines both hate crime and the white racist hate movement as a part of the larger system of privilege and oppression. Hate crime and the white-supremacist movement are interconnected in various ways. While most individuals who carry out hate crimes are not members of specific white-supremacist organizations, the line between the two is blurry. The white-supremacist movement provides the underpinning ideology and overtly encourages individuals to commit hate crimes. Furthermore, the meaning of "membership" in the white-supremacist movement is not so clear. Today, their greatest presence is on the Web and the Internet, where they receive broad exposure. Far more people are exposed to and partake in white-supremacist discourse on the Web than actually formally join an organization. Finally, and most importantly, the white-supremacist movement and hate crimes share a similar space at one end of the continuum of race and gender power and inequality in the United States. In a racist, patriarchal culture such as this, joining a white-supremacist organization or committing a hate crime fulfills similar purposes. They are both extreme displays of white masculine power in a landscape characterized, historically and up to the present, by pervasive race and gender inequality.

PRIVILEGE

The performance of hate is not just about the oppression of target groups, but equally about the privilege of its perpetrators. Privilege is the flip side of oppression. Privilege confers power, dominance, resources, and rewards

(McIntosh, 2003). One of the most significant features of privilege is that those who experience it do not have to think about it. They have the privilege of obliviousness. While those who experience oppression and inequality are confronted with this reality on a daily basis, those who experience privilege are often unaware of the workings of oppression and privilege and do not see how it affects their own lives.

Whiteness and masculinity are two of the most salient privileged classifications in our society. To be white and male is to have greater access to rewards and valued resources simply because of one's group membership. Focusing on the victims of racism and sexism, historically many scholars have failed to explore the way race and gender shapes the lives of those in the dominant groups. The experiences of white males have been taken as the norm, assumed to be free from the fetters of race and gender. This approach has limited our understanding of race and gender *privilege*, relieving whites of responsibility for racism, and men for responsibility for patriarchy. This perspective makes a sociological understanding of racist and sexist systems and culture almost impossible to understand. As Toni Morrison (1993) maintains, we need to examine "the impact of racism on those who perpetuate it" (p. 11). The invisibility of whiteness serves to "reinforce the existing racial understandings and racial order of society" (Doane, 2003, p. 11). Making whiteness and masculinity visible allows us to examine the ways in which all white men gain benefits from their race and gender, expanding the discussion beyond the actions of prejudiced individuals to examine institutionalized, systemic oppression and privilege (Feagin, 2001).

Bringing the concept of privilege into the discussion of hate activity thus has two direct results:

1. It reveals that hate crime is as much about the perpetrator, perhaps more so, than about the victim. It shifts our focus from the victim classifications to the perpetrators and the culture that breeds them. Most research on oppression has long focused primarily upon the victims of oppression, and this has been true in the study of hate crime as well. As Jenness (1999) observes, the social constructionist approach in the study of hate crime has examined the social processes by which certain kinds of people become recognizable. In this process, certain people are constructed as worthy of legal recognition as a result of being constructed as a category of "hate crime victim" (Jenness, 1999). However, the performance of hate crime and hate activity tells us as much about the construction of the privileged subject and the society that produces. And it is this knowledge that will be most valuable in combating such violence.

2. The second implication is that gender is made central to the analysis. The concept of privilege is a theoretically important tool for understanding the motivation behind hate activity. The white-supremacist movement and hate crime activity are the realms of primarily privileged people:

white men. Yet people of privilege often do not realize the extent to which inequality is still pervasive. Looking at life from their own narrow experience, they fail to recognize that their experiences are not universal and common, but instead the result of their privileged status. As a result, privileged people often become angry when confronted by the fact of their privilege, having been taught to see their own accomplishments as based on their own efforts and hard work alone. It is this anger that fuels much hate-motivated activism.

The organized white racist movement has traditionally attracted and represented the position and interests of men, and the vast majority of hate crimes are committed by white males. Historically, gendered analyses have been applied to movements of women, reflecting the cultural assumption that only women are gendered, and men reflect universal, nongendered, interests. The fact that the organized racist movement is made up primarily of men, however, is also an issue of gender. A perspective that brings privilege into the picture pushes us to ask why it is that men are primarily responsible for hate crime and hate group activity. What does masculinity have to do with it?

Definitions of hate crime emphasize that they involve acts of violence and intimidation; target and speak to an entire group; and are usually directed at members of oppressed groups. Analyzing issues of privilege shifts our focus away from the victims, to the perpetrators, and reveals that hate activity is largely an issue of identity and power. It is an exercise of power, aimed at securing and extending white, patriarchal authority and privilege. It is a process of "masculine reassertion," according to Michael Kimmel (2003).

The remainder of this chapter examines feminist perspectives and research that expand our understanding of hate activism. Reviewing the work of scholars bringing privilege and gender into the analysis reveals that hate activism is

1. part of the larger culture of privilege and oppression
2. tied to the political and social context
3. part of the construction of masculinity, privilege, and power

PART OF THE LARGER CULTURE OF PRIVILEGE AND OPPRESSION

Many hate crime scholars recognize the significance of the broader cultural context. "Hate crimes have a basis in what the members of a society are normally taught when they are growing up" (Levin & McDevitt, 2002, p. 51; see also Hamm, 2002). As Perry (2001) concludes, "Hate crime is not abnormal, rather, it is a normal (albeit extreme) expression of the biases that are diffused throughout the culture and history in which it is embedded" (p. 37). It is not the bias that is unique, only the outright violence.

Bias-motivated violence is one important piece in the tool kit for maintaining relations of inequality. As Gregory Herek (1991) argues in his research on hate crimes against gays and lesbians, violent behavior is simply an extension of institutionalized inequality and pervasive negative attitudes. Similarly, Tracy Isaacs (2001) observes that pervasive mainstream negative attitudes underlie the performance of hate crimes; "for example, homophobia is not restricted to gay bashers. Nor are racist attitudes restricted to perpetrators of racist crimes" (p. 31).

The importance of the larger culture is especially true when we examine gender-motivated violence, and this helps explain why violence against women is less visible as a hate crime. Samuels and Samuels (2008), in their research on sexual assault at the U.S. Air Force Academy, argue that the "culture of gender inequality, and specifically male privilege, allowed rape, sexual assault, and sexual harassment to occur" (p. 578). Perry's (2001) research amply demonstrates that "cultural permission to hate and to victimize women is typically bestowed upon men. Abundant myths, stereotypes, images, and ideologies simultaneously support gendered and unequal relations of power" (p. 103).

Jackson Katz (2006) also argues that "violent individuals must be understood as products of a much larger cultural system" but makes the crucial observation that "here is the paradox: this very normality makes it harder to see just how pervasive the problem is" (p. 153). The sheer pervasiveness and normality of gender inequality and violence against women renders gender-motivated hate crime invisible. This contributes to our understanding of why gender has been excluded from so many hate crime statutes. As sociologist Allan Johnson (2008) writes, "Whose interests does sexism support, and what kind of social order does it perpetuate? From this perspective misogyny and other forms of sexism are more than mistaken ideas and bad attitudes. They are part of a cultural ideology that serves male privilege and supports women's subordination" (p. 534). Yet in a society where gender inequality and male privilege is invisible, it is extremely difficult to see the ways in which violence against women reinforces the cultural devaluing of women. As Katz argues, "News accounts of gang rapes and countless other sexual abuses should be seen as part of a normative cultural pattern. Sexual violence, in short, is part of a broader cultural pattern in which masculinity comes to be linked with power and control over women" (p. 154). According to Franklin (2004), "Young men ritualistically enact an exaggerated version of the gender-role norms expected of men in hypermasculine social environments. Their victims serve as almost interchangeable dramatic props in their performance" (p. 26).

Jenness (2004) explores this issue in her research on hate crime, arguing that gender has generally been excluded precisely because gender-based hate crimes are so common and pervasive. This exclusion further contributes to the invisibility of violence against women. Indeed, gender inequality is so pervasive in part because it still so often remains invisible. If we see hate crimes as an extremist act, carried out by a racist, or a homophobe, we can punish the criminal and vindicate the wider society of racism or homophobia. However, if we have to define every man who batters his wife, every young man who rapes a girl, as a perpetrator of hate crime, the numbers of hate crimes would jump astronomically, and it would no longer be possible to see hate crimes as an aberration in an otherwise egalitarian, democratic society.

Much of the very widespread crimes against women are, therefore, rarely seen as hate crimes. For example, Isaacs (2001) observes that the same kinds of negative attitudes about women as a group underlie domestic violence as the negative attitudes underlying other forms of hate crimes. Isaacs makes the important point that it is thus not only the individual perpetrators, but the communities of which they are a part, that are responsible for the crime.

The pervasiveness of gender inequality at the same time contributes to the prevalence of hate activism. Literature on social movements has revealed "that strategies using frames that 'resonate' with preexisting belief systems will be more effective . . . Frames that are consonant with the ideas that are already widespread in society may be more effective because they evoke ideas that are familiar and compelling to the society's members" (Einwohner, Hollander, & Olson, p. 691). The implication of this body of work is that if our goal is to decrease hate crime, we must attack the culture of privilege and oppression itself, not simply condemn the act of overt violence and its perpetrators.

THE LARGER POLITICAL AND SOCIAL CONTEXT: PRIVILEGE IN CRISIS

As Charles Gallagher (2003) observes, many young, white men, particularly in the working class, are anxious: "They believe the American dream of social mobility has stopped or at least stalled with their generation" (p. 315). Economic restructuring, globalization, and technological breakthroughs have had dramatic effects on industrialized nations and are accelerating the deterioration of a world many have taken for granted (Bonanno, Busch, Friedland, Gouveia, & Mingione, 1995; Jobes, 1997; Maalouf, 2000).

The advances of the civil rights, women's, and gay and lesbian movements have been perceived by many white men as attacks against them. White male privilege no longer proceeds unquestioned. As a result of these social and cultural dislocations, in conjunction with increasing globalization, declining economic opportunities and real wages, and increased unemployment, many people feel insecure about their futures. For white men in particular, having been raised with a sense of entitlement to the American Dream, this insecurity can translate into a profound sense of loss. We have witnessed a widespread backlash, evident most recently in attacks against affirmative action and undocumented immigrants. Susan Faludi has documented the breadth of this backlash, ranging from film and television portrayals, to the growth of a reactionary men's movement, which includes groups like the Promise Keepers and the Million Man March. According to Sine Anahita (2006), "As white men feel embattled, and see their personal and structural status dissolve, many turn to reactionary social movements to help them find new masculine identities" (http://findarticles.com/p/articles/mi_qa3719/is_200607/ai_n16855774/pg_2?tag=artBody;col1).

Kimmel (2003), Connell (2005) and other sociologists have concluded that the gender order, and masculinity in particular, is in crisis. We are facing "a historic collapse of the legitimacy of patriarchal power and a global movement for the emancipation of women . . . feminist movements throughout the world have challenged and contested men's institutional power and the ideas that support this power" (Messner, 1997, p. 10). This sense of victimhood can be sustained only by embracing the myth that white men experienced no privilege to begin with, and operated on a level playing field. Starting from that assumption, they see now themselves under attack.

Targeting white men who perceive their power and privilege as declining, the white-supremacist movement encourages them to interpret these shifts as a personal attack. Crime, immigration, integration, affirmative action, education: whatever is focused on is defined as part of a multipronged assault on whites. For example, an article in the white-supremacist publication *White Patriot* asserts that "the White people of America have become an oppressed majority. Our people suffer from discrimination in the awarding of employment, promotions, scholarships, and college entrances" (cited in Ferber, 1998). Anahita (2006) concludes, "rightist movements such as the global skinhead movement effectively exploit beliefs about a crisis of white masculinity and the need to affirm traditional manhood by creating discourses that explain white men's problematic situation in terms of not only race, but gender and sexuality."

As Ezekiel (1995) suggests, "white rule in America has ended, members feel. A new world they do not like has pushed aside the traditional one they think they remember" (p, xxv). Hate groups present themselves as the answer to America's current social problems by promising to empower white men. Thus, the discourse of the movement has been able to attract some of the disillusioned who now believe that their interests are not being represented by mainstream politicians.

The same dynamics also underlie the phenomenon of hate crime. Indeed, we find that, according to Kimberly A. Vogt (2004), "members of society who are disenfranchised or are experiencing eroding social status are at the greatest risk of offending" (p. 167). According to Vogt,

> members of historically dominant social groups such as males, Europeans . . . enjoy social rights and privileges (power) solely because of their membership in that particular group . . . When we feel that we are losing social

status or power, we fight to retain it. [Individuals often turn to violence] because an individual feels that his or her position in the social structure, or his or her access to scarce resources, is being threatened [such as] the loss of a high-paying manufacturing job, the perception that social status has been eroding for people like myself, or perceived competition from new-comers . . . are viewed as threatening. (p. 165)

White-supremacist Web sites proclaim that their goal is to reclaim what they believe is rightfully theirs. According to hate crimes scholars Jack Levin and Jack McDevitt (2002), "resentment can be found, at least to some extent, in the personality of most hate crime perpetrators. The interchangeability of victims gives us a clue that this resentment may be immense and that it likely serves a deep-rooted psychological need" (p. 51).

Within this social, political, and cultural context, both bias-motivated violence and the continuing activism of the organized white-supremacist movement should be viewed as strategies, embraced to advance the goals of white supremacy and patriarchy.

MASCULINITY, PRIVILEGE, AND POWER

Randy Blazak (2004) argues that both microlevel psychological and macrolevel sociological reasons attract men to the movement, and most of these revolve around issues of masculinity. The macrolevel forms of strain identified by Blazak include changing constructions of masculinity and femininity, loss of social status by white males, and the lack of advocacy groups or movements representing white men. Responding to what is perceived as a threat to both racial and gendered certainties, the contemporary white-supremacist movement is primarily preoccupied with rearticulating white male identity and privilege. Masculinity must be performed; it can never be proven once and for all. It must be demonstrated again and again, and is always vulnerable and at risk. Each of these forms of micro- and macrolevel strain are highly gendered, emphasizing that individuals are attracted to the politics of hate for gender-based reasons and may join the movement to prove their masculinity by talking about, and occasionally acting out, a violent masculinity.

Karen Franklin (2004) argues that "one function" of hate violence "is the garnering of social status by individuals who are cut off from other means of achieving it" (p. 26). According to Martin Oppenheimer (2005), "[for] those who don't prove their masculinity in the various ways a culture has told them it must be done . . . [this] translates into violence when men feel their masculinity has been challenged" (p. 25). Hate activism attracts white men by seemingly offering them the chance to prove their masculinity. White-supremacist ideology encourages males to become "real" men by standing up and protecting white women, reasserting their place in the natural hierarchy, and taking over the world (Ferber, 1998; Kimmel & Ferber, 2000).

Hate crimes are not primarily about hate, but about the construction and maintenance of identity and privilege. Identifying the "other" is central to supporting our own sense of identity: we understand who we are in relation to who we are not. Hate crimes reveal an underlying "fear of losing something—jobs, neighborhood, prestige, values, tradition, power. The 'other' becomes the source of this fear, and is hated" (Oppenheimer, 2005, p. 5). Research by both Herek (1987) and Franklin (2004) examine the ways in which bias-motivated behavior "helps individuals affirm their identities by expressing personal values" and helps individuals to "win membership in a social group by denigrating" (Franklin, 2004, p. 27). those constructed as outsiders. Franklin (2004) found that males, for example, "reported assaulting gays in order to prove their toughness and heterosexuality" (p. 28).

Contemporary white-supremacist discourse relies upon both cultural and biological justifications for both racial and gender inequality. Ferber (1998, 2004) and Perry (2001) both argue that the construction of dichotomous gender and racial differences produces the illusion of inherent superiority and inferiority. White men are constructed as essentially distinct and superior to men of color and to all women. The emphasis upon essential racial and gender differences is a constant theme in white-supremacist discourse. According to David Duke, in an interview conducted for *Contemporary Voices of White Nationalism in America*, "Science has been uncovering these differences dramatically over the last few decades. They exist in physiological areas, cultural areas, and in actual physical areas. We have these great differences between the races, and knowledge of these differences has been suppressed" (Swain, 2003, p. 173). Statements such as this are abundant, and as feminist scholars have noted, discussions of racial and gender differences are often intertwined. The naturalization of gender differences is frequently used to justify the naturalization of racial differences, and vice versa. For example, white-supremacist authors argue that one sign of white superiority is the "unparalleled natural beauty of its women." On the other hand, they argue for the superiority of men over women, because women are the breeders of the race, whose reproductive capacities *must* be controlled by men (Daniels, 1997; Dobratz & Shanks-Meile, 2004; Ferber, 1998, 2004; Perry, 2004; Rogers & Litt, 2004).

White women are seen as the key to reproducing the white race, whose population is depicted as declining and under siege, and changing racial demographics are believed to be undermining white power. Perry (2004) has explored the particular "politics of reproduction" so central to the movement, focusing specifically on abortion, homosexuality, and miscegenation, three highly gendered issues which preoccupy white-supremacist discourse and are central to the goal of preserving the white race. Much of the discourse of hate groups is preoccupied with women as breeders, who must be controlled to secure the reproduction of the race. Black and Latina women are also depicted as breeders, but seen as a threat to white power and white economic entitlement. They are stereotyped as hypersexual welfare queens, and black and Latino men are constructed as dangerous, violent, hypersexual beasts (Daniels 1997; Ferber, 1998, 2004). It is white males who are given responsibility for controlling not only white women, but men and women of color as well (Ferber, 1998).

Numerous scholars argue that white-supremacist ideology reiterates and extends the historical construction of white male entitlement and examines they way in which interracial sexuality is constructed as a threat to white masculinity. Daniels (1997), Ferber (1998), and Perry (2004) highlight the white-supremacist obsession with interracial relationships. This threat is summarized in a typical article that proclaims: "White men are discovering that some of their rightful biological partners are becoming hideous to behold. The skin of these women still gleams like ivory, their bodies as voluptuous as ever. The hideousness comes from the male hand intertwined with one of theirs. The hand is black" (*National Vanguard*, 1979, p. 11, cited in Ferber, 1998). This discourse suggests that interracial sexuality threatens white masculinity and privilege, and white men are encouraged to stand up and become real men by joining this movement, and reasserting white, masculine privilege.

If we ignore the issue of gender, we cannot comprehend just why miscegenation is such a threat to white supremacy. Gender shapes this obsession. It is only white women who are obsessed over. Images of white women and black men fill the publications and Web sites of white-supremacist groups, and in the final scenes of *The Turner Diaries*, white women who were involved in interracial relationships are hung during the bloody "Day of the Rope," yet the issue of white men in relationships with women of color is rarely ever discussed, and when it is, excuses are made for their actions, blaming white women for becoming too feminist.

Hate crimes are encouraged as a strategy among white men in the movement to keep people in their "proper places." Both the white-supremacist movement and hate crimes are about maintaining the constructed matrix of domination, as Patricia Hill Collins (2000) calls it, where white men are set squarely atop the hierarchy. Just as important to keeping the oppressed in their proper places is the performance of white masculinity. Performing hate crimes is one means whereby individuals perform their race and gender, and assert and maintain their superiority and privilege (Perry, 2001).

Blazak (2004) argues that both white-supremacist organizations and hate crime provide opportunities for men to perform masculinity. For example, he observes that the "inability to express aggression in a culture that decries violence causes strain. Hate groups provide an outlet for aggression" (p. 163). They also allow men to perform their masculinity in a myriad of other ways. In the white-supremacist movement, tactics, behaviors, displays, and activities often take gendered forms. Men in the movement often adopt highly masculinized wardrobes, tattoos, boots, and so on. While these vary among the specific organizations, the images and performances are often highly masculine and warriorlike (Kimmel & Ferber, 2003). Anahita (2006) finds that concern over appropriate masculine appearance pervades online discussion among skinheads. Gendered tactics such as these are connected to the construction of gendered identities. Movement members select and perform specific, gendered identities, which is one means of performing masculinity.

Research by Kimmel and Ferber (2000) explores the particular gendered identity for men constructed throughout the movement's literature, as well as in the carrying out of hate crime and terrorist activity. Their work highlights several gendered themes: the experience of humiliation, the attempt to recover something that is believed to have been lost, and the attempt to reassert masculinity. For example, in their analysis of the Oklahoma City bombing, they examine Timothy McVeigh's need to prove his masculinity, to prove that he was a "real man." Elsewhere Kimmel (2003) examines the ways in which men in far-right hate groups deploy masculinity to not only understand their situation in the world, but as a tool for attacking their "enemies," and as a means of recruiting other young men.

As James Messerschmidt (1993) argues, violence is commonly perceived as a means of proving one's masculinity. Throughout white-supremacist discourse and discussion, men are invited to take up arms to defend both their ideals and their manhood (Ferber, 1998). Violence is one means of fulfilling this role. Numerous scholars have argued that the performance of hate provides men with an opportunity to prove their masculinity. In examining hate crimes motivated by gender and sexual orientation (antigay violence and group rape), Franklin (2004) argues that both are commonplace mechanisms for young men to assert and demonstrate their masculinity for others. Group rape, like other hate crimes, usually is perpetrated by young men, and the victims are usually unknown or only casual acquaintances. Franklin (2004) observes that violence against women and gay men "are ideal ways for young men to visibly demonstrate their masculinity, which includes heterosexuality as a central element" (p. 25). Supporting this contention, Anahita (2006), in her research on white-supremacist blogging, concludes that hypermasculinity and heteronormativity are "two of the most important attributes for virtual skinheads to embody. Establishing a collective identity based on hypermasculinity and heteronormativity is one of the most important objectives of the virtual skinheads."

CONCLUSION

As this brief overview makes clear, there is abundant research to support the argument that gender is central to hate activism. Hate crime is a socially constructed classification, and we, as researchers, contribute to that construction. It is our task to critically interrogate its construction and reconstruct it in ways that further the goal of social justice. While gender has been largely excluded from the legislative and judicial constructs, research and analysis of hate crime and hate group activity should not ignore gender. We, as researchers, are involved in the process of framing what constitutes hate crime and hate activity, and must examine the consequences of our constructs.

Giving gender-motivated violence less attention in discourse around hate crime reinforces gender inequality. Surely one of the greatest insights of privilege studies is its revelation of the invisibility of whiteness and masculinity, and the ways in which this invisibility serves to reproduce and naturalize white privilege. In the same manner, gender-blind analyses of hate groups and hate crime are abetting the erasure of the reality of gender-motivated violence and gender inequality in U.S. society.

Further, the research examined in this chapter leads to the conclusion that hate crime and hate activism must be understood within the larger context of inequality that pervades U.S. society. They exist at one end on a continuum of privilege. It is not simply this one manifestation that must be interrogated, but the entire system of privilege and oppression. Allan Johnson (2005) argues that one of the ways that we deny that privilege exists, or minimize its impact, is to blame it on the actions of certain "racist" individuals. This is the strategy taken by our legal system: we deny the culture of privilege and oppression, and blame hate crime and hate activism on the actions of a limited number of "sick" individuals. Not only does this approach leave the system of privilege and oppression unexamined, but it is also bound to fail in its efforts to curtail the occurrence of hate crime. It simply does not work to argue that hating certain people enough to attack them is wrong, in a culture where we cultivate that very hatred to begin with. If we are serious about protecting people from violence and crime simply because of their group identities, then we must also take seriously their right to equality in the home, workplace, and other social institutions.

REFERENCES

Anahita, S. (2006). Blogging the borders: Virtual skinheads, hypermasculinity, and heteronormativity. *Journal of Political and Military Sociology, 34*(1), 143–164.

Blazak, R. (2004). Getting it: The role of women in male desistance from hate groups. In A. L. Ferber (Ed.), *Home grown hate: Gender and organized racism,* (pp.161–179). New York: Routledge.

Bonanno, A., Busch, L., Friedland, W., Gouveia, L., & Mingione, E. (Eds.). (1994). *From Columbus to Conagra: The globalization of agriculture and food.* Lawrence, KS: University Press of Kansas.

Collins, P. H. (2000). *Black feminist thought: Knowledge, consciousness, and the politics of empowerment* (2nd ed.). New York: Routledge.

Connell, R. W. (2005). *Masculinities* (2nd ed.). Berkeley: University of CA Press.

Daniels, J. (1997). *White lies: Race, class, gender and sexuality in white supremacist discourse*. New York: Routledge.

Doane, A. W. (2003). Introduction. In Doane, A. W., & Bonilla-Silva, E. *White out: The continuing significance of race* (pp. 3–18). New York: Routledge.

Doane, A. W., & Bonilla-Silva, E. (2003). *White out: The continuing significance of race*. New York: Routledge.

Dobratz, B. A., & Shanks-Meile, S. L. (2004). The white separatist movement: Worldviews on gender, feminism, nature, and change. In A. L. Ferber (Ed.), *Home-grown hate: Gender and organized racism* (pp.113–141). New York: Routledge.

Einwohner, R. L., Hollander, J. A., & Olson, T. (2000). Engendering social movements: Cultural images and movement dynamics. *Gender and Society, 14*(5), 679–699.

Ezekiel, R. S. (1995). The racist mind: Portraits of American neo-Nazis and Klansmen. New York: Viking.

Faludi, S. (1991). *Backlash: The undeclared war against American women*. New York: Doubleday.

Feagin, J. R. (2001). Racist America: Roots, current realities, and future reparations. New York: Routledge.

Ferber, A. L. (1998). *White man falling: Race, gender and white supremacy*. Lanham, MD: Rowman and Littlefield.

Ferber, A. L. (2004). *Home-grown hate: Gender and organized racism*. New York: Routledge.

Franklin, K. (2000). Antigay behaviors by young adults: Prevalence, patterns and motivators in a noncriminal population. *Journal of Interpersonal Violence, 15*(4), 339–362.

Franklin, K. (2004). Enacting masculinity: Antigay violence and group rape as participatory theater. *Sexuality Research & Social Policy, 1*(2), 25–40.

Gallagher, C. (2003). White reconstruction in the university. In M. S. Kimmel & A. L. Ferber (Eds.) *Privilege: A reader* (pp. 299–318). Cambridge, MA: Westview.

Hamm, M. S. (2002). *In bad company: America's terrorist underground*. Boston: Northeastern University Press.

Herek, G. M. (1987). "Can functions be measured? A new perspective on the functional approach to attitudes." *Social Psychology Quarterly, 50*, 285–303.

Herek, G. M. (1991). Stigma, prejudice and violence against lesbians and gay men. In J. C. Gonsiorek & J. D. Weinrich (Eds.), *Homosexuality: Research implications for public policy* (pp. 66–80). Newbury Park, CA: Sage.

Isaacs, T. (2001). Domestic violence and hate crimes: Acknowledging two levels of responsibility. *Criminal Justice Ethics*, summer/fall, 31–43.

Jenness, V. (1999). Managing difference and making legislation: Social movements and the racialization, sexualization and gendering of federal hate crime law in the U.S. 1985–1998. *Social Problems, 46*(4), 548–571.

Jenness, V. (2004). The dilemma of difference: Gender and hate crime policy. In A. L. Ferber (Ed.), *Home-grown hate: Gender and organized racism* (pp. 181–203). New York: Routledge.

Jobes, P. C. (1997). Gender competition and the preservation of community in the allocation of administrative positions in small rural towns in Montana: A research note. *Rural Sociology, 62*(3), 315–334.

Johnson, A. (2005). Privilege, power, and difference. New York: McGraw Hill.

Johnson, A. (2008). Feminism and feminists. In A. L. Ferber, C. Jimenez, A. O'Reilley Herrera, & D. Samuels (Eds.), *The matrix reader: Understanding the dynamics of privilege and oppression* (pp. 523–543). New York: McGraw-Hill.

Katz, J. (2006). *The macho paradox: Why some men hurt women and how all men can help.* Naperville, IL: Sourcebooks.

Kimmel, M. S. (2003). Globalization and its mal(e)contents: The gendered moral and political economy of terrorism. *International Sociology, 18*(3), 603–620.

Kimmel, M. S., & Ferber, A. L. (2000). Reading right: The western tradition in white supremacist discourse. *Sociological Focus, 33*(2), 193–213.

Levin, J., & McDevitt, J. (2002). *Hate crimes revisited: America's war on those who are different.* Cambridge, MA: Westview.

Maalouf, A. (2000). *In the name of identity: Violence and the need to belong.* New York: Penguin Books.

McIntosh, P. (2003). White privilege and male privilege. In M. S. Kimmel & A. L. Ferber (Eds.). *Privilege: A reader.* Boulder, CO: Westview Press.

McPhail, B. A. (2002). Gender-bias hate crimes. *Trauma, Violence and Abuse, 3*(2), 125–143.

Messerschmidt, J. (1993). *Masculinities and crime.* Lanham, MD: Rowman and Littlefield.

Messner, M. (1997). *Politics of masculinities: Men in movements.* Thousand Oaks, CA: Sage.

Morrison, T. (1993). *Playing in the dark: Whiteness and the literary imagination.* New York: Vintage.

Nyatepe-Coo, & D. Zeisler-Vralsted (Eds.), *Understanding terrorism: Threats in an uncertain world.* Upper Saddle River, NJ: Pearson.

Oppenheimer, M. (2005). *The hate handbook: Oppressors, victims, and fighters.* Lanham, MD: Rowman and Littlefield.

Perry, B. (2001). *In the name of hate: Understanding hate crimes.* New York: Routledge.

Perry, B. (2004). "White genocide": White supremacists and the politics of reproduction. In A. L. Ferber (Ed.), *Home-grown hate: Gender and organized racism* (pp. 75–95). New York: Routledge.

Rogers, J., & Litt, J. S. (2004). Normalizing racism: A case study of motherhood in white supremacy. In A. L. Ferber (Ed.), *Home-grown hate: Gender and organized racism,* (pp. 97–112). New York: Routledge.

Samuels, D., & Samuels, S. (2008). In A. L. Ferber, C. Jimenez, A. O'Reilly Herrera, & D. Samuels (Eds.), *The matrix reader: Understanding the dynamics of privilege and oppression* (pp. 579–583), New York: McGraw Hill.

Southern Poverty Law Center. (2001, Winter). Discounting hate. *Intelligence Report.* Montgomery, AL: Author.

Swain, C. M. (2003). *Contemporary voices of white nationalism in America.* Cambridge: Cambridge University Press.

Van Brakle, M. (2007). *Hate crimes legislation is on the move.* Footnotes, *35*(7), 3.

Vogt, K. A. (2004). Hate crime as a reaction to the terrorist attacks of September 11, 2001. In A. A. Nyatepe-Coo and D. Zeisler-Vralsted (Eds). Understanding terrorism: Threats in an uncertain world. Upper Saddle River, NJ: Pearson.

CHAPTER 6

FEMALE-PERPETRATED HATE: A CONTENT ANALYSIS OF HATE INCIDENTS

Tammy L. Castle

Research on hate or bias crime, crime motivated by the perpetrator's bias toward the victim, has slowly increased over the years (Gerstenfeld, 2004; Perry, 2003). The study of female participation in hate crimes, however, remains confined to investigations of the role of women or female participation in organized hate groups and activities (see Blee, 1996, 2002; Ferber, 2004; Hamm, 1993; Moore, 1993). Although an understanding of female participation in organized hate groups is imperative, the lack of research attention to female-perpetrated hate incidents is significant since most hate crimes are not committed by members of organized hate groups (Dunbar, 2003; Levin, 2002; Levin & McDevitt, 1993).

The few studies on hate crimes that do mention female offenders simply note the number as minute (Dunbar, 2003) or discuss the female role as secondary, whether in the context of as bystander to the event or providing support to a male offender (Bufkin, 1999). Even if the number of female perpetrators in hate incidents is relatively small, an examination of their role is crucial, as scholars have noted an increase in violent hate activities by females (Blee, 2002; Perry, 2004). So that the validity of this statement can be addressed, a discussion of hate crime statistics is essential.

HATE CRIME STATISTICS

The Hate Crime Statistics Act, passed in 1990, required the Federal Bureau of Investigation's (FBI) Uniform Crime Reporting (UCR) program to collect data on criminal offenses motivated by bias or hate because of race, religion, sexual orientation, or ethnicity (disability was added in 1994). The FBI, under the direction of the Attorney General, prepares an annual report on bias or hate crimes from information received by participating law enforcement agencies. Like the UCR, the annual statistics are influenced by the number of participating law enforcement agencies. Since the number of agencies varies from year to year, the FBI cautions against comparisons. For example, in 2005 a total of 7,163 hate crime incidents were reported by 12,417 agencies. In 2006, more agencies reported (12,620) and the number of incidents increased to 7,722. The media widely reported that hate crime incidents increased by almost 8 percent that year (FBI, 2008).

Even with the lack of consistency in reporting, the UCR *Hate Crime Statistics* compiled by the FBI is still one of the best sources of hate crime incidents (McDevitt, Balboni, Bennett, Weiss, Orchowsky, & Walbolt, 2003). The annual report includes information about the type of bias motivation (by race, religion, sexual orientation, ethnicity/national origin, or disability), type of offense (by crimes against person or crimes against property), victim type (by individuals, businesses or financial institutions, government, religious organizations, or other), and offenders (by race and crime category). One weakness with this reporting method is that there is a proportion of hate crime incidents that go unreported to the police; thus, those incidents are not captured in the official statistics. Furthermore, research has found that the majority of agencies report that zero hate crimes took place during the year, even though some police officers believed that a hate crime had been reported and investigated in their jurisdiction (McDevitt et al.).

In addition to the UCR, the FBI has a second crime reporting system, the National Incident Based Reporting System (NIBRS), which includes more detailed information, such as the victim's and offender's gender, age, and relationship (FBI, 2007). Although the number of agencies reporting to NIBRS has grown (4,200 reported in 2003), there are more than 17,000 law enforcement agencies in the nation (Strom, 2001). Therefore, researchers also must rely on victimization surveys for information on hate crimes.

The National Crime Victimization Survey (NCVS) is a biannual report on crime conducted by the Bureau of Justice Statistics (BJS) under the U.S. Department of Justice. The NCVS surveys a random sample of households, approximately 77,600 people, about crime experiences, and the statistics are compared with information from the UCR. These comparisons allow researchers to provide more accurate crime statistics in the United States by highlighting crimes not reported to the police. In 2000, the BJS began to include questions about hate crime victimization in the biannual survey (Harlow, 2005). The NCVS closely resembles the information obtained from NIBRS, as information about the victim's race, age, gender, motivation, etc. is included.

A number of different advocacy groups and nonprofit organizations also compile information on hate incidents. For example, the Anti-Defamation League (ADL) uses information provided by the FBI to construct tables comparing hate crime statistics for the last 10 years. The ADL also posts media articles related to hate incidents, as well as resources on data collection and federal and state hate crime laws. Furthermore, the ADL provides educational information on how to combat bias and hate crimes in various agencies (ADL, 2008).

The purpose of this chapter is to examine female participation in hate incidents, utilizing information provided by another advocacy group, the Southern Poverty Law Center (SPLC). According to the Web site,

> The Southern Poverty Law Center was founded in 1971 as a small civil rights law firm. Today, SPLC is internationally known for its tolerance education programs, its legal victories against white supremacists and its tracking of hate groups.
>
> Located in Montgomery, Alabama—the birthplace of the Civil Rights Movement—the Southern Poverty Law Center was founded by Morris Dees and Joe Levin, two local lawyers who shared a commitment to racial equality. Its first president was civil rights activist Julian Bond.
>
> Throughout its history, SPLC has worked to make the nation's Constitutional ideals a reality. The SPLC legal department fights all forms of discrimination and works to protect society's most vulnerable members, handling innovative cases that few lawyers are willing to take. Over three decades, it has achieved significant legal victories, including landmark Supreme Court decisions and crushing jury verdicts against hate groups. (SPLC, 2008, para. 1–3)

The SPLC also has several other programs, including Teaching Tolerance, which provides educational resources for schools and community centers, and the Intelligence Project.

FEMALE PARTICIPATION IN HATE CRIMES

As mentioned above, two official reporting systems collect information on the gender of the offender in hate crime incidents, NIBRS and the NCVS. The most recent report from NIBRS (*Hate Crimes Reported in NIBRS*, 1997–99) identified 2,976 hate incidents with 3,072 known offenders (Strom, 2001). Of the known offenders in all crimes, 17 percent were female (11% white, 5% black, 1% other); however, statistics on the gender/race of offender was missing in 14 percent of data. Gender also is divided by crime category, with females committing 17 percent of violent offenses (10% white, 6% black, 1% other) and 18 percent of property offenses (15% white, 2% black, 1% other). Regarding 808 arrestees, females accounted for 15 percent of all offenses

(9% white, 5% black, 1% other), 16 percent of violent offenses (8% white, 7% black, 1% other) and 14 percent of property offenses (11% white, 1% black, 2% other). Information about gender by type of bias motivation or offense type was not reported (Strom, 2001).

The first report to include questions about hate crime from the NCVS (*Hate Crime Reported by Victims and Police*) reported an annual average of 191,000 hate incidents from July 2000 to December 2003 (Harlow, 2005). The offender information in the NCVS is provided when "the victim was present, knew the offender, or learned something about the offender after the incident" (Harlow, 2005, p. 7). For crimes of violence motivated by hate, 21.2 percent were committed by females and 6.6 percent were committed by both males and females. Of the hate crimes committed by only females, 68.8 percent were motivated by race, 22.6 percent by association, and 37.1 percent by ethnicity. The category of association was included as "the victim's association with persons who have certain characteristics, for example, a multiracial couple" (Harlow, 2005, p. 3). Ten or fewer cases committed by females were motivated by sexual orientation (7.3%), perceived characteristics (8.3%), religion (14.8%), and disability (8.4%). Furthermore, 10 or fewer cases were committed by both males and females based on race (35.9%), association (51.5%), ethnicity (14.1%), sexual orientation (38.3%), perceived characteristics (7.6%), religion (6.2%), and disability (37.0%). Finally, 41.0 percent of the incidents involved female offenders and female victims. Ten or fewer cases involved female offenders and male victims (6.1%), as well as both male and female offenders and male victims (4.5%) and female victims (9.3%).

The BJS also offers a comparison of the hate crime victimizations from the NCVS (July 2000—December 2003) and NIBRS (2002). For the period of study, 21.2 percent of NCVS and 16.5 percent of NIBRS offenders were female. In addition, 6.6 percent of NCVS and 7.2 percent of NIBRS offenders included both males and females. Although helpful, fewer agencies participate in NIBRS than in the UCR. For this reason, the biannual NCVS is better than NIBRS in providing information about victimization and hate crime incidents, since the number includes incidents that go unreported to the police.

The collective knowledge on female-perpetrated hate incidents is influenced by the limitations inherent in official statistics. The purpose of this exploratory study was to examine the involvement of females in hate incidents through information provided by an advocacy group, the SPLC.

METHODS

This study is exploratory in nature, as relatively little is known about female participation in hate incidents. Secondary data were utilized for this purpose and were obtained from the SPLC's Intelligence Project. According to the Web site (www.splcenter.org), the Intelligence Project was started in

1981 as a method of monitoring the activities of the Ku Klux Klan. By 1998, the project expanded intelligence gathering to include other hate groups and extremist activities beyond the KKK. The Intelligence Project also "publishes the *Intelligence Report*, a quarterly magazine updating law enforcement, the media, and the public on the activity it investigates" (SPLC, 2008, p. 2). In addition, the Intelligence Project compiles a list of hate incidents on a weekly (Hatewatch Weekly) and annual (Hatewatch for the Record) basis (SPLC, 2008).

The annual lists of hate incidents are available on the Web site from the year 2003 to the present. A total of 1,699 incidents are listed by year (362 in 2003, 558 in 2004, 246 in 2005, 247 in 2006, 286 in 2007). Under each year, the incidents are listed by city and state in descending order, based on the date that the hate incident was originally published by Hatewatch Weekly. Furthermore, each incident also is listed by category, which includes arson, assault, cross burning, harassment, intelligence, intimidation, leafleting, legal developments, murder, rally, threat, and vandalism (see Appendix A for an example of an incident from each category).

Sample

So that the sample could be obtained, all of the incidents were examined to determine whether the perpetrator(s) was (were) known. If the perpetrator(s) or the gender of the perpetrator(s) was (were) unknown, the incident was excluded from the sample. Regarding the various categories, two were excluded ("intelligence" and "rally") because the incidents consisted of reports on various activities of known hate group affiliates, as well as hate group rallies held during the year. Moreover, the incidents listed under the category "legal developments" involved updates on cases from previous years (see Appendix A, for example). After these incidents were excluded, the sample contained a total of 428 incidents from the five-year period.

Results

Table 6.1 provides the total number of incidents per year, as well as the gender of known offenders involved in each incident. During the five-year study there were 384 (90%) incidents involving male offenders, 25 (6%) incidents involving female offenders, and 19 (4%) incidents involving both male and female offenders.

Since female involvement in hate incidents was the focus of the study, each incident also was classified based on type. Table 6.2 depicts the number and type of female-perpetrated hate incidents by year. Alone, females were involved in seven types of hate incidents during the five-year period of study (see Appendix B for a full description of each incident). The two most

Table 6.1   Number of Hate Incidents by Gender and Year ($N = 428$)

Year	Male only	Female only	Both
2003	101	1	5
2004	82	6	6
2005	48	5	1
2006	57	0	1
2007	96	13	6
Total[a]	384	25	19

[a]$N = 428$.

Table 6.2   Number of Female-Perpetrated Hate Incidents by Year ($N = 25$)

Type of offense	2003	2004	2005	2006	2007
Arson	0	0	0	0	0
Assault	0	2	2	0	9
Cross burning	0	0	0	0	0
Harassment	0	1	0	0	0
Intimidation	0	1	0	0	0
Leafleting	0	0	0	0	1
Murder	0	0	0	0	1
Threat	0	0	1	0	0
Vandalism	1	2	2	0	2
Total[a]	1	6	5	0	13

[a]$N = 25$.

common hate incidents were assault and vandalism. Hate related assault was committed by females in 2004 ($n = 2$), 2005 ($n = 2$), and 2007 ($n = 9$). Vandalism was reported in 2003 ($n = 1$), 2004 ($n = 2$), 2005 ($n = 2$), and 2007 ($n = 2$). Two incidents of harassment and one incident of intimidation were reported in 2004. One incident involving a threat was reported in 2005, as well as one incident of leafleting in 2007. Furthermore, one incident of bias-related murder was reported. Overall, the most incidents were reported in 2007 (52%) and 2004 (24%).

Regarding hate incidents with both male and female offenders, as was the case with female-perpetrated incidents, assault was the most common, as illustrated in table 6.3. Assault was reported in 2003 ($n = 2$), 2004 ($n = 3$), 2006 ($n = 1$), and 2007 ($n = 5$). Harassment was the second-most common

Table 6.3   Number of Female- and Male-Perpetrated Hate Incidents by Year ($N = 19$)

Type of Offense	2003	2004	2005	2006	2007
Arson	0	0	1	0	0
Assault	2	3	0	1	5
Cross burning	0	0	0	0	0
Harassment	1	2	0	0	1
Intimidation	0	0	0	0	0
Leafleting	0	0	0	0	0
Murder	1	0	0	0	0
Threat	0	0	0	0	0
Vandalism	1	1	0	0	0
Total[a]	5	6	1	1	6

[a]$N = 19$.

Table 6.4   Type of Bias Motivation for Female- and Male-and-Female-Perpetrated Hate Incidents 2003–2007 ($N = 44$)

Bias Motivation	Female only	Male and Female
Race	12	12
Religion	6	0
Sexual orientation	2	2
Ethnicity/National origin	2	3
Disability	1	0
Homeless	1	0
Unknown	1	2
Total[a]	25	19

[a]$N = 44$.

type of incident reported in 2003 ($n = 1$) and 2004 ($n = 2$). One incident of arson and intimidation was reported in 2005. Two incidents of vandalism were reported in 2003 and 2004. Furthermore, one bias-related murder was reported in 2003.

The bias motivation for each group also was examined. Table 6.4 describes the type of bias motivation present in hate incidents with female involvement during the five-year period of study. Of the hate incidents, race was the most common motivation in both the female-only (48%) and male-and-female-perpetrated (63%) incidents. Religion was the second-most common bias motivation for females only (24%), and ethnicity/national origin was second for the sample of male and female (16%) perpetrators.

Additional information was cited in some of the incidents, such as the number and age of the perpetrators. Of the female-only incidents, 40 percent ($n = 10$) listed multiple perpetrators. Moreover, 23 incidents listed the ages of the perpetrators; 43.5 percent ($n = 10$) were under the age of 18. In the sample of both male and female perpetrators, the age of the females was listed in 16 incidents; and 25 percent ($n = 4$) were under the age of 18.

DISCUSSION

Of the hate incidents examined, males continue to be the primary perpetrators (90%), although the gender gap is not as wide in official statistics (64.7% male and 35.3% female; Harlow, 2005). Regarding type of offense, assault was the most common crime reported with female involvement. These numbers mirror those reported in *Hate Crime Statistics, 2006*, where 60 percent of crimes reported were "crimes against persons," and of these, over half (53.5%) were assaults, although the number of female perpetrators remains unknown, as the UCR does not record the offender's gender. In NIBRS, females were responsible for 17 percent of violent offenses and 18 percent of property offenses (Strom, 2001). Are females perpetrating violent hate crimes at higher rates than in the past? The answer to that question is beyond the scope of this study, but the number of female-perpetrated violent incidents reported here warrants further consideration.

In addition to the number of females involved in hate incidents, causality beyond bias motivation remains to be explored. Interviews with females arrested and/or convicted of hate crimes may yield valuable insights into possible motivation behind the hate incident. According to Levin and McDevitt's (1993) typology, offenders commit hate crimes for purposes of thrill-seeking, defense against perceived intrusions, retaliation, and ridding the world of a particular group of people. Does this typology also apply to females? Future researchers should focus on eliciting this kind of information through qualitative methods.

Limitations

One of the strengths of relying on secondary data is that "it is cheaper and faster than collecting original data" (Maxfield & Babbie, 2005, p. 347). A limitation of secondary data, however, can be the lack of systematic collection. Although both the FBI and BJS collect hate crime statistics, the information on offenders is limited. The UCR *Hate Crime Statistics* is the best source but provides no information on the gender of the perpetrator. This method is supplemented by NIBRS, even though fewer agencies contribute.

Due to a lack of detailed information on female perpetrators of hate crime, the researcher chose to use information provided by a nonprofit group, the SPLC. The SPLC's Hatewatch Weekly does not systematically collect data on hate crime incidents, making the sample obtained from the organization incomplete. The sample does not include all hate incidents during the five-year period in which the perpetrator(s) was known, and the amount of detail included in each incident varies; thus, conclusions are tentative.

CONCLUSION

Since research on female-perpetrated hate incidents is virtually nonexistent, our understanding of the nature of female offenders remains inadequate. The following exploratory study attempted to add to the scant literature by examining female-perpetrated hate incidents using data obtained from one organization, the SPLC. Although official statistics continue to be the best source of information on hate incidents, relatively little can be gained from them other than a description of the number and type of crimes perpetrated by women. Additional studies on female perpetrators of hate incidents will be necessary for a more comprehensive understanding of this population and the nature of their crimes.

APPENDIX A

Examples of Type of Hate Incident (www.splcenter.org)

Arson

Queens, New York—Kevin McKenna, 35, was charged with allegedly setting fire to a van bearing Korean lettering because he hated Asian immigrants.

Assault

Tarpon Springs, Florida—Three men allegedly attacked a group of people they believed were gay outside a Greek restaurant. The men also allegedly made antigay remarks and warned the group not to return to the area. Michael Kitsos, 21, was charged with a hate crime for allegedly participating in the beating, and John A. Himonetos, 21, and Stamatios N. Kannis, 22, were charged with three counts of misdemeanor battery and two counts of felony aggravated battery.

Cross Burning

Trenton, Georgia—Eric Sullivan, 25, Jerrell Garner Jr., 29, Stacy Jones, 30, Steven Jones, 41, Jeremy Sims, 28, and Billy Wells, 31, were each charged with one count of terroristic threats and acts for allegedly burning a cross in a person's yard.

Harassment

Gloucester Township, Pennsylvania—James R. McGee, Brad A. Carr, and Francis J. Tinney, all 19, were charged with bias intimidation for allegedly verbally harassing a group because of the members' sexual orientation.

Intelligence

Johnson City, Tennessee—Gregory Allen Freeman, 45, was charged with aggravated assault and felony reckless endangerment for allegedly firing a gun in the air during a Ku Klux Klan initiation ceremony.

Intimidation

Cuyahoga Falls, Ohio—William Fowler, 43, was charged with ethnic intimidation and criminal damaging for allegedly using racial slurs toward a co-worker and burning a cross at the man's workstation.

Leafleting

Raleigh, North Carolina—White supremacist William Franklin Brown, 41, was charged with littering for allegedly dumping a barrage of white-supremacist leaflets onto the lawns of a neighborhood.

Legal Developments

Elkhart, Indiana—Alex Witmer, 22, received the maximum, 65-year prison sentence for the 1999 racially motivated killing of a black man.

Murder

Washington, D.C.—Antoine Jacobs, 22, was charged with first-degree murder while armed, and hate and gender bias for allegedly killing a Hispanic man who dressed as a woman.

Rally

Eddyville, Kentucky—Members of the Imperial Klans of America rallied.

Threat

The Bronx, New York—A group of men allegedly threatened to shoot an Asian man while yelling racial slurs.

Vandalism

Palm Beach, Florida—Five black swastikas were spray-painted on the walls and furniture was slashed at a Jewish residence.

APPENDIX B

Description of Hate Incidents with Female Involvement (2003–2007; www.splcenter.org)

2003

Vandalism

Middletown, New Jersey—A 16-year-old girl was sentenced to 60 days in jail for her role in several bias crimes targeting a Catholic church.

2004

Assault

Hudson, New York—A 24-year-old black woman, Latisha E. Diaz, allegedly attacked a white woman because of her race.

Ithaca, New York—Four black females, LaToia Harris, 23, Tieara E. Leckey, 21, and two 14-year-olds were charged as juveniles with third-degree assault. Harris and Leckey were charged with second-degree harassment for allegedly assaulting a white girl in November.

Harassment

Buffalo, New York—Two teenage sisters were allegedly threatened and chased by a car. The car had two white females inside who allegedly yelled obscenities and made references to the teenagers' Islamic background.

Intimidation

East Brunswick, New Jersey—Michelle Dixon, 40, was convicted of conspiracy to commit first-degree bias intimidation and second-degree robbery for robbing a man with epilepsy and a mental disability.

Vandalism

Montpelier, Vermont—Sarah Abair, 22, and Tonya Richards, 17 were arrested for allegedly drawing swastikas on a temple with anti-Semitic epithets, sentenced to 90 days in jail, and ordered to serve 80 hours each of community service and to complete educational sessions on tolerance provided by the Jewish Federation.

Queens, New York—Yolanda Moorjaney, a 31-year-old white woman, was charged with criminal mischief as a hate crime for allegedly scrawling racist graffiti on a school's bathroom wall.

2005

Assault

Brooklyn, New York—Four teenage girls, three black and one Hispanic, allegedly attacked two white teenage girls.

Plymouth, Massachusetts—Erin Monaghan, 25, was charged with a hate crime after she allegedly punched a 14-year-old girl who was dressed in the traditional plain clothing of her fundamentalist Christian sect.

Threat

Bannockburn, Illinois—Alicia Hardin, a black 19-year-old woman, was charged with disorderly conduct and a hate crime for allegedly mailing racist threats to fellow minorities at Trinity International University because she was homesick and wanted to convince her parents the campus was dangerous.

Vandalism

Upper Deerfield, New Jersey—Shenina Ware, 30, was charged with two counts of bias intimidation and two counts of criminal mischief after she allegedly wrote racial slurs and drew swastikas at two residences.

Palm Desert, California—Two 13-year-old girls were arrested for, and allegedly confessed to, hate crimes involving the vandalism of 12 houses and vehicles.

2006

No reports

2007

Assault

Lewiston, Idaho—Jill Grant, 40, was charged with felony malicious harassment after she allegedly kicked a 13-year-old Native American girl several times in the head and stomach after Grant and several others shouted "white power." Grant's daughter, 21-year-old Ashley Grant, is being sought for allegedly beating the girl.

West, Texas—A Latino man was allegedly beaten and kicked by four teenage girls who say they are white supremacists.

Nutley, New Jersey—Kerri A. Livesay, 34, was charged with simple assault and a bias crime after allegedly screaming curses and assaulting a teen wearing traditional Muslim garb at a store.

Wichita Falls, Texas—Vera Fay Labs, 37, was charged with assault-bias/prejudice after she allegedly used racial slurs and assaulted her cellmate because the woman was black.

Palm Springs, California—A black man and a black woman were allegedly stabbed behind a coffeehouse by a self-proclaimed member of a white-supremacist group. Mandie Kearns, 28, was charged with suspicion of assault with a deadly weapon and a hate crime.

Oakhurst, California—Donna Hubbard received three years of formal probation and 400 hours of community service for weapon possession charges. Hubbard was also accused of assaulting and yelling racial slurs at a Jewish woman.

San Mateo, California—Tiffany Adler, 20, was charged with suspicion on two counts of misdemeanor hate crime and two counts of misdemeanor battery for allegedly throwing apples and asparagus while yelling a racial slur at a gay couple.

Des Moines, Iowa—Jassimen Dobbins and Angela Wade, both 19, were charged with first-degree burglary and third-degree arson for allegedly beating a gay teenager in December with a bottle, stabbing him with a fork, and stealing $5, his ATM card, and his driver's license before setting his bag on fire.

Portland, Oregon—Four black girls (Chelsea Rivers, 14; Rinita Low and Brianna Streeter, both 13; and Mary Michelle Blackshear, 16) were charged with robbery, intimidation, and assault for allegedly attacking and robbing a 16-year-old white girl because of her race.

Leafleting

Crystal Lake, Illinois—A 16-year-old girl was sentenced to 14 days in jail and one year of probation and ordered to write letters of apology for distributing antigay fliers outside a high school in May.

Murder

Queensgate, Washington—Donald Francis, a 44-year-old apparently homeless man, was shot, allegedly by a woman from whom Francis asked money. Geraldine Beasley, 62, was charged with murder.

Vandalism

Wanaque, New Jersey—Three teenage girls were charged with criminal mischief, harassment, and bias intimidation for allegedly vandalizing the home of an Asian man with ketchup, white rice, dishwashing detergent, and an epithet directed at Chinese people.

Redding, California—Swastikas were spray-painted on a garage, a mailbox, and a street. Racial epithets were also spray-painted on the mailbox. A 14-year-old girl was charged with suspicion of vandalism and committing a hate crime.

APPENDIX C

Description of Hate Incidents with Male and Female Involvement (2003–2007; www.splcenter.org)

2003

Assault

Plymouth, Massachusetts—Jacob Stanton, 17, and his mother, Cynthia Stanton, were charged with a hate crime by means of threatening to commit a crime and assault to intimidate after they allegedly used racial slurs and assaulted a woman, her daughter, and two others.

Queens, New York—George Fortunato, 60, and his wife, Jacqueline, 58, were sentenced to anger management and ethnic sensitivity training after they pleaded guilty to assaulting an Asian woman in January.

Harassment

Madison, Wisconsin—Kasey Bieri, 22, and Matthew Genack were charged with disorderly conduct as a hate crime after Bieri allegedly spit on an interracial couple and Genack tried to provoke a fight.

Murder

San Francisco, California—Dominique England, 23, Jeanne Sorja, 29, and Daymon Schrock, 20, were charged with murder, conspiracy, kidnap, torture, and a hate crime after allegedly killing a bisexual man.

Vandalism

Anoka, Minnesota—A 16-year-old boy and a 14-year-old girl were taken into custody for allegedly spray-painting a racial epithet on a garage.

2004

Assault

Middletown, Ohio—Michael Ray Miracle, 40, and Eric Fugate, 22, were charged with arson and aggravated menacing by ethnic intimidation in connection with a cross burning at a black family's residence. Misty Miracle, 19, was facing assault charges in connection with an alleged attack that preceded the cross-burning incident, and two juveniles were being held on the same charges.

Milford, Massachusetts—Shirley A. Aldrin, 32, and Roger Britton, Jr., 33, allegedly attacked a gas station attendant who is an American citizen born in Iraq.

Government Camp, Oregon—Four men and one woman allegedly attacked two gay men in what deputies are calling a brutal hate crime.

Harassment

East Haven, Connecticut—David Hoadley, 43, and Nancy Smyth, 51, both white, were arrested after an alleged racial confrontation with a black man.

Staten Island, New York—Josephine Laringa, 24, and Kimberly Albertson and David Egan, both 25, were charged with reckless endangerment as a hate crime for allegedly shouting racial slurs at a black and Hispanic couple last September.

Vandalism

Manlius, New York—Amy Maestri, 17, and Paul A. Doughty and Suong T. Phan, both 16, were charged with two felony counts of criminal mischief and one misdemeanor count of criminal mischief for allegedly scrawling graffiti at two schools and a home.

2005

Arson

Indianapolis, Indiana—Five members of a gang called 2–1 FATAL allegedly set fire to a home to prevent a black family from moving in. Michael Litel, 40; Doris Litel and Dennis Craig, both 29; Richard D. Hacker, 22; and James Holwager, 25, were charged with gang activity, arson, and criminal recklessness.

2006

Assault

Long Beach, California—Ten black youths, nine of them females, ranging in age from 12 to 17 years old, were charged with a hate crime attack after they allegedly attacked a group of white girls and shouted racial slurs.

2007

Assault

Big Creek, West Virginia—Frankie Brewster, a 49-year-old white woman, was charged with kidnapping, sexual assault, malicious wounding, and giving false information after she and several others allegedly tortured a black woman and called her racial epithets. Brewster's son, Bobby R. Brewster, 24, was charged with kidnapping, sexual assault, and malicious wounding and assault during the commission of a felony in connection with the incident. Danny J. Combs, 20, also was charged with malicious wounding, battery, and assault during the commission of a felony; and Alisha Burton and George Messer, both 27, were charged with battery and assault during the commission of a felony.

West, Texas—Stephen Ray Chapman, 34, was charged with engaging in organized criminal activity and aggravated assault with a deadly weapon after he allegedly beat a Latino man. Maria Lee Wooten, 33, was also charged in connection with the incident.

Westminster, California—Justin Louis Mullins, 23, Cheyne Danica Wilson, 25, and James Joseph Kelly, 26, were charged with felony aggravated assault with a hate crime enhancement after they allegedly pulled a Latino man out of his car and beat and kicked him while yelling racial slurs.

New York City—Two white men and two white women allegedly yelled anti-Chinese remarks and assaulted a group of Asian men.

Greenville, North Carolina—Tiffany Dawn O'Neal Maxwell, 36, Wallace Eugene Woodard III, 25, Dustin Grey Frick, 18, and a 16-year-old boy, all alleged members of a white-supremacist group, were arrested for kidnapping, assault inflicting serious injury, and conspiracy to commit murder. Woodard was also charged with communicating threats.

Harassment

Southington, Connecticut—Three teens, a 14-year-old and a 15-year-old boy and a 14-year-old girl, were charged with first-degree breach of peace, second-degree criminal mischief and second-degree harassment after they allegedly left suspicious packages spray-painted with hate messages at six houses.

REFERENCES

Anti-Defamation League. (2008). *Combating hate.* Retrieved February 7, 2008, from http://www.adl.org.

Blee, K. M. (1996). Becoming a racist: Women in contemporary Ku Klux Klan and Neo-Nazi groups. *Gender and Society, 10,* 685–697.

Blee, K. M. (2002). *Inside organized racism: Women in the hate movement.* Berkeley: University of California Press.

Bufkin, J. L. (1999). Bias crime as gendered behavior. *Social Justice, 26,* 155–176.

Dunbar, E. (2003). Symbolic, relational, and ideological signifiers of bias-motivated offenders: Toward a strategy of assessment. *American Journal of Orthopsychiatry, 73,* 203–211.

Federal Bureau of Investigation.(2007). *Hate crime.* Retrieved February 7, 2008, from http://www.fbi.gov/hq/cid/civilrights/hate.htm

Ferber, A. L. (2004). *Home-grown hate: Gender and organized racism.* New York: Routledge.

Gerstenfeld, P. B. (2004). *Hate crimes: Causes, controls, and controversies.* Thousand Oaks, CA: Sage.

Hamm, M. (1993). *American skinheads: The criminology and control of hate crime.* Westport, CT: Praeger.

Harlow, C. W. (2005). *Hate crime reported by victims and police.* Washington, DC: Bureau of Justice Statistics Special Report (NCJ 209911).

Levin, J. (2002). *The violence of hate: Confronting racism, anti-Semitism, and other forms of bigotry.* Boston: Allyn & Bacon.

Levin, J., & McDevitt, J. (1993). *Hate crimes: The rising tide of bigotry and bloodshed.* New York: Plenum.

Maxfield, M., & Babbie, E. (2005). *Research methods for criminal justice & criminology* (4th ed.). Belmont, CA: Thomson-Wadsworth.

McDevitt, J., Balboni, J., Bennett, S., Weiss, J., Orchowsky, S., & Walbott, L. (2003). Improving the quality and accuracy of bias crime statistics nationally: An assessment of the first ten years of bias crime data collection. In B. Perry (Ed.), *Hate and bias crime: A reader* (pp. 77–89). New York: Routledge.

Moore, J. B. (1993). *Skinheads shaved for battle: A cultural history of American skinheads.* Bowling Green, OH: Bowling Green State University Press.

Perry, B. (2003). *Hate and bias crime: A reader.* New York: Routledge.

Perry, B. (2004). "White genocide": White supremacists and the politics of reproduction. In A. L. Ferber (Ed.), *Home-grown hate: Gender and organized racism* (pp. 75–95). New York: Routledge.

Southern Poverty Law Center. (2007). *HateWatch: For the record.* Retrieved September 24, 2007, from http://www.splcenter.org/intel/hatewatch/fortherecord.jsp

Southern Poverty Law Center. (2008). *Advocates for Justice and Equality.* Retrieved February 7, 2008, from http://www.splcenter.org/center/about.jsp

Strom, K. J. (2001). *Hate crimes reported in NIBRS, 1997–99.* Washington, DC: Bureau of Justice Statistics Special Report (NCJ 186765).

CHAPTER 7

BEHAVIOR OR MOTIVATION: TYPOLOGIES OF HATE–MOTIVATED OFFENDERS

Christopher Fisher and C. Gabrielle Salfati

Horrific incidents of violence motivated by hate against particular groups of individuals mar the history of modern society. Some of the more severe examples of these events include post–Civil War lynchings of African Americans in the United States; the rise of the Nazi state in Germany; the ethnic cleansings in the Balkans, Rwanda, and the Sudan; the rising tide of anti-Semitism in Europe at the end of the twentieth century; and the September 11 terrorist attacks (Green, McFalls, & Smith, 2001; Richardson & May, 1999). There also have been innumerable, more confined incidents ranging in severity from simple harassment on school playgrounds to the deaths of an African American man dragged by a truck and a 21-year-old gay college student severely beaten and left to die crucified on a fence. Research suggests that there are both psychological and sociological variables involved in the formation and expression of the hate involved in all of these types of incidents; however, questions remain about why some individuals choose to violently express their hate and whether the same behavioral dynamics are involved in the expression of different kinds of hate (Allport, 1954; Ehrlich, 1990).

OFFENDER DATA AND TRENDS

Official collection of data on hate crimes in the United States began in 1991, following the passing of the Hate Crime Statistics Act (HCSA) in 1990. The Federal Bureau of Investigation (FBI) took on the responsibility of collecting and disseminating this data and incorporated the process into the preexisting Uniform Crime Report (UCR). Before and after the passage of the HCSA, numerous advocacy groups assumed the task of collecting victim-, offender-, and situational-related data to supplement the data officially collected by the government. Almost the entire body of research devoted to the investigation of who commits hate crimes has found that these offenders tend to be young males, acting as part of a group—but not as a part of an organized hate group—who come from middle-class families, have no criminal record, victimize targets of convenience, and are complete strangers to the individuals they victimize (Bufkin, 1999; Cotton, 1992; Craig, 2002; Franklin, 1998, 2000; Harry, 1990; Kuehnle & Sullivan, 2001; Mason, 1997; Maxwell & Maxwell, 1995; Reasons & Hughson, 2000; Richardson & May, 1999; Van de Ven, Bornholt, & Bailey, 1996).

Research carried out through the cooperation of the New York City Police Department found that 80 percent of the hate crime offenders handled by the department were adolescents (Cotton, 1992, p. 3000). Another study based on data collected in New York City found that individuals under the age of 21 committed more hate crimes than those individuals over 21, and that up to 71 percent of the crimes included in the study sample were committed by individuals under the age of 20 (p. 36). It is important to consider the average age of offenders given that research has found that when adolescents—the most common offenders—engage in hate crimes, they tend to physically victimize their targets (Maxwell & Maxwell, 1995).

Group dynamics, including the number of offenders and the ratio of offenders to victims, are central components of the process of hate crimes (Bufkin, 1999; Franklin, 2000; Reasons & Hughson, 2000). Bufkin's research found that multiple perpetrators are involved in 48 percent of hate crimes, and in only 22 percent of nonhate crimes (p.161). Craig (2002, p. 87) and Franklin (2000) assert that hate crimes are very much a group activity, citing official data as indicating that up to two-thirds of reported hate crimes are committed by two or more people. In their study examining hate crime in New York City, Maxwell and Maxwell (1995) found that the average number of offenders was usually higher than one offender for all types of hate incidents/crimes. The fact that most hate crimes involve multiple offenders is important because research has found that the higher number of perpetrators involved in a violent crime, the more severe the crime (Craig, 2002).

A majority of the research indicates groups of hate crime offenders are typically complete strangers to their victims, particularly in incidents involving youth offenders and youth victims (Maxwell & Maxwell, 1995). Specifically, Reasons and Hughson found that around 41 percent of offenders were complete strangers (2000, p. 140), with 67 percent of offenders under the age of 30 known to the victim and only 21 percent of offenders under the age of 18 known, it appears that the younger the offender, the more likely they are to victimize a stranger (Reasons & Hughson, p. 140). It also has been found that when assailants are known to the victim (e.g., friends, relatives, and lovers) hate crimes are less likely to be reported, but more likely to be extremely violent (Kuehnle & Sullivan, 2001).

The main body of research on hate crime incidents—in an effort to legitimize the study of hate crime as a unique type of event—has focused on how such incidents are different from nonhate crimes. These studies have found that up to three-fourths of hate-motivated assaults involve physical injury, while only 29 percent of nonhate assaults do (Bufkin, 1999, p. 162; Craig, 2002: 8049). Thirty percent of hate-motivated assaults are so severe that the victim requires hospitalization, while only 7 percent of nonhate assaults approach that level of severity (Bufkin, 1999, p. 162; Levin & McDevitt, 1993).

Overall, researchers have concluded that hate crimes are different on almost every factor (Mason, 1997; Maxwell & Maxwell, 1995). The differences that have been examined, however, are descriptive at best, and lacking when it comes specifically to hate-motivated homicide. Determining if the situational and behavioral dynamics of hate homicides differ based on the motivation and the location could significantly increase the understanding of these homicides and other hate-motivated crimes.

Summary of Trend Data

With data on hate crimes having been collected for over 16 years, trends are beginning to be discussed. These trends, however, are seen generally as tenuous, given that it is a relatively new field, and many researchers are unsure if the changes represent actual variation in hate crime or if they are results of ever-increasing attention to the problem. One consistent trend in the hate crime data is that racially motivated incidents and crimes are the most common. Interestingly, during the middle to late 1990s, official data indicated that hate crimes were increasing and that they specifically were increasing for incidents not motivated by racial hate (Anderson, Dyson, & Brooks, 2002). Groups particularly being victimized more frequently included Asians, Hispanics, and gays and lesbians. Overall, the end of the twentieth century was marked by a 3 percent decrease in hate crimes; however, at the same time antihomosexual hate crimes rose an astounding 81 percent (Reasons & Hughson, 2000). Following the September 11 terrorist attacks, hate crimes significantly increased, mostly attributable to the spike in anti-Arab/Muslim hate crimes following the attacks, but have leveled off in the years since. One of the more startling trends recently uncovered is that while hate crimes have been generally leveling off or decreasing, they have been increasing in intensity. The most recent FBI numbers indicate an 8 percent increase in hate-motivated crimes in 2006 (FBI, 2007). Other than research indicating that hate crimes are becoming more severe, which is based primarily on basic official data, patterns of severe hate violence have not been addressed. With studies showing that hate crimes are changing—both intensifying and diversifying—it is becoming increasingly important to understand how the dynamics of the most violent form of hate differ for various hate motivations.

Although these data and trend analyses provide a description of who the typical hate crime perpetrator is, they do not grant the kind of insight useful for making the subtle distinctions between these offenders—who overall have been found to be remarkably similar—that would be required of a criminal investigator or psychologist charged with the task of differentiating hate-motivated offenders based on crime-scene evidence. With only this type of data at hand, if an investigator or psychologist were trying to generate a description of the likely suspect of a hate crime, that description, or profile, would apply to a majority of the entire country's male population in high school and college.

Acknowledging that descriptions of the typical hate-motivated offender could move the research on hate crime only so far, some of the leading researchers in the field of hate crimes (Levin & McDevitt, 1993; McDevitt, Levin, & Bennett, 2002) developed typologies (or classification systems) of hate-motivated offenders with the goal of presenting means of capturing and understanding the often subtle differences between offenders and their crimes.

TYPOLOGIES AND PROFILING OF OFFENDERS

A typology, or classification system, is intended to group offenders together based on common underlying factors. The field of criminal justice includes a variety of typologies, ranging from those focused on individuals who offend against children, rapists, and stalkers to domestic and violent offenders. Generally, there has been a lack of a common reason for developing such typologies, with some created to help determine offender risk level, others to identify possible treatment options, and still others to provide an empirical basis for profiling offenders based on crime-scene evidence. According to Hood and Sparks (1970), a good typology "should separate offenders or kinds of behavior into types which have different theoretical explanations appropriate to them" (p. 124).

The notion of typologizing offenders has its roots in the work of Cesare Lombroso in 1876 and his student Enrico Ferri in the early 1900s. Lombroso acknowledged that his work—grounded in anthropometric measurements—on the biological and typological theory of criminals, which resulted in a schema of six types, was limited in its ability to identify either the motivation or causation of the offender's behavior. Ferri expanded two of Lombroso's existing types and added a seventh, but did not drastically alter the methods used for establishing the classification scheme. As criminal justice research matured and became more rigorous during the next 100 years, the main

criticism of these early typologies focused on the lack of any empirical testing in their development. As a result, the typologies that sprung from their
work began to incorporate the empirically obtained data into their conceptualization and testing.

The likely hundreds of typologies that were crafted after the initial work
of Lombroso and Ferri have addressed issues ranging from offender risk assessment to appropriate offender treatment options. Specific to the current
discussion is the use of typologies as the basis for classifying types of offenders either to improve our understanding of the motivation of the offender
(i.e., why the offender committed the specific act) or to provide insight into
the behavioral aspects associated with the overall style of the offense so that
a type of offender can be linked to his or her respective type of crime—the
process commonly referred to as profiling.

While violent crime has decreased throughout the United States since the
early 1990s, there is a continued need to better understand the behavioral dynamics of violent crime. According to the FBI's UCR, violent crime dropped
precipitously in the United States at the end of the 1990s and over the past
few years, declining 3.2 percent in 2003 alone (FBI, 2004). This reduction of
violent crime, however, was marred by an increase in homicide and by a continuing decline in homicide clearance rates (FBI, 2004; Wellford & Cronin,
1999). In recognition of these facts, researchers have continued working
to improve the understanding of the interrelations between offender, victim, and situational variables and how that information can assist homicide
investigators. These efforts have included developing more sound methods
of connecting offender crime-scene behaviors and offender characteristics
expressed at crime scenes with offender background characteristics. Understanding the evolution of homicide classification frameworks into one of the
current systems, which is based on the expressive/instrumental dichotomy
(Salfati, 2000), is a necessary step in comprehending how to apply the same
methodology in examining hate-motivated crimes, including homicides.

Wolfgang (1958) and Block (1977)—recognizing that murder is an interpersonal event that is influenced by the individuals involved and their
relationship to each other—were some of the first social scientists to conduct studies on homicides and those who are involved in them. These early
explorations of this extreme expression of aggression primarily focused on
offender demographics, the relationship between the offender(s) and the
victim(s), and the method of killing. Psychiatrists, often using convenience
samples or other methodologically questionable techniques, attempted to
develop typologies of murderers, but these classifications often lacked a theoretical underpinning (Bromberg, 1961)

The FBI can be credited with laying the groundwork for the process of linking the patterns present in offender crime scene behaviors to the background
characteristics of the offenders (Ressler, Burgess, & Douglas, 1988). This early

work by the FBI focused on developing a profiling classification for sexual homicides, namely the organized/disorganized typology. As with any new area of research, however, this work represented a foundation that needed to be scientifically evaluated. The FBI expanded the scope of homicide research by focusing on the behavioral aspects of homicide that had been ignored by earlier researchers. They developed a classification system where crime-scene behaviors were used to categorize the homicide scene as organized or disorganized. Researchers who have evaluated the FBI's original system found that its various methodological issues—lacking details helpful to investigators and relying on volunteers which presented a biased sample, and restricted its contribution to the field mainly to the concept of treating crime-scene behaviors as a unit of analysis (Canter, Alison, Wentink & Alison 2004; Salfati, 2000; Santilla, Canter, Elfgren & Hakkanen, 2001). Furthermore, as Canter et al. (2004) showed in their initial evaluation of the FBI typology, many of the differentiating behaviors—those behaviors relied on primarily to distinguish between types of offenders who were generally similar—were common to a majority of offenders, and therefore unsuitable differentiators. Overall, these previous classification systems, while helpful in adding to what is known about the behavior of violent offenders, did not provide a rigorously empirically-based model to connect crime-scene behaviors to different types of offenders or to the background characteristics of offenders.

Empirically-based models using crime-scene behaviors form the basis of the investigative psychology approach to understanding and classifying crime scenes. Advocates of this approach have attempted to develop an understanding of violent crime through examinations of the psychological and behavioral dynamics that play a role in incidents of extreme aggression. Such an understanding would be more systematic and empirical than approaches employed by other researchers, including the FBI (Buss & Shacklerford, 1997; Santilla et al., 2001). These efforts to better understand violent crime have two stages: developing a description of the main characteristics of crime scenes and connecting these crime-scene characteristics to offender characteristics (Salfati, 2000; Salfati & Canter, 1999). The key concept in this approach to research is the idea that an offender's actions, or general themes of criminal behavior, at a crime scene can assist researchers and law enforcement personnel in identifying the offender's specific background characteristics (i.e., aspects of the offender's background that could help identify a type of person who would share those characteristics; Canter, 2000; 1994; Salfati, 2000). The relationship between the offender and victim also is important. Since aggression, and therefore homicide/murder, is understood to be an interpersonal interaction, the relationship between the actors is a significant factor in the dynamics of the incident (Wolfgang, 1958). This contention finds support in homicide data, which consistently shows that stranger homicides are much less frequent than homicides between individuals who know each other. The degree of the relationship also has been found to affect the incident, with better-known offenders engaging in homicides expressing higher levels of emotion (Gillis, 1986).

In a study clearly showing this type of approach is possible, Salfati and Canter (1999) established three distinct themes of single victim–single offender stranger homicides: expressive (impulsive), instrumental (opportunistic), and instrumental (cognitive). Expressive homicides included random, varied violent offender behaviors, with offenders who had a history of violence. Instrumental (opportunistic) homicides had offenders who viewed their victims as means to an end. The opportunistic offender picked victims who they thought would make it easy to achieve their goal of obtaining property or even sex. Such offenders usually were found to be unemployed, had previous burglary/theft convictions, knew their victims, and lived close to where the crime occurred. Cognitive homicides were characterized as highly forensic, with the offender frequently trying to hide evidence of the crime. Such offenders are routinely violent in their lives because they view other people only as obstacles preventing them from reaching their goals. Relationship with the victim is not a factor, as who the victim is not key to defining these types of offenders.

This style of research often uses Multidimensional methodologies such as Smallest Space Analysis (SSA) and Multidimensional Scaling Analysis (MSA) to examine and test the theoretically hypothesized typologies. SSA analyses hold that the system of behavior is best understood if the relationship between every variable and every other variable is examined (Shye, Elizur, & Hoffman, 1994).

Homicide researchers have dramatically advanced this new method of analyzing violent crimes, finding that there are specific themes of behavior at crime scenes that are mirrored in past behaviors. These similarly styled behaviors allow investigators to use the crime scene to identify potential suspects. Other research has found that this approach works cross-nationally and for other types of violent crime such as serial rape and serial homicide, while ongoing work is evaluating its utility cross-culturally (Salfati & Dupont, 2006; Salfati & Haratsis, 2001). Hate homicide, lacking such a systematic analysis of the behavioral and situational dynamics involved, needs to be examined in a similar manner.

Typologizing Hate Crimes

The idea of classifying hate crimes has not been completely overlooked. Some of the primary researchers of hate crime realized that a classification system of types of hate crime could greatly assist in understanding and even investigating such crimes. Levin and McDevitt (1993) are responsible for a significant portion of the research that seeks to explain why some individuals act out their bias attitudes. Their work has focused on developing the main classification of hate crimes, which primarily has focused on understanding offender motivations, including thrill-seeking, mission, defensive, and retaliatory. While this classification system is broad enough that it most likely captures all hate crime offenders, does not specify mutually exclusive types and still paints the typical hate crime offender as someone who is not part of normal, everyday culture (Perry, 2001). While this sort of system does explain, at least at the general individual level, what gives rise to the criminal expression of hate in specific incidents, it provides a limited framework and information that could help investigators. Law enforcement personnel unfortunately do not have the luxury of access to the offender's mind when they are investigating a case with an unknown offender; therefore, making connections between psychological motivations and crime-scene behaviors would become guesswork instead of an empirically based process.

THE MCDEVITT, LEVIN, AND BENNETT TYPOLOGY

McDevitt, Levin, and Bennett (2002) have been working on their classification system since Levin and McDevitt's earlier work in 1993, and have revised the system from the original three divisions—excitement/thrill, defensive, and mission hate crimes—to the most recent four-division model, which added the additional category of retaliatory hate crime. The original and revised schemes were based on case files for hate crimes reported between July 1991 and December 1992 to the Community Disorders Unit of the Boston Police Department, which is manned by experienced police investigators specially trained to investigate hate crimes in Boston.

McDevitt, Levin, and Bennett (2002) approached the construction of their more recent typology based on underlying theories present in the work of several other hate crime researchers, as well as their original work, all of which had investigated how hate-motivated crimes are justified in the minds of those who commit them. Out of this research, which found that hate crimes are explained away in the minds of offenders in a variety of very similar ways, Levin and McDevitt (1993) postulated that violent hate crime offenders could be classified according to what motivated them to commit specific incidents of hate-motivated crime. They acknowledge that bigotry is the underlying motivation for all hate crimes; however, they stress that aside from the base motivation, every offender is different in respect to the specific situational and psychological variables that lead them to violently act out that bigotry. It is these differentiating variables that offer theoretical support to the hypothesis of McDevitt, Levin, and Bennett that the location of a hate crime, the situational factors surrounding the commission of the crime, and how the offender commits the crime all can be used to determine the motivation of the offender, and thus, some of the characteristics of the offender.

McDevitt, Levin, and Bennett (2002) present their types of hate crime as follows: *thrill* hate crimes, where the offenders commit the crimes simply for the excitement or thrill of the act; *defensive* hate crimes, where the offenders see themselves as defenders of neighborhoods or resources; *mission* hate crimes, where the offenders take it as their mission to rid the world of individuals or groups they believe are evil or undeserving; and *retaliatory* hate crimes, with the offenders responding to a real or perceived affront to them or their group. These types will be fleshed out further when they are defined for analysis later in this chapter.

While most hate crime research has not focused specifically on violent hate-motivated crimes, the general body of research has found that each of the motivations suggested by McDevitt, Levin, and Bennett (2002) are present across the spectrum of hate crimes. Researchers focused on the nexus of limited economic opportunities and hate behavior (Green, Glaser, & Rich, 1998) have theorized that some hate offenders commit their crimes to protect or *defend* those opportunities; general hate crime research has found both that many hate-motivated offenders commit their crimes because they believe that minority victims represent easy opportunities to commit a crime simply for the *thrill* of it and that many hate-motivated crimes spur on *retaliatory* crimes, which are responses to real or rumored offenses against a specific person or group; and some individuals focused on understanding the beliefs and behaviors of organized hate groups have described the motivation of individuals who belong to these groups as *mission*-based, with the intention to purify the earth. Obviously, the motivations themselves have theoretical support; however, the supposition that crime-scene information can reveal an offender's motivation, as well as the approach used to test that supposition, does not share the same theoretical support. Concerns about the theoretical support and real-world usefulness of a typology directly tied to offender motivation, combined with additional questions surrounding the approach used to develop the typology, made it obvious that the McDevitt, Levin, and Bennett typology—the main hate crime typology available in the literature—needed to be empirically tested to determine if it could successfully distinguish hate-motivated crimes into meaningful categories.

Critique of the McDevitt, Levin, and Bennett Typology

In determining the situational factors and crime-scene behaviors that are indicative of each motivation type of hate crime, McDevitt, Levin, and Bennett (2002) admit that many of the variables they identified were not exclusive to one motivation category. It is, however, this lack of exclusivity that gives rise to the main criticism of this type of classification (e.g. Canter & Wentick, 2004). If variables that are apparent at a crime scene are associated with multiple motivations, then they offer little help in distinguishing one crime from another. Aside from issues surrounding the creation of the list of factors/behaviors associated with different motivations, there is a theoretical problem with formulating a crime-scene-related classification scheme that is based on the motivation of the offender. When an investigator begins examining a crime scene, particularly a homicide scene such as all of the scenes analyzed in the current research, there are only observable crime-scene variables with which to work—unless there is a witness or a surviving victim (Salfati, 2000).

Even if all of the motivations were exclusive in terms of their associated situational/behavioral factors and the motivation for a crime could be discerned based on the presence of certain groups of those factors, a question about the usefulness of using such a typology as a basis for crime-scene investigation. Motivation is important when it comes to understanding why someone committed a crime, but without many unobservable factors, which could rarely be present, investigators might not be able to routinely narrow down the types of offenders who could have committed that crime based solely on knowing the motivation (Canter & Wentick, 2004).

It is also not clear from the McDevitt, Levin, and Bennett (2002) model how the information gleaned from the case files was used to develop the classification scheme. The process was described generally as based on the connection between case-file information and information gathered from the offenders about their motivations. With the motivation for each crime known, the most common characteristics across each motivation were grouped together to develop attack characteristics representative of each type. The problems with this process are that it once again bases the development of this type of classification scheme on a top-down model where incident characteristics are matched to a later-known motivation, and that it results in typologies that share multiple attack characteristics; it is, therefore, nearly impossible to connect crime scenes exclusively to one type of offender based on perceived motivation because some crime scenes will have offenders who share characteristics and behaviors from more than one type. At many crime scenes there may be only a select few of the possible observable attack characteristics present, and if there are too many nonexclusive variables in the typology, it is possible that a crime scene would have a majority of its observable characteristics be variables that are also associated with another motivation type. This would leave the typology useless for an investigator unless the investigator somehow became aware of nonobservable attack characteristics.

McDevitt, Levin, and Bennett (2002) have dealt with these issues by focusing on the presence or absence of one or two particular crime-scene characteristics that may distinguish hate crimes; however, most of these characteristics could be described as precipitating factors that would not be readily apparent from the evidence available at some crime scenes. They state that whether a fight occurred before a hate-motivated assault helps to distinguish *defensive* vs. *retaliatory* incidents; however, as discussed previously, it would not be apparent routinely to a homicide investigator if a fight occurred beforehand unless there were witnesses or a surviving victim. There needs to be a set of criteria that can distinguish offenders when a variety of features that are present are typical of several types of hate crime.

There are other concerns about the formulation of the typology. One of these is the lack of direct empirical testing of the typology. There is no way to know if any of the definitive characteristics McDevitt, Levin, and Bennett (2002) cite as useful for determining hate crime type predictably co-occur. There have been no statistical differentiations of the types to support if there are even simple differences in the frequencies of specific behavioral occurrences across the four categories of hate-motivated crimes; rather, the model is supported by describing how examples of different types of crimes—such as a hate-motivated assault that was clearly an attempt by the offender to retaliate against being insulted—are used to illustrate how the behaviors that occurred in that particular incident can be distinguished from similar behaviors in another assault motivated by a desire purely for excitement/thrill. Relying on this sort of distinction instead of on empirical testing means that there is no objective framework for determining when a hate-motivated offense would be classified as one of the four types.

Overall, these issues make it very difficult to operationalize the crime-scene characteristics that could be used to empirically test the model in question. The McDevitt, Levin, and Bennett (2002) model has helped investigators understand the dynamics of hate-motivated crimes, particularly those where there are victims, witnesses, and offenders to speak with. In order to further adapt this model for use in actual investigations, further empirical testing and a greater focus on objective observable behaviors is still needed.

AN EMPIRICAL MODEL OF HATE-MOTIVATED HOMICIDE

Following the work of Salfati (2000) and Canter and Wentick (2004), Fisher (2007) sought to establish an empirically derived and validated typology of hate-motivated homicides using various Multidimensional Scaling techniques. One of the primary stages of that research was the empirical testing, by way of SSA analyses, of the applicability of the McDevitt, Levin, and Bennett (2002) hate crime typology—generally based on hate-motivated assaults—to hate-motivated homicides. Fisher's analysis focused heavily on describing and understanding how the McDevitt, Levin, and Bennett hate crime types overlap in terms of crime-scene attack characteristics and how, if at all, the types can be distinguished. The analysis generally can be grouped in response to the two challenges outlined in the previous critique of the typology: analyses undertaken to identify and understand the behaviors

McDevitt, Levin, and Bennett linked to their types, as well as those that would theoretically fit within those types and provide a basis for empirical testing, and determining the existence of exclusive types empirically linked to the behaviors hypothesized to be associated with them.

Defining and Understanding the Variables and Their Distributions

McDevitt, Levin, and Bennett (2002) did not specifically outline a method for operationalizing the crime-scene variables supporting their bias-crime typology that would allow a researcher to test the scheme. As a result, Fisher (2007) developed a list of observable crime-scene behaviors based on comparisons of descriptions of such behaviors in hate crime and homicide research to the McDevitt, Levin, and Bennett typology to determine which variables would best represent the traits suggested by the typology. Because Fisher's work focused specifically on understanding the crime scene itself as it relates to bias homicides, it should be noted that only variables that could objectively be gleaned from the crime-scene evidence were included because variables such as whether the offender lured the victim or the offender was on drugs would be indeterminable without access to witnesses or the offender. The variables that were operationalized based on the typology descriptions and chosen to be included in the analyses can be found in Table 7.1 and are described in full in Table 7.2. The process of selecting the variables and allocating them to the appropriate motivation(s) is discussed in detail in the following section.

Variable Selection Criteria for Each Type

The variables for each type were conceptualized through an examination of hate crime research as well as general violence/homicide research (Fisher, 2007). The work of Canter and Wentick (2004) was used as a guide in developing the methods for the study, given that those researchers faced similar challenges in defining a set of behavioral variables that were not directly discussed by the creators of the typology under examination. As noted in Tables 7.1 and 7.2, those variables that are marked with an asterisk came directly from the information included in the McDevitt, Levin, and Bennett (2002) study. Only two variables outlined in the McDevitt, Levin, and Bennett typology were not covered by the included behaviors—commitment to bias and deterrence. These were not included because they are not objectively observable crime scene behaviors (Fisher, 2007). There were very few objectively observable crime-scene behaviors discussed in either the original or revised typologies; therefore, most of the behaviors that are included in Fisher's work were added based on research findings suggesting their

Table 7.1 Bias-Motivated Homicide Types with Variables Selected for Each

	Thrill	Retaliatory	Defensive	Mission
Offenders	Multiple*	Single*	Multiple*	Multiple*
Location	Outside	Outside, victim residence	Outside	Inside, victim residence
Wounding Method	Manual*, blunt*, knife* multiple wounds	Blunt*, firearm* single wound	Manual*, blunt*, knife* multiple wounds	Firearm*, knife* multiple wounds
Control/ Preparation	Binding and gagging, strangulation	None	None	None
Treatment of the body/ Awareness of Evidence	Postmortem activity, sexual behavior, forensically aware offender, covering body, property stolen, spent time at crime scene	Forensic evidence, body left at murder site	Body left at murder site	Forensically aware offender, body left at murder site
Weapon	Weapon to*, from*	Weapon to*	Weapon from*	Weapon to*
Wound Location	Face, torso, pelvis	Torso, head	Limbs, torso	Neck, head, pelvis
Precipitating and hate factors		Frequent hate crimes, locality, bias object*, bias symbol*	Locality, frequent hate crimes, bias object*	Holiday, bias object*, frequent hate crimes, bias symbol*

* Derived from McDevitt, Levin, and Bennett (2002) study.

association with behaviors that were compositionally similar to the behaviors described by McDevitt, Levin, and Bennett. The variables for each type were conceptualized as described below.

Thrill-Related Hate Crimes

The crime scenes of thrill-related hate crimes are described as instances of perpetrators leaving their turf in search of a victim in an area or particular location where individuals of a particular racial, ethnic, religious,

Table 7.2   Definitions of Variables Selected for Analysis

Variable definitions

1. injpelv: pelvis injured
2. injface: face injured
3. injhead: head (other than face) injured
4. injneck: neck injured
5. torso: torso (front or back) injured
6. Limbs: arms/hands or legs/feet injured
7. m_wnds: multiple wounds present
8. single: single wound present

9*. firearm: wound from a firearm
10. Cutting: wound(s) from a cutting instrument
11*. manual: victim killed manually
12*. bluntins: wounds from a blunt instrument
13. strangul: evidence of strangulation
14*. weapto: weapon brought to scene
15*. weapfrom: weapon came from scene
16. Bin_gag: victim bound and/or gagged
17. murdsite: body found at murder site
18. outside: body found outside
19. vicres: body found in victim residence
20. forevid: forensic evidence at scene
21. ForOff: forensically aware offender tampered with potential evidence
22. pm_treat: post-mortem treatment of body, including dismemberment
23. Covering: body covered partially or completely
24. Sex_tot: sexual behavior toward/with victim
25. propstol: property stolen from scene or victim
26. spenttim: offender spent time at scene after murder
27*. multioff: evidence of multiple offenders
28*. viclocal: victim was in another group's "territory"
29*. freqhate: history of frequent bias crimes in the area
30. holiday: homicide occurred in conjunction with a significant holiday
31*. biasdraw: bias-related drawings or writings left at scene
32*. biasobj: bias-related object left at scene

* Derived from McDevitt, Levin, and Bennett (2002) study.

or sexual orientation group are known to be found. These targeted victims are not chosen randomly; instead, they are selected because they represent or are thought to represent an out-group. The offenders engage in these incidents to seek out a cheap thrill, to gain bragging rights among their peer group, and mostly to derive a sense of power and/or control (Franklin, 2000).

They derive pleasure from inflicting pain on the victim, and, in a sense, controlling the victim. As a result, the killer may not seek a quick death, instead wishing to enjoy the pain and suffering for as long as possible by restraining and torturing the victims. Methods of killing may include strangulation, beating, or stabbing. Continuing the desire for control and power, the offender may engage in sexual activity with the victim while the victim is still alive (Canter & Wentick, 2004). Postmortem the offender may still desire the ability to control the victim, and therefore become concerned with concealing the crime and dispose of or hide the body—either by covering, isolating, or concealing it—and remove any weapons. Some offenders may remove particular body parts to maintain the sense of control and power. These murders have a very professional feel to them, including evidence that the offender was cognizant of forensic evidence (Canter & Wentick).

Mission-Related Hate Crimes

Mission-motivated crime scenes are described as well planned and particularly focused on the actual act of killing the victim (Canter & Wentick, 2004; McDevitt, Levin & Bennett, 2002). There is no desire to engage in postmortem activities such as torture, dismemberment, or sexual activity. Methods of killing are all designed to achieve the end of the victim's life as quickly as possible (Canter & Wentick). Based on the description provided by McDevitt, Levin, and Bennett, and following the work of Holmes and Holmes (1998), Fisher (2007) concluded that it was likely that mission-oriented offenders would remove the weapon from the scene to reduce the chance of their identity being revealed or because of possible symbolic meanings of the weapon. There was an inherent difficulty in connecting objective crime-scene characteristics to the mission motivation because of how strongly that type was based on a particular motivation. That is, while a retaliatory hate crime could be said to be based on a particular motivation, in reality it can be seen as an attempt to restore self-esteem or honor that has been diminished because of a real or perceived affront. Mission-motivated hate crimes, however, are all about achieving an end—riding the world of an evil group—so that a lot of the behaviors that theoretically are associated with such crimes (hate group membership, personal writings, etc.) would not result in observable crime-scene characteristics (Canter & Wentick; Fisher).

Defensive-Related Hate Crime

Defensive-type offenders engage in activity designed to restore honor or dignity (McDevitt, Levin, & Bennett, 2002). These are not quick crimes or kills, and the method of offending is often very severe—the thought being that a message needs to be sent to other out-group members by violently injuring the victim. The particular victim is not important; rather, it is only necessary that the victim is or is perceived to be a member of the group the offender believes is invading his or her turf or stealing his or her resources (Franklin, 2000).

Retaliation-Related Hate Crime

Retaliatory hate-motivated crimes are incidents where the offenders are responding to real or perceived affronts to the honor of their group (McDevitt, Levin, & Bennett, 2002). These incidents are distinct from those where the offenders are responding to the mere presence of a group or individual, such as is the case with defensive hate crimes. When these types of hate-motivated crime reach the level of murder, they often involve quick-kill weapons and techniques, as the main goal is to kill the individual(s) who committed the initial incident (Dunning, 2000).

METHODS

Considering the success of Canter and Wentick's (2004) methodology in testing the Holmes and Holmes (1998) serial-murder typology, Fisher (2007) employed the same methodology in his examination of the McDevitt, Levin, and Bennett (2002) typology. Their hate crime typology, which primarily included assaults, was not formulated specifically for hate-motivated homicides; however, if a typology of hate-motivated crime is to have universal value, it should apply to all levels of hate crime. The first step in the analysis—identifying those variables that overlapped across multiple types (see Table 7.3)—has already been discussed in the general critique of the typology. Identifying the high-frequency variables delineated the general core of hate-motivated homicides and clarified which behaviors would be most helpful in the distinguishing of the homicides (see Table 7.4). With the high-frequency variables addressed, the hate crime typology was tested by examining the frequency of co-occurrences among every variable included in the analysis to determine, beyond simple frequencies, whether the presence of certain variables together at a crime scene could be used to determine if that crime scene is indicative of a specific classification of hate-motivated crimes consisting of psychologically similar behaviors. Producing all of these frequencies would be rather simple, but interpreting them would be a monumental task; therefore,

Table 7.3   Variables Cross-Referenced by Each Type

	% of crime scenes	Thrill	Retaliatory	Defensive	Mission
Multiple offenders	42.9	✓		✓	✓
Multiple wounds	44	✓		✓	✓
Blunt instrument	26.4	✓	✓	✓	
Injury to torso**	71.4	✓	✓	✓	
Outside**	80.2	✓	✓	✓	
Frequent hate	15.4		✓	✓	✓
Bias object	2.2		✓	✓	✓
Weapon to scene**	80.2	✓	✓		✓
Murder site**	84.6		✓	✓	✓
Forensic aware offender	17.6	✓			✓
Injury pelvis	14.3	✓			✓
Manual wounding	23.1	✓		✓	
Cutting	25.3	✓		✓	
Weapon from scene	25.3	✓		✓	
Forensic evidence**	65.9		✓	✓	
Victim residence	14.3		✓		✓
Bias drawing	5.5		✓		✓
Injury to head	42.9		✓		✓
Firearm**	51.6		✓		✓
Strangulation	3.3	✓			
Binding/Gagging	4.4	✓			
Spent time at crime scene	13.2	✓			
Covering body	6.6	✓			
Property stolen	25.3	✓			
Injury to face	28.6	✓			
Postmortem treatment of body	12.1	✓			
Sexual treatment	9.9	✓			
Injury limbs	29.7			✓	
Holiday	5.5				✓
Injury to neck	23.1				✓
Single wound	29.7		✓		
Victim locality	7.7		✓		
Total		19	14	13	14

** Crime Scene Behavior Occurred in over 50 percent of all the cases.

Table 7.4 Frequencies of Selected Variables Across Sample

Crime scene variable	Frequency	Grouping
Body found at murder site	85%	
Weapon brought to scene	80%	
Body found outside	80%	High frequency (>50%) (i.e., cannot be used to classify scenes)
Wound to torso	71%	
Forensic evidence found	66%	
Firearm used	52%	
Multiple wounds	44%	
Multiple offenders	43%	
Injury to head	43%	
Injury to limbs	30%	
Single wound	30%	
Injury to face	29%	Medium frequency (20–50%)
Blunt object used	26%	
Property stolen	25%	
Weapon from scene	25%	
Cutting victim	25%	
Manual wounding	23%	
Injury to neck	23%	
Forensically aware offender	18%	
Frequent bias crimes in area	15%	
Murder at victim residence	14%	
Injury to pelvis	14%	
Offender spent time at scene	13%	
Postmortem treatment of body	12%	
Sexual behavior	10%	
Victim in "other" locality	8%	Low frequency (<20%)
Covering of body	7%	
Bias-related drawings	6%	
Holiday significance	6%	
Binding and gagging	4%	
Strangulation	3%	
Bias-related object	2%	

SSA was the methodology of choice because it allows the frequencies of co-occurrences of all the variables to be displayed and interpreted in a geometric space, and it was the technique utilized by Canter and Wentick (2004). Using SSA to analyze crime-scene actions through the analysis of behavior frequencies and the use of SSA models to uncover behavioral themes have also been used successfully in numerous other studies (Canter et al., 2004; Canter & Heritage, 1990; Canter & Wentick; Salfati, 2003; 2000; Salfati & Canter, 1999).

SSA represents every crime-scene variable as a point in space, where the amount of distance between any two points represents how frequently they co-occur, with points that are closer together having higher correlations with each other. There is an inherent regional hypothesis with the SSA methodology: characteristics of each type of hate crime should be found in distinct regions of the SSA geometric space.

The testing of the hypotheses involves a visual examination of the SSA geometric plots, which, if the typology is valid, should reveal four distinct regions with variables corresponding to the four types of bias crime outlined by McDevitt, Levin, and Bennett (2002). The lack of any identifiable regions would indicate a lack of support for the four-type model, while the presence of one or two regions would provide limited support for the classification scheme. If the SSA space does not reveal a corresponding four-region model, it still can be directly examined to determine a more applicable model identifying the main distinctions among bias crimes (Canter & Wentick, 2004).

THE DATA

Fisher's (2007) work was based on 91 hate-motivated homicides reported to the FBI's UCR program.[1] These 91 hate-motivated homicides represented approximately two-thirds of all of the hate-motivated homicides that were reported between 1991 and 2002 to the FBI, following the passage of the HCSA of 1990. Homicides committed prior to 1991 were not included because they were not officially classified as hate crimes. Specifically, the data for this research were taken from closed, fully adjudicated state and local cases that were contributed from law enforcement agencies from around the country for the purpose of research. All identifiers, including names of victims, suspects, offenders, officers, departments, and correctional agencies, were removed. Only aggregate data were reported on. A randomization of the cases was not possible given the nature of the data collection; however, a review of the states from which the cases came showed that the cases came from 32 states and represented all regions of the country. There were no areas of the country that were uniformly not submitting cases, and there were no years in the study that were disproportionately missing cases.

The classification of these cases as hate-motivated homicides by the investigating agencies was structured according to several legal definitions. According to the UCR data collection guidelines, the crime of "murder and non-negligent manslaughter [is] defined as the willful (non-negligent) killing of one human being by another. Not included in this definition are deaths caused by negligence, suicides, or accidental deaths. Attempts to commit murder are classified as aggravated assaults" (FBI, 2003, p. 497). The FBI, according to the HCSA, defines a hate crime as any criminal offense that is "motivated, in part or in full, by prejudice based on race, religion, sexual orientation, or ethnicity, including where appropriate the crimes of murder and non-negligent manslaughter; forcible rape; aggravated assault, simple assault, intimidation; arson; and destruction, damage or vandalism of property" (FBI, 2003, p. 3). In September 1994, the Violent Crime Control and Law Enforcement Act amended the HCSA to include bias against individuals with disabilities.

SSA Results

An SSA was run and produced an association matrix of each variable across the 91 homicide cases. The Guttman-Lingoes coefficient of alienation is an indication of how well the spatial representation produced by the SSA fits the co-occurrences as represented in the association matrix. The smaller the coefficient of alienation is, the better the fit of the plot to the original matrix (Borg & Lingoes, 1987). This three-dimensional SSA showed a coefficient of alienation of .142 in 28 iterations, indicating a good fit for this type of data. The results of the analysis were clearest when the projection of the first dimension against the second dimension for the three-dimensional solution was examined, so that configuration is used in this study (see Figure 7.1).

A visual examination of the SSA plot in Figure 7.1 showed a general clustering of almost all of the variables in the upper half of the plot, which suggested that in relation to the variables included in the study, the 91 hate-motivated homicides were fairly similar (Fisher, 2007). Fisher tested the validity of the typology by examining each motivation type one at a time to determine if the behaviors identified as belonging to a specific type co-occurred at a high rate with the other behaviors associated with that motivation. For example, the figure relating to the discussion of the mission-motivated hate homicide crime scenes would have the variables hypothesized to be indicative of a mission-oriented crime represented in the plot by a unique symbol, while those not found in research to be associated with that motivation would be represented by another symbol. Overall, the figures revealed that the four distinct regions representative of the four McDevitt, Levin, and Bennett (2002) hate crime types were not present.[2]

Previous research in this paradigm by advocates of investigative psychology supports the concept that because individuals consistently behave the

Figure 7.1 Three-Dimensional (1st Vector v. 2nd Vector) Small Space Analysis Plot of Bias-motivated Crime Scene Behaviors with Frequency Contours (Coefficient of alienation = .142, 28 iterations)

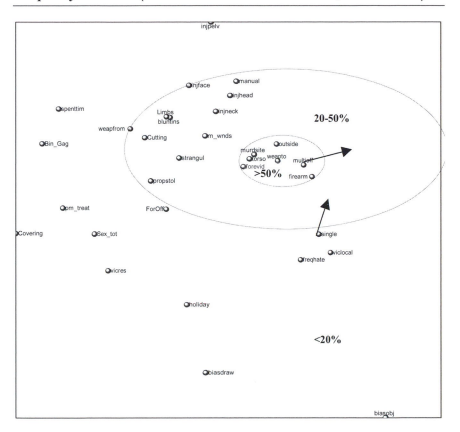

same way in similar contexts, behaviors displayed in crime scenes can be used to predict offender background characteristics, including offender–victim relationships (Canter et al., 2004; Farrington, 1991; Salfati, 2000, 2003; Salfati & Canter, 1999). Farrington's study found that even individuals who were identified as the most aggressive delinquents remained the most aggressive throughout their lives. This consistency leads to the links between crime-scene behaviors and offender characteristics becoming investigative tools. It also becomes possible to differentiate between offenders engaged in the same offense based on actions during the crime and their background characteristics (Donald & Wilson, 1999).

The Thrill Hate Murder

A majority of the observable crime-scene behaviors could be associated with the *thrill* type (Fisher, 2007) (see Figure 7.2). A majority of the

Figure 7.2 Three-Dimensional (1 v. 2) Small Space Analysis Plot of Bias-motivated Crime Scene Behaviors: Thrill Killer Variables Highlighted with Triangles (Coefficient of alienation = .142, 28 iterations)

thrill-type variables focused on how and where the victim was wounded. There was one group of thrill variables, which was slightly removed from the main group, located primarily in the upper-left quadrant of the plot (i.e., sexual behavior, postmortem treatment of the body, covering of the body, and removal of forensic evidence), which formed a slightly distinct type of thrill hate-motivated homicide—a type more concerned with the actual body of the victim as opposed to simply the act of committing the aggression. These victim-associated behaviors suggested that in these thrill homicides there is a sexual/control motivation underlying the overall desire for excitement and/or power (Fisher).

The tight grouping of thrill variables occupied about half of the plot, again indicating that the thrill type dominates the overall classification system. This predominance of thrill-related variables does not support a typology where thrill is just one of the classification types; however, it is not surprising, considering that McDevitt, Levin, and Bennett (2002) found that, based on their typology, two-thirds of all bias-motivated crimes are thrill crimes.

The Retaliatory Hate Homicide

The right side of the plot contained 10 variables indicative of retaliatory hate crimes (see Figure 7.3). As opposed to the thrill homicides, the retaliatory crime-scene variables did not focus on aspects of the victim—specifically the victim's body; rather, they portrayed an incident that was centered on a quick kill related to the atmosphere of an area being charged with hate—that is, these murders involved hate-related objects and drawings and took place in areas that had frequent bias crime/incident activity and/or are locations

Figure 7.3 Three-Dimensional Small Space Analysis Plot of Bias-motivated Crime Scene Behaviors: Retaliatory Killer Variables Marked with Triangles

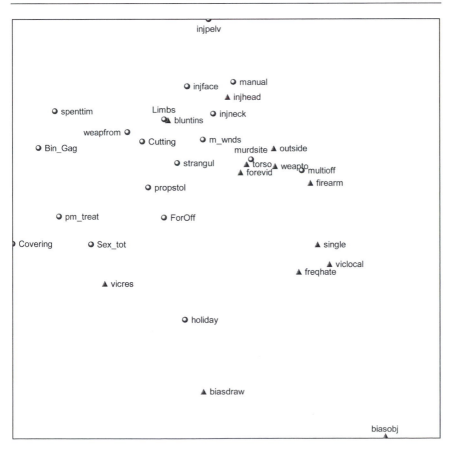

where the victim was not necessarily a common sight (i.e., the victim was seen in a location/neighborhood where someone like the victim was not normally seen). One such incident involved a shooting among two groups of young adults who had been exposed to ongoing racially tinged arguments about the use of a hate-related symbol at a community sporting event.

The clear divide between the thrill- and retaliatory-related variables suggested what may be an important distinction between hate-motivated homicides: some are acts designed to achieve a sense of power/control/excitement (i.e., thrill homicides where the offender quickly dominates the victim through overwhelming force or through direct control of the victim's body), and others are acts committed to restore a sense of self-esteem/honor (i.e., retaliation homicides where the offender is primarily motivated by a desire to repay some perceived wrong). With the retaliatory-related variables focused more on quickly killing a specific victim who had, in some way, interacted with an area and group of offenders who were primed as a result of ongoing bias-related incidents/beliefs that may have resulted in an affront to the offender's or offenders' honor, as opposed to the thrill-related variables centering on wounding and controlling the victim, the plot indicated that there were at least two themes of bias-motivated homicide that could be distinguished based on an analysis of variable co-occurrence. It should be emphasized, however, that the general lack of variable exclusivity across types makes any distinction questionable.

The Mission Hate Homicide

The mission-killing variables crossed both sides of the plot and were not confined to one particular region (see Figure 7.4). The variables encompassed the wounding behaviors/locations associated with thrill killings and the hate atmosphere of the crime-scene variables connected to the retaliatory killings. This again highlighted one of the main issues with their typology: there is an exceptional amount of *variable sharing* among the typology's four motivations, which results in an absence of a discernable thematic region of crime-scene behaviors associated with mission-motivated hate crimes (Fisher, 2007).

The Defensive Bias Murder

Much like the mission hate crime scenes, the defensive hate crime scenes were mostly confined to the right side of the SSA configuration (see Figure 7.5). These defensive crimes scenes were characterized by a slightly different set of wounding behaviors, which were less focused on quickly killing the victim, as well as a lack of concern about forensic evidence left at the crime scene. Defensive hate murders were associated with multiple wounds sustained from blunt or cutting instruments, and the offenders leaving possible forensic

Figure 7.4 Three-Dimensional Small Space Analysis Plot of Bias-motivated Crime Scene Behaviors: Mission Killer Variables Highlighted with Triangles

evidence undisturbed at the scene—indicating a lack of planning or concern about being connected to the scene.

RESULTS SUMMARY

In general, there appeared to be two subgroupings of thrill behaviors—those indicative of intent to interact with the victim's body (i.e., sexual behavior, post-mortem treatment of the body, covering the body, binding/gagging, strangulation) and those illustrative of a desire simply to act out aggression. The thrill variables highlighted the key issue with the McDevitt, Levin, and Bennett (2002) typology: there is too much overlap between thrill-related behaviors, which seem to be the core of bias-motivated homicide, and the other types. The retaliatory

**Figure 7.5 Three-Dimensional Small Space Analysis Plot of
Bias-motivated Crime Scene Behaviors: Defensive Killer Variables
Highlighted with Triangles**

behaviors, represented by behaviors designed to quickly kill the victim, had more
of a connection to some of the bias-related elements (i.e., previous bias-related incidents), which showed that a key divide between hate-motivated homicides may
be whether the offender's actions were designed to achieve a sense of power/
control/excitement—as was the case with thrill-related homicides—or whether
the offender wanted to restore a sense of self-esteem/honor (Fisher, 2007).

The mission and defensive types, both of which overlapped thrill/
retaliatory as well as each other, could not be linked to specific sets of
behaviors; instead, all that could be concluded in relation to these types was
that mission-oriented homicides were associated with more hate-related behaviors (i.e., bias-related drawings, holidays, and objects), which was not surprising given that mission-oriented offenders are motivated by hate against a
group they believe to be less than human, or even evil (Fisher, 2007).

Figure 7.6 Overlay of Each Motivation's Space on the Three-Dimensional Small Space Analysis Plot of Bias-Motivated Crime Scene Behaviors

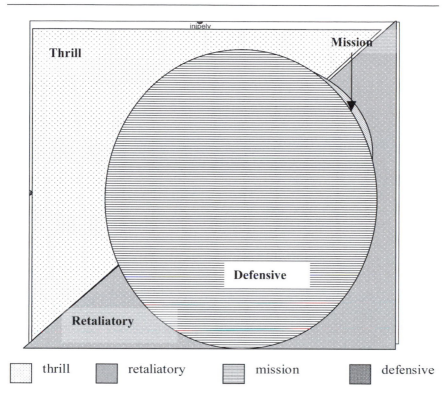

| ☐ thrill | ▨ retaliatory | ▤ mission | ▨ defensive |

Overall, the solution space could be divided in half by the *thrill* and *retaliatory* behaviors, with *mission* and *defensive* behaviors overlapping each other as well as the divide between *thrill* and *retaliatory*. Such an overlap of areas shows that as the model was defined, it would be difficult to classify a hate-motivated homicide based solely on observable crime-scene behaviors (Fisher, 2007) (see Figure 7.6).

DISCUSSION

The McDevitt, Levin, and Bennett Typology

The results of the SSA analysis supported the idea that high-frequency crime-scene characteristics cannot be used to distinguish between offenses based on the proposed typology and thus that with the level of detail about the motivations currently available, the McDevitt, Levin, and Bennett (2002) typology—at least in terms of observable crime-scene behaviors—is not an effective basis for a behavioral classification scheme. The solution space highlighted a divide between offenses with an element of power/control and of restoring a sense of self by retaliating or "getting the other guy back." The SSA analysis also showed that the other two proposed typologies (mission and defensive), may be subtypes of the two dominant styles, with, for example, some defensive hate homicides committed because of a need for power/control or excitement, and others to pay back a group that is perceived to be infringing on the dominant group's turf (Fisher, 2007).

This analysis of the McDevitt, Levin, and Bennett (2002) typology focused on both the strengths and weaknesses of their conceptualization of hate crimes. Before their work, no one had considered the idea that there were different motivations for hate crimes aside from the different sources of the hate (race, ethnicity, sexual orientation, etc.). Through their focus on elements of the crime, Levin and McDevitt, and later Bennett, began the development of a better understanding of the various motivations that could lead a potential offender to choose a specific type of person to victimize because of what they were perceived or known to represent. However, in this SSA analysis, a model of hate homicide emerges that may be focused more on the role that the victim serves for the offender. That is, in some hate homicides the offender may have chosen victims who were easy targets, which allowed them to attain a sense of power/control or general excitement/thrill, and in other hate-motivated homicides a particular individual may have been targeted because offending against that individual allowed the offender to take back honor that was perceived to have been taken previously. Given the high percentage of variables that were associated with multiple motivations, this distinction was not clear-cut; however, with the one distinct spatial divide being the distribution of the *thrill* versus *retaliatory* behaviors, and research (Franklin, 2000) finding that seeking out excitement or getting back at another group are frequent motivations for hate-motivated crimes, it is reasonable, acknowledging certain limitations, to find that *thrill* and *retaliation* may be the main underlying themes of behavior in hate-motivated homicides (Fisher, 2007) (see Figure 7.7).

Limitations

The main limitation confronting Fisher's (2007) analyses was that the behaviors included were mainly derived second-hand from descriptions of the typology's motivations. Very few of the behaviors were explicitly described by McDevitt, Levin, and Bennett (2002). Instead Fisher's work used similar studies and research on hate and violence to attempt to obtain agreed upon definitions of the components that McDevitt et al. highlighted as key to each of their types. This provided a first step in combining the behavioral approach with the motivational based model, a process which could be extended by collaborations between the two sets of approaches in the future.

Figure 7.7 Three-Dimensional Small Space Analysis Plot (1 v. 2) of Bias-motivated Crime Scene Behaviors: Grouping with Highlighted Motivating Bias (Coefficient of alienation = .143, 28 iterations)

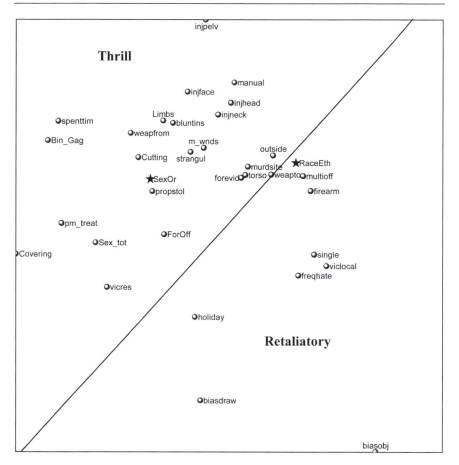

Other limitations also need to be addressed, such as that the data used in the analysis were collected primarily not for research but for police investigations, and therefore the potential for hate-specific and general mistakes in the data cannot be ignored. Additionally, because of this potential, it must be assumed that not all the information relevant to this analysis was relevant to the investigation, and therefore, if all information was accessible, the model might fit more clearly. The strength of the particular material used in this study, however, cannot be ignored. Research has shown that by limiting the detail of the information to the presence or absence of the variable in the case files, police records are very well suited for this kind of analysis (Salfati, 2000). The cases examined in these analyses were all homicide cases, while the typology was constructed with and for violent hate crime in general.

This should be remembered in any interpretation of the results. The work of McDevitt, Levin, and Bennett (2002) is the only typology that is based on the level of detail that is available in hate-motivated crime-scene case files, so it is important, even with the limitations, to determine whether it applies to all forms of violent hate crime. Nevertheless, it would be interesting to conduct this type of analysis using assault files instead of homicide files.

CONCLUSIONS ABOUT TYPOLOGIES OF HATE-MOTIVATED OFFENDERS

Fisher's (2007) SSA analysis of hate-motivated homicides revealed a general style or theme divide based on the crime-scene characteristics that could be associated with the McDevitt, Levin, and Bennett (2002) typology. Thus, the identification of this divide was only the first step in developing a model that could be used to differentiate between hate-motivated homicides. Fisher's research found that hate-motivated offenders interact with their victims in ways that either reflect a desire to participate in violence/aggression for thrill's sake, or to participate in violence/aggression to achieve some goal. However, because of the high level of crossover with the thrill-related behaviors, Fisher stressed that such a thematic divide should be seen as a suggestion, which needs to be further investigated with more refined sets of behaviors and other methodologies.

With the primary hate crime typology McDevitt, Levin, and Bennett (2002) examined to see whether it could successfully classify hate-motivated homicides, it appears that because hate crimes are uniquely defined by their motivations, it may not be possible to develop a behavior-based typology that would exclusively distinguish two hate crime scenes characterized by generally similar crime-scene behaviors. This raises the question of whether a typology of hate-motivated offenders can provide meaningful insight into hate crimes and those who commit them. It may be the case that the specific motivation of the offenders must be taken into account when interpreting how they interacted with their victim and the crime scene. This would mean, however, that any offender typology would simply be a method for organizing the known information about offenders associated with a particular motivation instead of a technique for profiling potential offender types based only on observable crime-scene behaviors. Future analyses should examine whether regular homicide classification schemes can consistently distinguish among the behaviors in relation to the bias with which they are most associated. The regular homicide classification systems, which have been found to be valid and exclusive, provide an outline of the process for continuing the investigation of whether thrill/retaliatory is the primary classification. All of this work, however, will always be built on the groundbreaking work of Levin and McDevitt, and with Bennett, who took the first steps toward understanding hate crime from a typological perspective.

NOTE

1. The authors would like to express their gratitude to the Federal Bureau of Investigation's (FBI) Behavioral Science Unit for coordinating access to the data used for the current study. Authors' opinions, statements, and conclusions should not be considered an endorsement by the FBI for any policy, program, or service.

2. For a more thorough explanation and illustration of this procedure, please read Fisher's (2007) complete work.

REFERENCES

Allport, G. W. (1954). *The nature of prejudice.* New York: Doubleday Books.

Anderson, J., Dyson, L., & Brooks, Jr., W. (2002). Preventing hate crime and profiling hate crime offenders. *The Western Journal of Black Studies, 26.*

Barnes, H., & Teeter, N. (1958). *New horizons in criminology.* (3rd ed.). New York: Prentice-Hall.

Block, R. (1977). *Violent Crime.* Lexington, MA: Lexington Books/D.C. Heath.

Borg, I. & Lingoes, J. C. (1987). *Facet Theory: Form and content.* New York: Springer-Verlag.

Bromberg, W. (1961). *The Mold of murder.* New York: Grune and Stratton.

Bufkin, J. (1999). Hate crime as gendered behavior. *Social Justice, 26,* 155–176.

Buss, D. M., & Shackelford, T. K. (1997). Human aggression in evolutionary psychological perspective. *Clinical Psychology Review, 17,* 605–619.

Byers, B., Crider, B., & Biggers, G. (1999). Hate crime motivation: A study of hate crime and offender neutralization techniques used against the Amish. *Journal of Contemporary Criminal Justice, 15*(1), 78–96.

Byrne, J., & Roberts, A. (2007). New directions in offender typology design, development, and implementation: Can we balance risk, treatment and control? *Aggression and Violent Behavior, 12,* 483–492.

Canter, D. (1994). *Criminal shadows: Inside the mind of the serial killer.* London: HarperCollins.

Canter, D. (2000). Offender profiling and criminal differentiation. *Journal of Legal and Criminological Psychology, 5,* 23–46.

Canter, D., Alison, L., Alison, E., & Wentick, N. (2004). The organized/disorganized typology of serial murder: Myth or model? *Psychology, Public Policy, and the Law, 10*(3), 293–320.

Canter, D., & Heritage, R. (1990). A multivariate model of sexual offence behavior: Developments in offender profiling: Part 1. *Journal of Forensic Psychiatry, 1,* 185–212.

Canter, D., & Wentick, N. (2004). An empirical test of Holmes and Holmes's serial murder typology. *Criminal Justice and Behavior, 31*(4), 489–515.

Cotton, P. (1992). Attacks on homosexual persons may be increasing, but many 'bashings' still aren't reported. *The Journal of the American Medical Association, 267,* 2999–3001.

Craig, K. (2002). Examining hate-motivated aggression: A review of the social-psychology literature on hate crimes as a distinct form of aggression. *Aggression & Violent Behavior, 7,* 85–99.

Donald, I. & Wilson, A. (1999). Ram Raiding: Criminals working in groups. In *The Social Psychology of Crime: Groups, Teams and Networks.* (Eds. D. Canter & L. Alison). Ashgate: Aldershot, pp. 189–246.

Dunning, E. (2000). Towards a sociological understanding of football hooliganism as a world phenomenon. *European Journal on Criminal Policy and Research, 8*(2), 141–162.

Ehrlich, H. (1990). The ecology of anti-gay violence. *Journal of Interpersonal Violence, 5,* 359–365.

Farrington, D. P. (1991). Antisocial personality from childhood to adulthood. *The Psychologist, 4,* 389–394.

Federal Bureau of Investigation. (2004). (Annual) *Uniform crime reports.* Washington, DC: Author.

Federal Bureau of Investigation. (2007). (Annual) *Uniform crime reports: Hate crime reporting statistics.* Washington, DC: Author.

Fisher, C. (2007). Extreme prejudice: A behavioral analysis of bias-motivated homicides. UMI Dissertation.

Franklin, K. (1998). Unassuming motivations: Contextualizing the narratives of antigay assailants. In G. Herek (Ed.), *Stigma and Sexual Orientation: Understanding Prejudice Against Lesbians, Gay Men, and Bisexuals* (pp. 1–23). London: Sage.

Franklin, K. (2000). Antigay behaviors among young adults: Prevalence, patterns, and motivators in a noncriminal population. *Journal of Interpersonal Violence, 15,* 339–362.

Gillis, A. R. (1986). Domesticity, divorce, and deadly quarrels: An exploratory study of integration-regulation and homicide. In T. Hartnagel & R. Silverman (Eds.), *Critique and explanation: Essays in honor of Gwynne Nettler* (pp. 133–147). New Brunswick, NJ: Transaction.

Green, D., Glaser, J., & Rich, A. (1998). From lynchings to gay bashing: The elusive connection between economic conditions and hate crimes. *Journal of Personality and Social Psychology, 75*(1), 82–92.

Green, D. P., McFalls, L. H., & Smith, J. K. (2001). Hate crime: An emergent research agenda. *Annual Review of Sociology, 27.* In D. Canter & L. Alison (Eds.), *The Social Psychology of Crime: Offender Profiling Series III* (pp. 479–504). Aldershot: Ashgate Publishing.

Harry, J. (1990). Conceptualizing anti-gay violence. *Journal of Interpersonal Violence, 5,* 350–358.

Holmes, R. M., & Holmes, S. T. (1998). *Serial murder* (2nd ed.). Thousand Oaks, CA: Sage.

Hood, R., & Sparks, R. (1970). *Key issues in criminology.* New York: McGraw-Hill.

Ituarte, S. (2000). *Inside the mind of hate.* UMI Dissertation.

Kuehnle, K. & Sullivan, A. (2001). Patterns of anti-gay violence: An analysis of incident characteristics and victims reporting. *Journal of Interpersonal Violence, 16,* 928–943.

Levin, J., & McDevitt, J. (1993). Hate crimes: The rising tide of bigotry and bloodshed. New York: Plenum Press.

Levin, J., & McDevitt, J. (2002). *Hate crimes revisited: Americas' war on those who are different.* Boulder, CO: Westview.

Mason, G. (1997). Heterosexed violence: Typicality and ambiguity. In *Homophobic Violence* (Eds. G. Mason & S. Tomsen). Hawkins Press. 15-32.

Maxwell, C. & Maxwell, S. (1995). Youth participation in hate-motivated crimes: Research and Policy Implications. Center for the Study and Prevention of Violence. Bolder: University of Colorado.

McDevitt, J., Levin, J., & Bennett, S. (2002). Hate crime offenders: An expanded typology. *Journal of Social Issues, 58*(2), 303–317.

Perry, B. (2001). *In the name of hate: Understanding hate crimes.* New York: Routledge.

Ressler, R. K., Burgess, A. W., & Douglas, J. E. (1988). *Sexual homicide: Patterns and motives.* Lexington, MA: Lexington Books.

Richardson, D. & May, H. (1999). Deserving victims?: Sexual status and the social construction of violence. *The Editorial Board of The Sociological Review,* 308–331.

Salfati, C. G. (2000). The nature of expressiveness and instrumentality in homicide. *Homicide Studies, 4,* 265–293.

Salfati, C. G. (2003). Offender interaction with victims in homicide: A multidimensional analysis of frequencies in crime scene behaviors. *Journal of Interpersonal Violence, 18,* 490–512.

Salfati, C. G., & Canter, D. V. (1999). Differentiating stranger murders: Profiling offender characteristics from behavioral styles. *Journal of Behavioral Sciences and the Law, 1,* 391–406.

Salfati, C. G. & Dupont, F. (2006) Canadian Homicide: An Investigation of Crime Scene Actions. *Homicide Studies. 10,* 118–139.

Salfati, C. G. & Haratsis, E. (2001). Greek homicide: A behavioral examination of offender crime-scene actions. *Homicide Studies, 5,* 335–362.

Santilla, P., Canter, D., Elfgren, T., & Hakkanen, H. (2001). The structure of crime-scene actions in Finnish homicides. *Homicide Studies, 5,* 363–387.

Shye, S., Elizur, D., & Hoffman, M. (1994). *Introduction to Facet Theory: Content Design an Intrinsic Data Analysis in Behavioral Research.* Thousand Oaks, CA: Sage.

Van de Ven, P., Bornholt, L., & Bailey, M. (1996). Measuring cognitive, affective, and behavioral components of homophobic reaction. *Archives of Sexual Behavior, 25,* 155–180.

Wellford, C. & Cronin, J. (1999). *An Analysis of Variables Affecting the Clearance of Homicides: A Multi-State Study.* Justice Research and Statistics Association, Washington DC.

Wolfgang, M. E. (1958). *Patterns in Criminal Homicide.* Philadelphia: University of Pennsylvania Press.

CHAPTER 8

THE BANALITY OF ANTI-JEWISH "HATE CRIME"

Paul Iganski

A "NEW ANTISEMITISM"?

Contemporary antisemitism provides such a conundrum that it demands—it begs—critical reflection. Jews are successfully integrated into the economic and social structures of Western European nations. Antisemitism, it had been thought, was banished to the social margins by decades of struggle against racism and for rights to equal treatment and protection from discrimination. Yet many Jews now believe that progress has gone into reverse. Numerous commentators have argued that a "new antisemitism" has been sweeping Europe, and there has been an industry of books analyzing the alleged problem (cf. Chesler, 2003; Finkelstein, 2005; Foxman, 2003; Harrison, 2006; Iganski & Kosmin, 2003; Rosenbaum & Ozick, 2004; Taguieff, 2004). Concerns about a resurgence of antisemitism in Europe have also prompted a number of official inquiries and reports by the international policy community. In addition to these reports, the Organization for Security and Cooperation in Europe (OSCE) held conferences on antisemitism in June 2003 in Vienna, in April 2004 in Berlin, and in June 2005 in Cordova. In June 2004,

This chapter further develops an analysis presented in chapter 2 of Iganski, P., *Hate Crime and the City* (Bristol, England: Policy Press, 2008). An earlier version of the chapter was presented in Iganski, P., *The Banality of Antisemitism* (American Society of Criminology 58th Annual Meeting, Los Angeles, California, 2006) and supported by a British Academy Overseas Conference Grant, which the author gratefully acknowledges.

the then United Nations Secretary General Kofi Annan hosted a UN seminar on antisemitism.

It became for a while the accepted wisdom in much of the commentary in the official reports and other publications on the alleged resurgence of antisemitism in Europe that much of the anti-Jewish hate crime is a manifestation of political extremism targeted against Jews. However, in taking the accepted wisdom to task, this chapter observes that many anti-Jewish incidents are committed by "ordinary" people in the context of their "everyday" lives. Given that observation, the chapter argues that much anti-Jewish hate crime is an indicator of the banality of antisemitism, in that many offenders are not prompted by a particular ideological conviction or volition but instead unthinkingly manifest a commonsense antisemitism.

"EXTREMISM," THE FAR RIGHT, MUSLIMS, AND ANTI-JEWISH INCIDENTS ON THE STREETS

According to what might be termed the "extremism thesis," the perpetrators of many of the recent attacks against Jews have not only included the old enemy from the far right. There has been apparently the more recent involvement of radical Islamists, and in addition many attacks against Jews have reputedly *in the main* been perpetrated by "Arab" or "Muslim" youths who are venting their hatred against Israel in particular, and against Jews in general. According to Professor Robert Wistrich, head of the Vidal Sassoon International Centre for the Study of Antisemitism at the Hebrew University of Jerusalem, "hate-mongering against Jews" is "mainstream in the Muslim world" (Wistrich, 2006). In this context, periods of escalation in the Israel–Palestine conflict trigger the venting of bigotry against Jews. Such a view is fuelled by newspaper reports, such as the one in the *Jewish Chronicle* in February 2006 (Peled, 2006), suggesting on the basis of polling evidence that one-third of British Muslims regard Anglo-Jewry as "a legitimate target as part of the struggle for justice in the Middle East" with almost half the respondents believing that "the Jewish community in Britain is in league with the Freemasons to control the media and politics."

A sharp rise in incidents against Jews that occurred in some European countries in April 2002, corresponding with the Israel Defence Force actions in Jenin on the West Bank, prompted the European Monitoring Centre on Racism and Xenophobia (EUMC) (now the European Agency for Fundamental Rights [FRA]) to investigate the phenomenon—the first time that it had specifically focused on anti-Jewish incidents since it was established in 1997. The EUMC commissioned the Center for Research on Antisemitism at the Technische Universität Berlin to carry out a study using information provided by the EUMC's 15 National Focal Points of its Racism and Xenophobia Network (RAXEN)—specially established consortia between academics, research organizations, and NGOs in each of the then 15 member states—offering an overview of antisemitism for their respective countries for the months of May and June 2002. The authors of the subsequent report concluded that

> For many antisemitic incidents, especially for violent and other punishable offences, it is typical that the perpetrators attempt to remain anonymous. Thus, in many cases the perpetrators could not be identified, so an assignment to a political or ideological camp must remain open. Nevertheless, from the perpetrators identified or at least identifiable with some certainty, it can be concluded that the antisemitic incidents in the monitoring period were committed above all either by right-wing extremists or radical Islamists or young Muslims mostly of Arab descent, who are themselves potential victims of exclusion and racism. (Bergmann & Wetzel 2003, p. 7)

The report included the United Kingdom, along with France, Belgium, and the Netherlands, as a country in which

> [T]he violent attacks on Jews and/or synagogues were reported to be committed often by members of the Muslim-Arab minority, frequently youths. The observers agree these are disaffected young men who themselves are frequently targets of racist attacks, i.e. here the social problems of these migrant minorities are obviously an essential factor for their propensity to violence and susceptibility to antisemitism. (Bergmann & Wetzel 2003, p. 27)

The attribution of culpability to Muslim youths sparked a controversy and allegedly led to the EUMC's decision not to publish the report. The authors subsequently released it for posting on the Internet. One of the authors, Werner Bergmann, claimed that the European Union "buried the research out of fear of civil war, and from excessive political correctness" (Sadeh, 2003). He suggested, "It was very difficult for them to accept the conclusions . . . They asked us again and again to re-write the drafts, to soften the conclusions, to balance the arguments" (UJA Federation Toronto,). The view that the report was suppressed was promulgated by a number of newspaper reports; among them it was claimed that an unnamed source connected with the EUMC said that "the directors of the EUMC had regarded the study as biased" and that "they had judged the focus on Muslim and pro-Palestinian perpetrators to be inflammatory" (UJA Federation Toronto,). The allegations of suppression, however, were "erroneous," according to the EUMC (2004, p. 10), which claimed that the report was inadequate, as the short time period covered and the peaking of incidents during that period distorted the picture of antisemitism that prevailed across Europe (pp. 9–10). Given these supposed limitations, the EUMC's National Focal Points were asked to report on a longer time period covering the whole of 2003 and to provide more detail about incidents than they had provided in the first exercise. A different scholar, Alexander Pollak, was commissioned to provide a critical appraisal and commentary on the information collected (2004, 10). The conclusion about the role of Muslim youths in the report that the EUMC published was more equivocal than the unpublished first report:

> In the course of the rise in antisemitic incidents in Europe over the last few years, there has been a shift in the public perception of the "typical" antisemitic offender from an "extreme right" skinhead to a disaffected young Muslim. Press reports perpetuate the assumption that the bulk of antisemitic attacks in Europe are committed by young men of immigrant and Muslim background. However, the NFP [National Focal Point] reports suggest a more complex picture than that. (p. 20)

However, in the case of anti-Jewish incidents in the UK it was far more certain in its conclusion:

> [F]rom the nature of the attacks within the period 2002–2003, the NFP states that it seems likely that the majority were carried out by far-right extremists whose political agenda is the intimidation of ethnic minorities, not the criticism of Israel's perceived human rights abuses. Nevertheless, the climate of hostility towards Israel provides such groups with a convenient cover. (p. 208)

However, when the then UK Foreign Office Minister Bill Rammell, speaking at an OSCE conference in Berlin in 2003, and informed by the EUMC evidence, echoed the view that far-right activists were behind the majority of anti-Jewish incidents in the UK, he came under fire from some Jewish communal leaders. The president of the Board of Deputies of British Jews responded that, "We do not accept that the evidence suggests that antisemitic attacks are predominantly coming from the right-wing" (Last, 2003). The following year, reports in the British press associated with the release of the Community Security Trust's annual report were claiming that *both* far-right and "Islamic extremists" were behind attacks against Jews (cf. Bennetto, 2004; Syal, 2004). (The Community Security Trust (CST) is an NGO that advises and represents Britain's Jewish community on matters of antisemitism, terrorism, and security.) Almost a year later, the U.S. Department of State's Report on Global Antisemitism (2005) concluded that

> In Western Europe, traditional far-right groups still account for a significant proportion of the attacks against Jews and Jewish properties; disadvantaged and disaffected Muslim youths increasingly were responsible for most of the other incidents. This trend appears likely to persist as the

number of Muslims in Europe continues to grow while their level of education and economic prospects remain limited.

Despite the alarm raised about the problem of a "new antisemitism" in Europe, however, opinion on whether there has been a resurgence of antisemitism on the streets is divided, and the lack of official data on the problem clouds the conclusions that can be drawn.

LESSONS FROM POLICE DATA ON ANTI-JEWISH INCIDENTS

While hate crimes against Jews figure prominently in the annual hate crime statistics published by the Federal Bureau of Investigation in the United States (U.S. Department of Justice, 2005), (and in 2005 anti-Jewish crimes accounted for one out of eight recorded bias-motivated incidents), in European countries by contrast, there are no routinely published official data on anti-Jewish incidents. In the UK—which has one of the most comprehensive arrangements in Europe for the collection of data on racist incidents—only a minority of police forces can specifically identify incidents against Jews captured in their recording systems (Iganski, 2007). However, the Community Security Trust (CST) has been systematically compiling reports of anti-Jewish incidents since 1984, gathered from victims, press reports, and the police (Whine, 2003). The CST has published an annual report on the incidents since 1998. While there have been evident fluctuations in the annual number of incidents recorded, the overall trend over time has been upward (see figure 8.1). In 2006 the CST recorded its highest yearly number of anti-Jewish incidents—594 in total (CST, 2007, p. 4).

As with all such recorded crime data, caution must be exercised in interpreting apparent trends because they may well reflect a greater propensity for victims to report incidents for a variety of reasons just as much as representing a real rise in incidents. Unfortunately, there have been no victimization surveys focusing on anti-Jewish incidents in Britain, and the annual British Crime Survey provides data of little value, given the small number of identifiable Jews included in the survey sample (as Britain's Jews constitute only approximately 0.5 percent of the population).

While the CST has been collecting data on anti-Jewish incidents for a longer period than police forces in Britain, it does not have the same investigative resources that police forces are able to employ, and so their information on perpetrators is limited. While not all police forces in Britain have the capacity to identify antisemitic incidents in their crime records, a few forces have recently carried out some detailed analyses of incidents. The first published police data on anti-Jewish incidents resulted from a research study of Metropolitan Police Service (MPS) data for London for the calendar years 2001

Figure 8.1 Antisemitic incidents recorded by the Community Security Trust

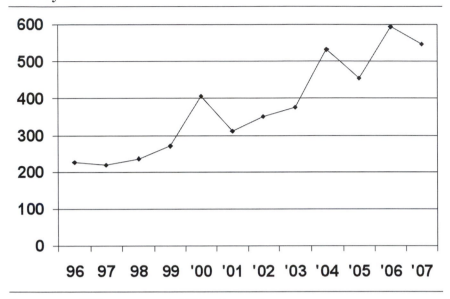

Data sources: CST 2006, page 15; CST 2008, page 21.

to 2004, reported in *Hate Crimes against London's Jews* (Iganski, Kielinger, & Paterson, 2005). The study carried out a quantitative analysis of all 1,084 incidents recorded during this time period. The quantitative data are limited but illuminating nevertheless. Where information was available, the majority (56.9%) of suspects were classified as "White European." (Although the MPS uses different ethnic group categories than those used in the 2001 population census, the proportion of white suspects clearly falls short of the proportion of the London population [71.2%] who classified themselves as 'white' in the census [Office for National Statistics, 2004, Table S104].)

Overall, the police data on the demographic characteristics of suspected offenders provide only a very broad-brush picture of the profile of the perpetrators of anti-Jewish hate crime. Nevertheless, the data do appear to strongly indicate that although black and Asian youths are overrepresented among offenders in comparison with their representation in the population at large, Muslim youths were certainly not responsible for *the majority* of incidents in the time period in question, given that the majority of suspected offenders were white. White Muslims constituted only about 12 percent of the Muslim population in England and Wales, according to the 2001 census (Peach, 2006, p. 632).

The research reported in *Hate Crimes against London's Jews* (Iganski et al., 2005) also analyzed in-depth the crime reports for a subsample of 156 anti-Jewish incidents. The crime reports were analyzed systematically, with a separate reading of each report by each member of the research team followed by a group discussion of the case. The initial discussions allowed the team to identify inductively a coding frame to unravel the situational dynamics of incidents. The coding frame consisted of a list of sensitizing questions to assist in the interrogation of the contextual information (see Iganski et al., appendix B, pp. 99–102). The subsample included 110 incidents recorded as "antisemitic incidents" by the MPS in April and May 2002. This period represented the largest peak in incidents that directly corresponded to media coverage of the conflict between the Israel Defense Force and Palestinian nationalists in Jenin. For comparison, an additional sample of 46 incidents was used in the analysis covering all recorded incidents in November and December 2002 and in August 2003 to represent in the sample months of low and medium, as well as high, occurrence of incidents. Notably, only 20 percent of the incidents showed evidence of anti-Israeli sentiment, or sentiment drawing on the Arab-Israeli conflict more broadly, in the discourse of the offenders. The level of such discourse manifest in incidents was much lower—approximately 5 percent—in months where there were fewer incidents.

The geographical concentration of anti-Jewish incidents is also illuminating with respect to the role of political extremism behind incidents. Four London boroughs, Barnet, Hackney, Camden and Westminster, accounted for approximately 60 percent of the anti-Jewish incidents recorded by the MPS between 2001 and 2004. It is notable that in these four boroughs there had been relatively little activism by extreme-right political groups compared with some other London boroughs. The subsample of incidents from April and May 2002 also corresponded with the local elections held in the London boroughs and elsewhere in England and Wales on May 2, 2002. Sixty-eight candidates from the extreme-right British National Party (BNP) stood in the elections. It has been observed by scholars and other commentators that extreme-right activity provides a climate in which hate crime escalates. Notably, therefore, in relation to the occurrence of anti-Jewish incidents, there were no BNP candidates in the 2002 local elections in the four London boroughs, Barnet, Camden, Hackney and Westminster, that together accounted for the majority of anti-Jewish incidents recorded by the police. In other parts of London, BNP candidates gained 22 percent of the vote in the Northend Ward of Bexley, 21.7 percent in Hainault in Redbridge, and 17.4 percent in Downham in Lewisham. But Redbridge is the only one of these three London boroughs that has a particular residential concentration of Jews (Graham, 2005, p. 83). The absence of extreme-right electoral activity in those areas of London that accounted for the highest proportions of anti-Jewish incidents appears to accord with the conclusions made by the recent All Party Parliamentary Inquiry into Antisemitism about the threat of the far right to Jews, which run counter to the conclusion drawn by the EUMC, as noted above. Although the Inquiry observed that "[d]uring the twentieth century the far right was the dominant source of antisemitism in the UK" and that it continues to articulate conspiracy theories about Jews, it concluded that although "there is no room for complacency," "the overt threat from the far right toward Jews may not be as significant as it once was" (UK All Party Parliamentary Group Against Antisemitism, 2006, pp. 24, 26).

UNDERSTANDING EVERYDAY ANTI-JEWISH "HATE CRIME"

If the perpetrators of anti-Jewish incidents on London's streets are not in the main extremists or street-level political activists, who are they? That was one of the driving questions behind the qualitative analysis of the subsample of anti-Jewish incidents recorded by the MPS, and a goal was to determine the extent to which "extremists" might be involved as perpetrators of incidents against Jews. Prior to the research, there had been very little detailed analysis carried out about the characteristics and motivations of offenders in antisemitic incidents in Britain or elsewhere, and this was also the case concerning hate crime offenders in general. The research using the more recent MPS records proposed that given what can be drawn from reported anti-Jewish incidents in the press in which the offenders were connected with extremist groups, in addition to any explicit evidence that the offender was a member of an extremist organization, incidents involving "extremists" would be more likely to be motivated by anti-Jewish animus than by other reasons, more likely to have some degree of premeditation on the part of the offender, and more likely to be instances in which the victim and offender had no prior acquaintance with each other. These suppositions were clarified in consultation with members of the CST at a presentation of some of the early quantitative findings from the research.

At first sight, two-fifths of the incidents appeared to fit these broad criteria, and they ranged from serious assaults to minor criminal damage. In none of them, however, was there any explicit evidence that the offender was connected with an extremist group—although the absence of such evidence does not rule out the possibility, given that offenders do not generally purposefully leave behind evidence to identify themselves. Less than a quarter of the incidents involved face-to-face contact between the offender and the victim (Iganski et al., 2005, table F1, p. 115), and so the majority of the offenders were somewhat shy or timid bigots. In one case in which the offenders weren't reticent about revealing themselves—according to the crime report—"Arab-looking" suspects in a van called out to a Jewish man on the street, "Are you a Jew?" When the victim answered, "Yes," the offenders jumped out of the van and verbally abused and assaulted him. In another incident, an Orthodox Jewish man was attacked from behind by a group of "Arab-looking" suspects while walking from one synagogue to another. In both of these cases, the offenders clearly instigated the incident, and given the absence of any other information to the contrary in the crime reports, anti-Jewish animus seems to have been the driving motivation for action. There was no apparent evidence in the crime reports that the suspects were connected with extremist groups, but there was also no evidence to rule out the possibility. Assaults on victims—serious or otherwise—constituted only a small proportion (just over one-seventh) of the recorded incidents for the whole period 2001–2004 (Iganski et al., table D1, pp. 105–107). In other cases analyzed in the subsample, the offenders did not reveal themselves to their victims, but from the circumstances, the incidents were clearly premeditated, and judging by other evidence, such as the words used by the offenders, they were driven by anti-Jewish animus. For instance, in one case two messages were left on a synagogue voicemail stating, "Hello . . . F**k off, you Jewish cockney f****ing w***ers" and "Hello, it's Dr. Shlockel of the foreskin removal company. Err, I'm a bit short of business at the minute so I was wondering if you could send some dirty f***ing Jews our way to get their foreskins lopped off. Thank you." Malicious communications such as these constituted just under one-fifth of all incidents recorded for the period 2001–2004.

Other incidents in the subsample seemed to involve the indiscriminate targeting of Jews. For instance, in one case a swastika had been sprayed onto a garage door. The crime report stated, "There are no identifying numbers on the garage door although as the victim herself stated, there are a lot of Jewish people in the area and the suspect would probably have known there was a good likelihood of their victim being Jewish" (Iganski et al., 2005, p. 44). In some incidents a person's property was targeted, either as a proxy target for the victim or perhaps because of its symbolic value. For instance, a Jewish victim reported that religious symbolic scrolls (mezuzot) pinned to their front door had been burnt and damaged. Overall, acts of criminal damage constituted just over one-fifth of all recorded incidents for 2001–2004. For the two particular acts just mentioned, there were no indications in the crime reports to suggest that they were committed by individuals connected with extremist groups rather than being acts of routine vandalism in the neighborhoods concerned. However, as with the other cases, there was no evidence to suggest that extremists were not involved.

Other cases in the subsample of incidents were clearly opportunistic in that they involved chance, random encounters between offenders and subsequent victims, rather than being engineered by the perpetrators. In such incidents it was a case of being in the right place at the right time for the offenders to vent their bigotry or hostility, and for the victim, a case of being in the wrong place at the wrong time in the course of their everyday lives. One-sixth of all the incidents fell into this category. There were no indications that the incidents were premeditated in any way. A clear example is an incident in which, according to the crime report, five 15-year-old boys who were playing football in a park were approached by a group of older youths who acted aggressively. One said, "Look at those Jews" and "Why are you picking up your bags? We're not going to nick anything, you f***ing Jewish c**t." Two of the victims were then punched and kicked. In another incident, the victim was walking in the street and had a coin thrown at him by one of four youths. As he walked past, two youths stood in his way and said "Jew." In neither of these incidents was there any circumstantial evidence in the crime reports to indicate that the offenders' actions were preplanned in any way that they had set out to target Jews in anti-Jewish attacks.

The types of incidents just mentioned appeared to be instigated *because of* anti-Jewish animus, but whether or not that was the primary motivation for each offense was impossible to tell from the crime reports. After much debate about the matter of understanding offender motivations, however, the research team in the *Hate Crimes against London's Jews* (Iganski et al., 2005) project agreed that the thoughts inside an offender's head prompting the actions could not be reliably deduced from the textual information in the crime reports alone. The analysis was therefore confined to unfolding the circumstantial and situational dynamics of the incidents. It was very clear, though, that some incidents arose for *other reasons* than anti-Jewish animus. In a number of incidents, the offender and the victim first became embroiled in some kind of conflict, and the situation then became aggravated with anti-Jewish animus. The interaction between the soon-to-be-offenders and soon-to-be-victims started out as commonplace episodes in everyday life, but often ones in which offenders seemed to perceive that a wrong had been inflicted upon them. In one incident, a minicab driver asked a passenger to take his feet off the seat of the car. An argument then ensued and escalated to a point at which the driver pulled over and radioed the minicab office to ask for another driver to complete the journey. The passenger grabbed at and repeatedly punched the driver, shouting, "I know your type; you're a f***ing Jew. You are the embodiment of everything that is bad about Jews in this country" (Iganski, Kielinger, & Paterson, 2005, p. 46). In another case, a victim was verbally abused when he complained about a car blocking his exit from a car park. According to the crime report, "The suspect was sitting in his car arguing with a female passenger. The suspect's car was stationary and blocking the road so the victim could not get by. The victim got out of his car and walked over to the suspect's car and asked the suspect to move his car. The suspect got out of his car . . . in a fighting stance position. He said to the victim, 'f***ing Jew, I'll spit on you,' and 'I'll get you'" (p. 46). Many incidents of this type will not be reported to the police, perhaps because they are seen by the victims as constituting part of the routine incivilities of everyday life.

It is notable that in each of these incidents just described, the offender seemed to perceive that a wrong had been inflicted upon him or her by the victim. It is tempting at first to think that the anti-Jewish animus voiced by the offender is solely an emotional outburst, an expressive act, provoked by the wrong that was perceived. However, in the time it took offenders to react arguably a decision, a "quick calculation" was still made about whether or not to react in a particular way—unless we are to believe that some people totally lack self-control and that situational constraints indicating what they may or may not get away with never have any bearing on them. It is possible that in the anti-Jewish incidents in question the offenders had taken the snap decision to restore justice as they see it by inflicting harm on the victim for the harm that they perceived had been inflicted upon themselves.

In each of the cases described, the victims and offenders were strangers to each other. By contrast, in other antisemitic incidents recorded by the MPS, there was a prior relationship between the offender and the victim that had since turned sour, and the offender's anti-Jewish animus appeared to surface as a consequence. One such incident involved an abusive phone call, believed to be from a former employer who was being taken to court by the victim for racial discrimination. In another case, an abusive and threatening voice mail was left on the victim's phone and was believed to be from a friend of an ex-girlfriend. As is the case with aggravated incidents, the anti-Jewish animus appears to have been used as a form of retaliation by the offenders against the victims.

A final group of antisemitic incidents recorded by the MPS appeared to have no tangible evidence of anti-Jewish animus; instead, the perception about the nature of the incident relied solely upon the interpretation made by the victim or another person, such as a police officer. One-fifth of the incidents fell into this category. In one such case a victim reported to the police that her garden fence had been damaged: the fence bordered a pedestrian shortcut used frequently after pub closing time and was thus a potential location for antisocial behavior. There were no indications at all to suggest that anti-Jewish animus was involved in any of the damage caused. The victim, however, believed that it was, stating that two years earlier she had discovered "NF" (the initials of the far-right National Front party) spray-painted on the fence. There were, however, no indications of any connection between the two incidents, and in the second incident the offender left no graffiti or any other signs or symbols that might be interpreted as "antisemitic." In another incident reported to, and recorded by, the police as "antisemitic," a brick was thrown through a shop window that had several Jewish signs in it. The responding police officer—by the account in the crime report—interpreted the incident as being antisemitic, owing to the prevailing state of tension in the Israeli–Palestinian conflict and also because there was no obvious source for the brick in the immediate vicinity of the shop, suggesting that some element of deliberation was involved on the part of the offender.

However, it was also recorded in the crime report that six other obviously Jewish shops in the vicinity of the targeted shop remained undamaged. In both of the incidents just discussed, it is difficult to determine whether anti-Jewish animus was involved.

THE BANALITY OF ANTI-JEWISH SENTIMENT

In commenting on the prevailing social climate affecting Jews in France a few years ago, sociologist Pierre-André Taguieff (2004) proposed that

> things have reached the point where we might reintroduce the old term "banalization." It is exactly as if many different attitudes and manifestations of Judeophobia had become banalized, as if they fitted so well into the ideological scenery that they were no longer perceptible. (p. 3)

Arguably, it is the banalization of anti-Jewish sentiment that this chapter illuminates and that sentiment *is perceptible* through the evidence of anti-Jewish incidents. Some incidents manifest an animus that is an overspill of tensions concerning the Israeli–Palestinian conflict. But those incidents constitute a minority of anti-Jewish incidents recorded by the MPS. Furthermore, the qualitative data on incidents presented in this chapter appear to undermine the view that many of the incidents against Jews on the streets in Europe are committed by "extremists" and by disaffected Muslim youths. Admittedly, and as is the case for racist incidents more generally, a singular pattern of victimization cannot be expected to occur across European countries, as incidents are mediated by local circumstances. But it is clear in the case of anti-Jewish incidents in London, where two-thirds of Britain's Jews reside, that when the situational contexts and the dynamics of incidents are unfolded, there is little apparent evidence that political extremism has been at work. This is not to argue that offenders affiliated with extremist groups and also Muslim youths have not been involved, or that individual Jews or Jewish communal property has not been targeted in premeditated attacks, as the evidence shows otherwise. But such incidents appear to be in the minority. Instead, the majority of incidents provide an indicator of the banality of antisemitism in that the incidents in question are not prompted by a particular ideological conviction or volition, but instead in their expressive character they display a thoughtless and "commonsense" antisemitism that lies beneath the surface of cognition for many individuals. It rises to the surface for some people when the opportunity to vent their simmering bigotry presents itself, and it is often triggered by a grievance, an irritation, or conflict: things that are commonplace in everyday life but present a particular reflex opportunity when a Jewish person is involved. Arguably, this is no different from the occurrence of "hate crime" more generally.

REFERENCES

Bennetto, J. (2004, February 20). Anti-Semitic assaults near record levels. *Independent*. Retrieved October 16, 2008 from, news.independent.co.uk

Bergmann, W., & Wetzel, J. (2003). *Manifestations of Anti-Semitism in the European Union*. First Semester 2002, Synthesis Report on behalf of the European Monitoring Centre on Racism and Xenophobia. Berlin, Germany: Zentrum für Anti-Semitismusforschung/Center for Research on Anti-Semitism, Technische Universität Berlin.

Chesler, P. (2003). *The new Anti-Semitism*. San Francisco, CA: Jossey-Bass.

Community Security Trust. (2006). *Antisemitic incidents report 2005*. London: Author.

Community Security Trust. (2008). *Antisemitic incidents report 2007*. London: Author.

European Union Monitoring Centre. (2004). *Manifestations of anti-Semitism in the EU 2002–2003*. Vienna: Author.

Foxman, A. H. (2003). *Never again? The threat of the new anti-Semitism*, New York: HarperCollins.

Graham, D. (2005). A snapshot profile of London's Jewish population. In P. Iganski, V. Kielinger, & S. Paterson (Eds.), *Hate crimes against London's Jews* (Appendix A, pp. 83–98). London: Institute for Jewish Policy Research.

Harrison, B. (2006). *The resurgence of anti-Semitism: Jews, Israel, and liberal opinion*. Lanham, MD: Rowman & Littlefield.

Iganski, P., Kielinger, V., & Paterson, S. (2005). *Hate crimes against London's Jews*. London: Institute for Jewish Policy Research/Metropolitan Police Service.

Iganski, P., & Kosmin, B. (Eds.). (2003). *A new anti-Semitism? Debating Judeophobia in 21ˢᵗ century Britain*. London: Profile Books.

Iganski, P. (2007). Too few Jews to count? Police monitoring of hate crime against Jews in the United Kingdom. *American Behavioral Scientist, 51*(2), 232–245.

Last, J. (2003, May 14). "Hate's from right" comment shocks leaders. *The Jewish News*.

Office for National Statistics. (2004). *CD supplement to the National Report for England and Wales and key statistics for local authorities in England and Wales*. Newport, Wales: Author.

Peach, C. (2006). Muslims in the 2001 census of England and Wales: Gender and economic disadvantage. *Ethnic and Racial Studies, 29*(4), 629–655.

Peled, D. (2006, February 10). Third of Muslims view UK Jews as "legitimate target." *Jewish Chronicle, 10*. Retrieved December 22, 2008 from www.thejc.com

Rosenbaum, R., & Ozick, C. (2004). *Those who forget the past: The question of anti-Semitism*. New York: Random House.

Sadeh, S. (2003, November 25). Researchers blast EU for 'burying' anti-Semitism study. Haartez. Retrieved December 20, 2008 from, http://www.ujafed.com/page.aspx?id=52012

Syal, R. (2004, February 15). Prominent Jews targeted by Muslims and the far right. *The Daily Telegraph*. Retrieved October 16, 2008, from www.telegraph.co.uk

Taguieff, P. A. (2004). *Rising from the muck: The new anti-Semitism in Europe*. Chicago: Ivan R. Dee.

UJA Federation Toronto. Retrieved October 16, 2008, from http://www.jewish-toronto.com/page.aspx?id=52012

U.K. All-Party Parliamentary Group Against Antisemitism. (2006). *Report of the All-Party Parliamentary inquiry into anti-Semitism.* London: The Stationary Office.

U.S. Department of Justice, Federal Bureau of Investigation. (2005). *Hate Crime Statistics, Table 1.* Retrieved August 14, 2007, from http://www.fbi.gov/ucr/hc2005/table1.htm

U.S. Department of State. (2005). *Report on global anti-Semitism.* Washington, DC: Bureau of Democracy, Human Rights and Labor, US Department of State. Retrieved August 14, 2007, from http://www.state.gov/g/drl/rls/40258.htm

Whine, M. (2003). Anti-Semitism on the streets. In P. Iganski & B. Kosmin (Eds.), *A new anti-Semitism? Debating Judeophobia in 21ˢᵗ Century Britain* (pp. 23–37). London: Profile Books.

Wistrich, R. S. (2006, February 10). Naked Muslim hatred. *Jewish Chronicle*, p. 3. Retrieved 12/22/2008 from www.thejc.com

CHAPTER 9

THE MOST HATED MAN IN SWEDEN

Michael Kimmel

Kumla prison is an imposingly secure structure: squat thick windowless concrete bunkers in the middle of a vast flat field, two hours north of Stockholm. Kumla is the most secure prison in Sweden, and the one in which the 300 most-hardened criminals are sent. As is typical of maximum-security prisons, there are massive barbed-wire fences immediately around the prison walls, an open field of perhaps 100 feet, sort of a dry moat, followed by equally imposing electrified barbed-wire fences at the outer perimeter.

One enters a small room with secure lockers, where visitors place everything they brought with them. I took my pad and pen into the next room (metal detectors, guards behind thick Plexiglas) and after I passed through the metal detector, they took my pen and gave me one of theirs, and checked my blank pad for coded messages.

They then led me down a nice, bright hallway to a narrow room. The room was bright and cheery, with a window that looked out onto the prison garden, and curtains, a single bed (with a cotton blanket and pillow, and a rubber sheet covering the mattress), a table and chair. There was a bathroom with a shower. These were visiting rooms and one could hear the, ahem, conjugal visits that were taking place in the next room. There was an intercom on the wall that would ring the front desk to come and open the door, and a small red panic button next to it behind glass. But these were placed on the wall next to his chair, so that he would be sitting between me and those buttons. I was a bit anxious.

I had come to Kumla prison to meet Jackie Arklof, the most hated man in Sweden. Described as "the Charlie Manson" of Sweden, Arklof was a neo-Nazi and a leader of a small faction called the National Socialist Front.

In the late 1990s, to fund the purchase of weapons for their planned takeover of the Swedish state, Arklof led a series of daring bank robberies. Cornered by the police after one of these, Arklof shot and killed two police officers. He is serving a life sentence.[1]

During his trial, it was revealed that he was also wanted for war crimes by an international court investigating the excesses—torture, brutality— by Croat forces in Bosnia in the mid-1990s. He has pleaded guilty to these crimes as well. That sentence runs concurrently.

You probably imagine that Jackie Arklof is a hulking neo-Nazi skinhead, with a large, shaved head, cold, murderous eyes, and tattoos of swastikas covering his bare chest. At least I did.

I was utterly unprepared for the man who walked into the visiting room to greet me, and who was then locked into the room with me. Jackie is of medium height, with a powerful body-builder chest and a slim waist, and long delicate fingers. His bright eyes are direct, engaged, and lively, indicating a fierce intelligence. Within 30 seconds of his entrance, he was describing to me the books by Dostoevsky and Coetzee he'd been reading. Of Dostoevsky, Jackie says, he advocated violence, was passionate and political in his youth, but then, in prison, he rethinks his positions and repents "with real agony." He laughs. "Hey, that sort of sounds like me."[2]

Have I mentioned that Jackie Arklof is black?

Yes, it's true. Scandinavia's most feared neo-Nazi murderer is black. Well, actually of mixed-race ancestry: his mother was Liberian and his father British. He was born in Monrovia and, at age 2, adopted by a Swedish family. And there lies the beginning of his story.

How did a mixed-race Swedish immigrant become the most feared neo-Nazi in Scandinavia? The answer has a lot to do with racism—ironically, not the traditional anti-Semitic racism of the German Nazis of the mid-twentieth century, but the undercurrents of racism that infect even the most egalitarian European societies today.

ALIENATION AND ACCEPTANCE

Jackie Arklof grew up in Ankarsund, a small town of 100 in northern Sweden—a village whose inhabitants had never seen a black person. Indeed, it's likely that no one in the whole province had ever seen a black person. He was, for certain, the only black person then living in the entire province. His parents were relatively well-off; his father was a prosperous farmer with thousands of chickens, and his mother was a music teacher. Although remote and inexpressive, they also made him feel safe.

At least at home. At school it was entirely a different story. Ever the outsider, he was always getting into fights. "I was bullied a lot," he says, "but the truth is I also bullied right back."

He described himself as a "willful learner"—he learned "whatever I wanted" but "not what they told me I had to learn." By high school he had become fascinated with the Nazis. "It wasn't the ideology that interested me," he said. "It was the military machinery, the warfare." Jackie was fascinated by military history; indeed, he asked me to send him some scholarly books on the military technology of the Thirty Years War.

If the military enthralled him, Nazism was a simple protest, a "way to get attention." As he said, "I was always angry, and I needed an outlet for my hate. It just kept growing, the hate."

These three forces—interest in the military, his growing hate, and the painful racism of rural Sweden—led him to overcompensate. He identified as Swedish, meaning he disidentified as a person of color. "I have to be more white than the other whites," he said. "I knew the Nazis had a racialist ideology that wouldn't include blacks. But I wasn't black. I was Swedish. I was going to show other Swedes that I was even more Swedish than they were. I actively opposed immigrants, complained constantly about refugees. They were parasites, taking *our* jobs."

After high school and an industrial/technical college career, he decided that what he really wanted was a military life. Recruited into the Swedish army, he quickly excelled. He became a Ranger, approved for Special Forces, the Swedish equivalent of the Green Berets.

"The problem for me, though, was that there were no wars. Sweden's such a nice country, they never fight anyone. I didn't want to just be in the military; I wanted to fight in a war.

"I was a warrior looking for a war," he says. And he found one.

From the Swedish army, he was recruited as a mercenary for the Croat army in 1993 and immediately was sent to the war in Bosnia. "It was great," he said. It was a real war, and real battles, and he felt immediately at home. It was among the Croats that he really learned about Nazism, he said. After all, the Croats had been Nazi sympathizers during the Second World War, unlike the Serbs, who were resisters and were slaughtered by the Reich.

Here, committing war crimes against the Muslim Bosnians, with these Croat soldiers, many who were the sons of real Nazis, whose racialist ideology completely detested blacks, he felt "truly accepted" for the first time in his life.

"It was the only time in my life that nobody called me a fucking nigger," he says.

"Sure, when they met me they were a little prejudiced," he adds. "But in the army, it's not who you are, it's what you do that counts. And they completely accepted me."

He pauses. "It's like the Norman Mailer novel, *The Naked and the Dead*," he says. "The tensions between the Italians and the Jews in the army." (Every time he cites literature I confess I am a bit nonplussed.)

Active with the Special Forces in Bosnia, he glosses over his own involvement. "Hell is a place on earth," he says somewhat cryptically. "I saw the
absolute worst that people can be to each other." It is the only time in the
conversation that he speaks in the third person, about others. There were
atrocities on both sides, he assures me, but he skirts away from confessing
the actual crimes in which he was a participant—or how willing a participant
he was.

In 1995, he was taken prisoner by the Bosnian army and spent the next
15 months in a Bosnian prisoner of war camp. Here were Bosnians, Serbs,
Croats—all together, and everyone got along extremely well.

BECOMING A SWEDISH NAZI

In August 1996, he was freed and repatriated to Sweden in a prisoner
exchange. He tried to return to civil society after his experiences in war. It
was impossible. He drifted from job to job, place to place.

"I had just been released from prison," he says, fully aware of the irony,
"but when I returned to civil society I felt like I was trapped in a cage, in a
box. I couldn't breathe."

He rented a cheap apartment in Ostersund, a small city in the center-
north of the country, and fell in with a group of neo-Nazis who were taken
with his military experience. "They saw me as a man of action, not words—a
man of deeds.

"And I took this northern Swedish idea of being a man to be what a real
man is." In the north, he explains, Swedish men are hard, lonely, stoic, inexpressive. They call Stockholm "Fjollholm"—literally "Fag-holm."

From 1996 to 1999, he become increasingly involved with the National
Socialist Front, a neo-Nazi faction in northern Sweden that was preparing
itself for the glorious and bloody takeover of the Swedish state. "Democracy
was all talk," he said; Sweden was "the bitch society, completely feminized.
Everything was corrupt, decadent, weak. Swedish men were weak cowards—
they didn't have the courage to stand up to the police or the immigrants, and
were just letting them roll over them. I thought, there must be one man who
is willing to stand up to them—and I thought it should be me. I could chan-
nel my anger, my hate, and stand up for Sweden.

"I believed that we, the Nazis, were the chosen people, the ones who would
sacrifice for them. We despised the Swedish people; at the same time as we
were willing to lay down our lives for them."

The Front planned its takeover of the Swedish government methodically,
carefully, and with paranoia given full reign. The militant faction of the IRA
was their role model, and they robbed banks to get money to buy weapons to carry out their terrorist attacks and assassinations (which did not
come to pass). On May 1, 1999, in Malexander, he and two comrades were

apprehended by the police after one such robbery; in the resulting shoot-out, it was Jackie who shot the two officers.

Since 2000 he has been serving a life sentence. In prison he began to realize the crazed depravity to which he had fallen. The Nazis were "crazy," he said. "No, I mean it. Seriously. They were so desperate for members they would take mentally retarded guys, alcoholics, and especially guys who you would say are paranoid and hysterical. Now they scare me."

More than that, though, he began to feel a deepening sense of remorse. "Where I used to feel hatred, that space inside me became increasingly filled with remorse and regret."

"At one point the hate becomes exhausted," he writes in academic article he has written of his experience. You feel empty and you have no energy left to hate. Hate changes from a driving force to a brake that leads to depression."[3]

Today, Arklof is filled with remorse. He quotes a Hebrew phrase: when you kill a man, you kill his whole world. "I didn't just kill those policemen; I killed their whole world. Their children, their wives, their relatives, their friends. I feel that every day." (Of course, he says, the fact that he killed two cops in a shoot-out has made him somewhat of a folk hero among other prisoners. He refuses any praise and tells inmates that he is "not a hero.")

Eventually, he reached out to EXIT, the organization in Stockholm that helps neo-Nazis "jump" from the movement. He has begun to work with them, and hopes that when he is released in another 15 years or so, that he will be able to work with EXIT to help others turn their lives around.

EXIT

As our interview winds down, Jackie takes out two thick loose-leaf binders he has brought to show me. Inside are printouts from the Web about Husserl and Wittgenstein. He has been reading Wittgenstein lately, he says, trying to understand the roots of violence and especially of racial and ethnic hatreds. He links antimodernism with economic displacement from globalization, and then links the feelings of invisibility ("being pushed aside") with arrogant invincibility.

I confess I was a bit taken aback having a conversation about Wittgenstein in the visiting room of a supermax prison with the country's most notorious murderer. I suspect this would be unusual in an American context. Jackie is pursuing a joint degree in history from the university at Upssala and in sociology from the university in Gavle. He reads constantly and conducts classes by telephone, correspondence, and with visiting instructors. His English is nearly flawless.

Jackie Arklof seems to express a contradiction—a black Swedish ex-neo-Nazi who fought with "white" Croats against "ethnic" Bosnians. And yet his life suggests some of the ways that race, class, gender, and nationalism can be combined in ways that are unexpected—to say the least. Seeing himself as a Swede, Jackie reacted to the racism he experienced by becoming "more Swedish" than the other Swedes—which led to his drift towards the anti-immigrant extreme right. His embrace by neo-Nazi Croat soldiers in the former Yugoslavia convinced him that "race" was more a social construct and that being a "man of action" was how one demonstrated one's capacity for comradeship.

Seeing the world through the single prism of race brought him face-to-face with his contradictions. He was naïve, set up by the officials in the movement, and abandoned by them as soon as they could run. But now, more thoughtful and introspective, he's come to also see how gender informed his choices about joining, how he needed to prove himself as a man, which led him to be manipulated. And he has come to see the route out of the movement through EXIT—and thus toward a very different definition of manhood. As our interview ends, I ask Jackie if there is anything else he wants to say. "When I was free on the outside I was mentally in prison," he says. "But now it's the other way around."

NOTES

My interviews with Jackie Arklof are part of a larger project on "Gender on the Extreme Right in the United States and Scandinavia." I am grateful to the Carnegie Endowment and the American Scandinavian Foundation for financial support, and to the members and staff of EXIT in Stockholm, and especially Robert Orell and Katja Wåhlström for their help in arranging interviews with Jackie and others, and to Klas Hyllander, Jens Malmstrom, and Jeppe Lyng for their logistical and linguistic help. For further information, see also Kimmel (2007).

1. A "life sentence" in Sweden typically runs about 20 years.

2. Unless otherwise noted, all quotations are from my interviews with Jackie Arklof.

3. "Nazismens inre verklighet: En sociologisk analys av drivkrafterna hos den harda karnan av dagens svenska nazister" ("The Inner Reality of Nazism: A Sociological Analysis of the Driving Forces that can be found in the Core of Swedish Nazi-members today"), 2004, p. 33. I am grateful to Jeppe Lyng for the translations from the Swedish.

REFERENCE

Kimmel, M. (2007). Racism as adolescent male rite of passage: Ex-Nazis in Scandinavia. *Journal of Contemporary Ethnography, 36*, pp. 202–218.

CHAPTER 10

SKINHEAD STREET VIOLENCE

Pete Simi

On the evening of October 16, 2002, a small group of skinheads was thrown out of a pool hall for starting a barroom brawl in Phoenix, Arizona. As the skinheads gathered in the parking lot, one of the leaders, Samuel Compton, began shouting "White Power! White Pride!" while goose-stepping around. Compton had just been released from prison for an aggravated assault charge and had recently written a letter to his ex-girlfriend warning what he might do to her new boyfriend: "I don't just hit, I want to bounce heads off of curbs and break teeth and bones. Put steel toe boots to his face"(Buchanan, 2003, p. 8). After a few goose-steps, Compton noticed Cole Bailey Jr., a 21-year-old white youth who was standing alone waiting for a taxicab. Reports indicate that Compton turned toward Bailey and asked him, "What the fuck are you looking at?" When Bailey responded, "Nothing, I'm just waiting for a cab," Compton walked over and punched him between the eyes with brass knuckles. The other skinheads joined Compton and began kicking Bailey repeatedly in the skull with their steel-toed boots while one of the female skinheads cheered them on. Bailey was taken to a hospital and pronounced dead a few hours later.

Images of shaven-headed, swastika-tattooed, jack-booted youth hurling racial epithets at Oprah Winfrey and breaking Geraldo Rivera's nose earned skinheads a "folk devil" (Cohen, 1980) status by the late 1980s. Skinheads, however, are, arguably, best known for hate violence targeting racial and other minorities. The Phoenix murder, though, reveals a larger trend in skinhead violence that is less often discussed. Racist skinheads are more likely to select targets based on convenience as opposed to carefully planned acts of violence that reflect their white-power beliefs (see also Blee, 2005). The focus here is on the relationship between skinheads and violence. Rather than catalogue skinhead violence, analysis is made of a sample ($n = 155$) of incidents of skinhead violence that occurred between 1988–1999 and 2006–2007, and ethnographic data collected between 1997–2004. I use these data to focus on the situational characteristics of skinhead violence (Katz, 1988), the ways in which skinhead violence is influenced by organizational factors, and the "subculture of violence" (Wolfgang & Ferracuti, 1967) that exists among skinheads.[1]

METHODS

Between 1999 and 2004, participant observation and in-depth interviews were conducted in a variety of settings in order to examine Southern California skinheads.[2] A snowball-sampling technique was used to locate skinheads in the Los Angeles area, obtaining data regarding 17 Southern California skinhead gangs and their members. Since 2004, collecting secondary data has continued through law enforcement interviews and analysis of watchdog reports and other secondary documents.

The analysis is based primarily on 127 interviews conducted with 43 current and former racist skinheads. These interviews were supplemented with data from interviews conducted with 14 law enforcement officers.[3] Most of the skinhead interviewees were male, reflecting the predominance of males in the skinhead subculture (Blee, 2002). No clear social-class pattern was found among interviewees, which is not surprising in view of the cross section of social classes represented among skinheads in general (Anderson, 1987; Hamm, 1993).

The range of events observed with skinheads in Southern California included house parties and other social gatherings, white-power music concerts, and 23 home visits ranging in length from one day to five weeks. Participant observation provided data regarding group practices and allowed me to build rapport with key informants who served as gatekeepers, introducing me to other skinheads and providing much-needed references for further interviews. Participant observation and interviewing allowed for close examination of a wide range of information, including how skinheads talk about violence and the extent to which violence is central to their daily lives.

The sample of violent incidents was primarily derived from secondary data sources, including official reports of antiracist watchdog organizations (e.g., the Anti-Defamation League), along with newspaper accounts and court documents.[4] A fourfold typology was constructed to characterize skinhead violence. The first dimension relates to motivation of the offender; to examine motivation, the incidents were coded in relation to bias motivation. The second dimension involves the incident's level of organization, ranging from spontaneous to planned. An incident could be coded as one of any four categories: (1) bias-motivated and planned (e.g., two skinheads who decided to murder an African American to demonstrate their commitment to the cause and drove to Wilmington, Delaware, and then Philadelphia, Pennsylvania, in order to find a victim); (2) bias-motivated and spontaneous (e.g., the murder of Ethiopian immigrant Mulugeta Seraw in Portland, Oregon, which started as a traffic altercation but escalated due to Seraw's race); (3) not bias-motivated and planned (e.g., the murder of a veteran Southern California skinhead who was killed by members of his own gang for talking to the local media about their activities); (4) not bias-motivated and spontaneous (e.g., the Phoenix murder described in the introduction).

HISTORY OF SKINHEADS IN THE UNITED KINGDOM

A significant component of skinhead culture is their appearance. Traditionally, skinhead style included closely cropped hair or a shaved head, work pants or denim jeans, Doc Marten steel-toed work boots, suspenders, and tattoos. Skinhead culture began in Great Britain and developed in two waves through the 1960s and 1970s. The first skinheads emerged in Great Britain in the late 1960s in response to deteriorating traditional working-class communities, stemming from a stagnating economy, competition with immigrants for scarce jobs, and withering neighborhood traditions. While they did not explicitly associate themselves with Nazism, they were ardently nationalist in political orientation and fervently opposed to foreign immigration, which was reflected by their affinity for violently attacking Pakistani immigrants, also known as "Paki-bashing."

While the first skinheads defined themselves along themes of nationalism, ultramasculinity, and working-class issues (e.g., lack of economic opportunity), they expressed political sentiments primarily through stylistic imagery; hence, they were not typically involved in traditional, organized political activities (e.g., unions, political parties, marches). This lack of politicization began to change as a second wave of English skinheads emerged in the late 1970s and tentatively became associated with the National Front (NF) and the British National Party (BNP), extreme right-wing political parties, who saw the utility of drawing disaffected white youth into their ranks (Brake, 1974; Clarke, 1976; Hebdige, 1979; Knight, 1982). The second wave of skinheads spread beyond Britain and emerged in several other European countries as well as in North America.

THE DEVELOPMENT OF AMERICAN SKINHEADS

Although the skinhead style spread to America through a process of international cultural diffusion, American skinhead gangs formed primarily in response to changes in local punk rock scenes. In the late 1970s, local punk rock scenes started getting "hardcore," which signaled a more violent and suburban trend in punk rock (Spitz & Muller, 2001). Hardcore referred to a faster style of music and a more hostile attitude, which was expressed through random violence directed at other punks during music shows. For younger suburban kids, hardcore aggressiveness provided an important security device from those antagonistic toward punk style. During this time, the skinhead style evolved from hardcore and, similar to hardcore, became a popular alternative to kids attracted to an ultra-aggressive style (Blush, 2001).

In the early 1980s, local youth cliques began forming skinhead gangs across the United States. The first skinhead gangs bonded around identity markers and shared interests (shaved heads, clothing styles, musical preferences, slang, tattoos, etc.). They built a collective identity with organizational names, initiation rites, semihierarchical social roles, and nonspecialized, "garden-variety" delinquency (e.g., vandalism, underage drinking, petty theft, and maybe most importantly fighting). Yet skinhead identity was also loose, unstructured, and tied to social gatherings that were relatively unregulated, allowing for the innovation needed to create oppositional identities.

CHARACTERISTICS OF SKINHEAD VIOLENCE

Since the late 1980s, as skinheads increasingly forged links with adult white-supremacist groups such as the White Aryan Resistance and Ku Klux Klan, observers have focused on the relationship between skins and hate violence (Hamm, 1993; Hicks, 2004). My examination of skinhead violence reveals that although approximately half of these incidents are related to ideology, slightly less than half of those are planned. More than half appear spontaneous, sparked by verbal exchanges that escalate, only in part because of skinhead beliefs, into violent offenses. A smaller number of incidents are split almost evenly between spontaneous, non-bias-motivated (26%) and planned and non-bias-motivated (23%).

Skinhead violence that is bias-motivated and planned tends to resemble two variants—"mission" and "defensive" (McDevitt, Levin, & Bennett, 2002). Mission violence refers to incidents where an offender's violence directly results from his/her beliefs, which have been held over a relatively long period of time. These offenders tend to view their violence as part of a larger political strategy. The Fourth Reich Skins in the early 1990s represent the mission type. Two of the leaders decided that a "racial revolution" was the only viable option for "saving the white race." Based on these ideas, Chris Fisher, 20, and Carl Boese, 17, began forming an active cell of skinheads with the goal of assassinating African American leaders and bombing synagogues in order to start the "race war." They practiced their training by exploding

Molotov cocktails on the front porches of members of a rival gang. Their larger plans of violence were interrupted as the group was dismantled when federal authorities indicted the two key leaders (Smith, 1994).

Defensive violence is the result of an immediate perceived threat to an offender's neighborhood or territory. Skinheads may perceive that someone is an outsider regardless of whether that person is a member of minority group. Further, skinheads are highly mobile, and their territorialism reflects this characteristic. Skinheads may claim a park in a neighborhood where none of their members lives. The park may simply be somewhere they enjoy hanging out. Skinheads also travel to areas knowing they will find "suitable targets" whom they perceive as outsiders.

For example, it became routine for skinheads in the 1980s and 1990s from northern and central Orange County, California, to travel to Laguna Beach, California (southern Orange County), in order to "gay bash." Interviews with skinheads reveal that this was a common practice.

> Oh yeah we used to go down to Laguna Beach all the time to gay bash. We really went after the scumbags down there . . . we'd chase 'em around with baseball bats and pipes. I remember one guy we were chasing all around, practically chased him off a cliff. That fag was scared shitless and we were just having a blast. (Orange County Skin interview, June 14, 2004)

These incidents reveal a need among the perpetrators to enact a "moral duty" where violence is not only justifiable; it is necessary. The preparation for this violence helps skinheads coalesce around a common goal: to eradicate "degenerate filth" from the world. Defensive acts of violence are similar to what Katz (1988) refers to as "righteous sacrifice," where the actors see their violence as obligatory.

ORGANIZATIONAL FACTORS AND SKINHEAD VIOLENCE

There is significant organizational variation among gangs (Fagan, 1989; Jankowski, 1991; Klein, 1995). The quantity and type of violence a gang participates in may reflect these organizational differences. In general, skinhead gangs are short-lived and have overlapping membership (e.g., sometimes a smaller skinhead clique will be composed completely of members from larger skinhead gangs). Most skinheads become involved between the ages of 12 and 19 (Moore, 1993; Wooden & Blazak, 2001), and they tend to coalesce around a unique music, style, argot, and set of practices that are autonomous and distinct from adult hate groups such as the Klan (Bjorgo, 1998; Wooden & Blazak). Skinhead gangs are typically organized at the state level (e.g., West Virginia Skinheads) or county and/or city level (e.g., Orange

County Skins, Las Vegas Skins), or they can even be neighborhood- and/or school-based (e.g., Milwaukee Eastside Bullies). One of the few exceptions is the Hammerskin Nation (HSN), an international skinhead organization, originally formed in 1988 in Dallas, Texas. Currently the HSN has five regional chapters in the U.S. (Northern Hammers, Midland Hammers, etc.) with an additional 10 chapters in other countries.

The skinhead gangs that were examined were not devoid of local, neighborhood-based forms of territoriality, as some observers contend (Hamm, 1993; Klein, 1995; Moore, 1993). They attempted to claim territory, which could be seen in their choice of gang names (Huntington Beach Skins, Chino Hills Skins, South Bay Skins, Norwalk Skins, etc.) and their claims of specific locations (such as parks or music clubs) through the use of graffiti "tags" and other more physically aggressive means. Of the 17 skinhead gangs studied, 13 attempted to claim territory by such methods as graffiti, hanging out, and/or accosting individuals who entered their turf.

There is significant diversity among racist skinheads (Simi, Smith, & Reeser, in press). Homeless "street skinheads" engage in relatively unplanned and disorganized criminal activity and spontaneous acts of unprovoked violence in order to meet basic survival needs (Baron, 1997). Some skinhead gangs like the Nazi Lowriders (NLR) or Public Enemy Number One (PEN1) are linked to prison gangs like the Aryan Brotherhood (AB), motorcycle gangs like the Hells Angels (HA), or street gangs from other racial/ethnic backgrounds, and their violence tends to reflect their involvement in profit-oriented criminal activity (Simi et al.). Within this type of skinhead gang, high levels of methamphetamine use and distribution mark their lifestyle. Members spend their days "tweaking" (getting high on methamphetamines) and traveling from one weekly motel to the next. These skinheads are also typically involved in home burglaries, "professional hits," credit card fraud, and embezzlement. Their violence is related to disputes involving money, drugs, and retribution for speaking to law enforcement.

SITUATIONAL CHARACTERISTICS AND A SUBCULTURE OF VIOLENCE

Subcultural explanations have played an important role in the criminological literature, helping explain the attributes and processes that integrate individuals into a group where the expression of violence is part of their "routine activities." Early subcultural researchers focused upon certain structural locations such as class status and/or poverty (Miller, 1958; Wolfgang & Ferracuti, 1967) while others focused upon geocultural factors (i.e., the Southern subculture of violence) to account for extreme levels of violence (Gastil, 1971). According to prior studies, gang members tend to participate in higher levels of offending, especially violent crime (see Thornberry,

2001, for a review of this research). The facilitation model suggests that the norms and group processes associated with gangs facilitate violent offending. Rather than sociopathic tendencies producing gang violence (Yablonsky, 1962), experiences related to gang participation encourage and reinforce violent behavior. In Vigil's (1988) study of "barrio gangs," he argues that violence is one of the "strongly embedded patterns requiring group effort and support" (p. 137). Although skinheads are not homogeneous or linked to a specific geographic region, subcultural explanations of violence provide important insights regarding the role of the skinhead group in producing and sustaining violent behavior. Skinhead violence provides a mechanism for achieving status within the group as well as a way to dramatically represent oneself (Blee, 2002; Katz, 1988; Moore, 1994). Rather than white-power beliefs driving them to carefully select targets that represent "racial enemies," their beliefs seem to have a more indirect effect on their violence. Their beliefs are an important part of their overall presentation of self, which is oppositional and embraces conflict.

While discussions of the frequency of skinhead violence must remain tentative, the intensity of skinhead violence is one characteristic for which there is ample anecdotal evidence. Skinhead violence typically occurs in exaggerated forms. Of the violent incidents analyzed, slightly more than 85 percent included weapons and resulted in injuries to the victims.[5] Several examples serve to illustrate this point. A group of Southern California skinheads surrounded a Native American man near the pier in Huntington Beach, California. After following him down the beach and taunting the man, two of the skinheads stabbed the victim 27 times, in what officers referred to as a "particularly frenzied attack" (Richardson 1998). During my interviews with the primary offender in the attack, he explained how his background with violence and his involvement with skins as a child prepared him for this type of violence as an adolescent.

> I started hanging out with my older brother and his skin friends when I was 12. They showed me how to fight. I was pretty small and needed to defend myself. They showed me how to use a knife. The more I hung out with them the more I started fighting. By the time I was 16 I was ready for WAR and I enjoyed it. (Skinhead letter, November 9, 2005)

In another example, a gang of skinheads outside of Boston showed up to a Halloween party and after being asked to leave returned a little later shouting, "You're gonna die," and wielding knives, chains, pipes, an ax handle, and a broomstick. The skinheads directed their anger toward 22-year-old Jayson Linsky, which resulted in skinhead leader John Tague fatally stabbing Linsky nine times (Rodriguez, 1997). Based on this account, skinheads seem to prefer an eclectic and creative range of weapons The Boston skins were asked to leave the party because they were acting like skinheads (i.e., shouting sieg heils). In other words, their core sense of self was rejected. The party-goers shamed the skinheads by asking them to leave. Individuals with weak ego defenses are more likely to respond aggressively to rejections of self such as this (Fleisher, 1995). Skinhead violence is reinforced by an emphasis on certain core "focal concerns" (Miller 1958). This last example illustrates skinhead perceptions about the importance of toughness and aggression. In the summer of 1993, Kenneth "German" Allen had just been paroled from a California prison where he'd served a sentence for aggravated assault as part of his attempt to hang an African American woman from a tree in San Jose, California. Shortly after his release Allen returned home to Southern California. Within a few months Allen and several other skinheads were hanging out at Huntington Beach. A staring match between one of the skinheads and an unknown beachgoer turned into a scuffle. When Allen, who was getting something from his car in the parking lot, saw the fight erupt he ran toward the scene with a tire iron and began assaulting the victim. Eventually Allen placed the victim in a choke hold from behind and then sliced the victim's throat with a straight razor that was in his back pocket. Two different skinheads explain that Allen's violence was a reasonable response to the situation and that once these conflicts emerge, there are "no limits."

> When Allen did that we all thought fuck yeah the guy got what he deserved—he brought his fists to a knife fight you know what I mean so no, no one was upset or thought Allen went too far. We all pretty much thought he just did what he had to and the guy shouldn't been fuck'n with him in the first place. (Hammerskin interview, February 23, 2002)

> You have to understand that when people look at fights like Kenny's they say shit like "those goddamn skinheads are just violent thugs or bullies" and they don't even look at what led up to a skinhead cutting someone's throat or whatever. That pisses me off because people don't know exactly what happened and most of the violence that I know about or have been around the people had it comin'. (WAR Skin interview, January 30, 1999)

Of the skinheads I have interviewed, most reject the notion of "fighting fair," a view that likely contributes to the excessive nature of skinhead violence. Instead, they typically advocated an "anything goes" approach to violence. One might assume this would translate into an affinity for using high-powered weaponry to fight. Although there are certainly skinheads who stockpile high-powered weapons and participate in terror plots that include bomb-making, most skinhead street violence is a result of interpersonal disputes and includes much less sophisticated weaponry. Skinheads' choice of weaponry may reflect a "tribal" (Etter, 1999) mentality that exists in their culture. Their violence is excessive and their weapons are primitive, a perfect combination for those who enjoy going to battle and inflicting bodily harm.

STATUS MANAGEMENT, TERRITORY, AND VIOLENCE

In addition to the high intensity of skinhead violence, it also typically occurs within a group context. The skinhead group not only improves "the odds" when fighting, but the group context is probably most significant because the group is an essential part of a dramaturgical performance (Goffman, 1959, 1963) that includes interactional ploys where actors attempt to manipulate situations in order to produce violence. Skinheads use verbal harassment as a precursor to violence. Some members of the group will begin the verbal harassment in what typically amounts to "set-up" questions (e.g., Are you white power? What race are you? Do you like skinheads?). Questions are asked until the "wrong" answer is given and at this point, one or more of the skinheads will initiate the violence.

During the 1980s, Eastside White Pride (EWP) began claiming Laurelhurst Park on the southeast side of Portland, Oregon, as their "turf." When members of EWP were gathered at the park, selected passersby were stopped, "questioned" about their racial heritage and political beliefs, and then usually assaulted. According to Anderson (1987), this was also true for the San Francisco Skins during the 1980s: "While most of these youths had lived in the 'Haight' only a short time, they came to see it as *their* neighborhood. The clearest declaration of their presence was the expropriation of Buena Vista Park, which became known as 'Skinhead Hill'" (p. 27). In the early 1990s, a patchwork of Southern California skinheads affiliated with several different gangs came together to form the Crazy Fuckin Skins/Confederate Front Skins (CFS) and began claiming a small city park in Orange County as their territory. They marked their territory by accosting strangers they perceived as "racially impure." This practice culminated in an incident where a multiracial group of three youths was held captive and beaten severely by CFS. One of the interesting things about this incident is that a relatively lengthy interactional exchange occurred prior to the beating. One skinhead leader questioned the victims about whether they were "antiracist" skinheads, and when they responded that they were not, the leader began questioning them about their views of white-power skinheads. Despite the victims trying to appease the skinheads by responding favorably (i.e., "We don't have problems with white-power skinheads") none of their answers seemed to help. The victims found themselves in a no-win situation. During the exchange, some of the other skinheads served as audience members and occasionally encouraged escalation toward physical violence with periodic shouts of "white power" and "beat the fuckers down."

What is interesting about this type of violence is that once skinheads initiate social contact, there is almost no way to de-escalate or diffuse the conflict. If the victim responds that they do not like white power, this is perceived as a challenge and an invitation to violence, while answers that are supportive or neutral are discarded as dishonest or irrelevant and thus also invitations to violence. In this respect skinhead violence seems to differ from other types of gang violence where situational conflicts are frequently diffused with various interactional ploys (Hughes & Short, 2005). The ethos placed on "violence for the sake of violence" within skinhead culture may prevent or reduce the possibility of avoiding violence once a conflictual situation emerges. This means that an individual who finds himself or herself pitted against a group of skinheads is literally facing a "fight or flight" situation. An interview with a WAR Skin provides insight about the group norms surrounding the use of violence:

> When we go out to a bar or whatever, we just don't want people staring at us, "you better turn the other fucking way or you're gonna get beat. Don't fuckin stare at us and you won't have any problems, don't try and be mister tough guy and show off for your girlfriend you know because if you pull that shit we will get violent; violence is necessary sometimes when you're dealing with scumbags, some people deserve to get the shit kicked out of them." (WAR Skin interview, March 21, 2000)

This comment illustrates Katz's (1988) notion of "badass":

> With friends, you generate a terrifying style, then take it to the street. When others curiously take note, you experience "agro"; suddenly, "they" are "screwing" you. Suddenly, the otherwise mundane phenomena of behavior in public are transformed into the stuff of mortal challenge. (p. 140)

At times skinhead violence has a curious relation to whether "outsiders" accept their presentation of self. For example, skinheads who accost someone in a park asking whether the person "likes skins" seem interested in the question of social acceptability. The murder in Phoenix described in the introduction was initiated when Compton asked the victim, "What the fuck are you looking at?" Bailey was in the wrong place at the wrong time and had the misfortune to stand in for society writ large. Bailey's answer was irrelevant because Compton already knew the answer. He had been making a spectacle of himself in the parking lot by goose-stepping around and for years before that night he had been tattooing swastikas and other symbols of hate all over his body. The skinhead style, including their violence, is if nothing else a rejection of conventional society. It is no coincidence that a skinhead's favorite pose during a photograph is flipping the camera off.

RECENT TRENDS IN THE SKINHEAD SCENE
AND THE FUTURE OF VIOLENCE

During the last two-and-a-half decades, the number of racist skinheads has ebbed and flowed. Recently, some observers report a resurgence of skinhead gangs. This resurgence has spurred the Anti-Defamation League to sponsor the Racist Skinhead Project, a national effort to monitor skinhead gangs across the country. Since their emergence in the U.S., skinheads have varied greatly from one region to another. This variety continues to be the case. In some skinhead scenes, emphasis is placed on retaining the "authentic" and traditional appearance of the skinhead style, while in other areas (most notably Southern California) some skinheads blend a traditional style with a more contemporary "gangsta" style (e.g., saggy pants, socks pulled up). Still other highly political skinheads encourage their "brothers" to grow their hair out and refrain from getting completely tattooed in order to infiltrate the system, which they argue is controlled by a "small cabal of Jews" who are secretly plotting to eradicate the "white race."

In some areas (e.g., Phoenix, Arizona) the skinhead scene continues to thrive despite a continuous implosion of specific groups. In other parts of the country, skinheads have developed ties to outlaw motorcycle gangs. A few of the areas where skinhead scenes are especially active include Southern California; Pennsylvania (especially the corridor between Philadelphia and Harrisburg); Portland, Oregon; Ohio; Indiana; and New Jersey.

Although skinhead violence during the early and mid-1980s was sometimes racially motivated, there is little evidence to suggest that these early skinhead gangs went beyond the long-standing pattern of white gangs' defense of racial neighborhood boundaries. Much skinhead violence was directed toward other subcultural groups (e.g., other skin gangs, punks, and surfers) that were also willing participants in the action. Skinheads defined their violence as a means of protecting themselves from aggressive nonskinhead groups. By the early 1990s, skinheads' political beliefs became more organized; their violence, however, remains largely spontaneous. Spontaneous violence loosely connected to ideology is likely to remain the most common type of skinhead violence. However, as gangs like PEN1 continue to grow, nonideological violence will also become more prevalent, as the last few years of data suggest.

NOTES

1. It is not to suggest that all racist skinheads are equally violent. In a forthcoming paper (Simi & Futrell, in press) the stigma management techniques used among skinheads and other white-power activists to "get by" in a world that is highly antagonistic to their identity without having to always resort to conflict is examined. In that paper, three factors are discussed (alcohol consumption, age, and number of Aryans present) that are

especially important in differentiating when Aryans display their identity nonviolently as opposed to using more aggressive means.

2.   During the course of fieldwork, interviews were conducted with skinheads in Chicago, Illinois; Dallas, Texas; Denver, Colorado; Detroit, Michigan; Las Vegas, Nevada; New York, New York; Philadelphia, Pennsylvania; Phoenix, Arizona; Portland, Oregon; Salt Lake City, Utah; and Seattle, Washington ($N = 18$). The data obtained from these interviews suggest important similarities in regards to how skinheads think about violence.

3.   This approach departs from previous studies of skinheads in that law enforcement data are combined with primary interviews of skinheads. Hamm (1993) did not conduct law enforcement interviews, and his interviews of skinheads were more akin to survey questionnaires, which are not well suited to obtaining historical data. Other researchers have claimed that because of the difficulty accessing skinheads it is necessary to rely primarily on secondary sources in order to compile a history of skinheads (see Blee, 2002; Wood, 1999).

4.   Two separate newspaper article searches were conducted on skinhead violence. The first search was drawn from the *Los Angeles Times*, the *Orange County Register*, the *Los Angeles Weekly*, and the *San Bernardino Tribune*. Data from these articles were supplemented with skinhead and law enforcement interviews and court documents. A national search for skinhead violence was conducted using the LexisNexis database and publicly available electronic and paper archives at the Anti-Defamation League and Southern Poverty Law Center. Data was retrieved on 620 incidents of skinhead violence and a subsample ($n = 155$) of these incidents was randomly selected and coded using both quantitative and qualitative content-analysis techniques.

5.   It is likely that the sample, however, is biased toward more serious incidents of violence.

REFERENCES

Anderson, E. (1987). *Skinheads: From Britain to San Francisco via punk rock*. Unpublished master's thesis. Pullman: Washington State University.

Baron, S. (1997). Canadian male street skinheads: Street gang or street terrorist? *Canadian Review of Sociology and Anthropology, 34*, 125–154.

Bjorgo, T. (1998). Entry, bridge burning, and exit options: What happens to young people who join racist groups. In J. Kaplan & T. Bjorgo (Eds.), *Nation and race: The developing Euro-American racist subculture* (pp. 231–258). Boston: Northeastern University Press.

Blee, K. (2002). *Inside organized racism: Women in the hate movement*. Berkeley: University of California Press.

Blee, K. (2005). Racial Violence in the United States. *Ethnic and Racial Studies, 28*, 599–619.

Blush, S. (2001). *American hardcore: A tribal history*. Los Angeles: Feral House.

Brake, M. (1974). The skinheads: An English working class subculture. *Youth and Society, 6*, 179–199.

Buchanan, Susy. (2003). "A Skinhead Slayer." *Phoenix New Times*, July 17, 2003. Retrieved November 2, 2008 from www.phoenixnewtimes.com/2003-07-17/news/a-skinhead-slayer

Clarke, J. (1976). The skinheads and the magical recovery of community. In S. Hall & T. Jefferson (Eds.), *Resistance through rituals* (pp. 99–102). London: Hutchinson.

Cohen, S. (1980.) *Folk devils and moral panics.* London: Macgibbon and Kee.

Etter, G. (1999). Skinheads: Manifestations of the warrior culture of the new urban tribes. *Journal of Gang Research, 6,* 9–21.

Fagan, J. (1989). The social organization of drug use and drug dealing among urban gangs. *Criminology, 27*(4), 633–669.

Fleisher, M. (1995). *Beggars and thieves: Lives of urban street criminals.* Madison: University of Wisconsin Press.

Futrell, Robert and Pete Simi. (2004). "Free Spaces, Collective Identity, and the Persistence of U.S. White Power Activism." *Social Problems, 51,* 16–42.

Gastil, R. D. (1971). Homicide and a regional culture of violence. *American Sociological Review, 36,* 412–27.

Goffman, E. (1959). *Presentation of self in everyday life.* Garden City, NY: Doubleday.

Goffman, E. (1963). *Behavior in public places: Notes on the social organization of gatherings.* New York: Free Press.

Hamm, M. (1993). *American skinheads.* Boston: Northeastern University Press.

Hebdige, D. (1979). *Subculture, the meaning of style.* London: Methuen.

Hicks, W. (2004). Skinheads: A three nation comparison. *Journal of Gang Research, 11*(2), 51–74.

Hughes, L., & Short, J., Jr. (2005). Disputes involving youth street gang members: Micro-social contexts. *Criminology, 43,* 43–76.

Jankowski, M. S. (1991). *Islands in the street: Gangs and American urban society.* Berkeley: University of California Press.

Katz, J. (1988). *Seductions of crime: Moral and sensual attractions of doing evil.* New York: Basic Books.

Klein, M. (1995). *The American street gang: Its nature, prevalence, and control.* New York: Oxford University Press.

Knight, N. (1982). *Skinhead.* London: Omnibus Press.

McCurrie, T. (1998). White racist extremist gang members: A behavioral profile. *Journal of Gang Research, 5*(2), 51–60.

McDevitt, J., J. Levin, & S. Bennett. (2002). Hate crime offenders: An expanded typology. *The Journal of Social Issues, 58,* 303–317.

Miller, W. (1958). Lower class culture as a generating milieu of gang delinquency. *Journal of Social Issues, 14,* 5–19.

Moore, D. (1994). *Lads in action: Social process in an urban youth subculture.* Brookfield, VT: Ashgate.

Moore, J. (1993). *Skinheads shaved for battle: A cultural history of American skinheads.* Bowling Green, OH: Bowling Green State University Popular Press.

Richardson, L. (1998, August 15). Huntington skinhead given life sentence. *Los Angeles Times,* B-1.

Rodriguez, C. (1997, December 5). Avowed skinhead guilty of murder at 1996 Norfolk party. *Boston Globe,* D-4.

Simi, P., Smith, L., & Reeser, A. (in press). From punk kids to public enemy number one. *Deviant Behavior, 29,* 1–22.

Smith, B. (1994). *Terrorism in America: Pipe bombs and pipe dreams*. Albany: New York University Press.

Spitz, M., & Muller, B. (2001). *We got the neutron bomb: The untold story of L.A. punk*. New York: Three Rivers Press.

Thornberry, T. (2001). Membership in youth gangs and involvement in serious and violent offending. In J. Miller, C. L. Maxson, and M. W. Klein (Eds.), *The Modern Gang Reader* (pp. 164–172). Los Angeles: Roxbury Publishing.

Vigil, D. (1988). *Barrio gangs: Street life and identity in Southern California*. Austin: University of Texas Press.

Wolfgang, M. & F. Ferracuti. (1967). *The subculture of violence: Towards an integrated theory in criminology*. London: Tavistock Publications.

Wood, R. (1999). The indigenous, nonracist origins of the American skinhead subculture. *Youth and Society, 31*(2), 131–151.

Wooden, W., & Blazak, R. (2001). *Renegade kids, suburban outlaws: From youth culture to delinquency* (2nd ed.). Belmont, CA: Wadsworth.

Yablonsky, L. (1962). *The violent gang*. New York: Penguin.

CHAPTER 11

ANTI-MUSLIM VIOLENCE IN THE POST-9/11 ERA: MOTIVE FORCES

Barbara Perry

It is always challenging to write with authority on the perpetrators of hate crime. We know very little about those who commit crime motivated by hostility, fear, or resentment of their victims. There are myriad reasons for this. First and foremost is that few such crimes are reported by victims. Where there is no documentation, there is no way to know about the offender. Moreover, even when the crime is reported to police, it may very well not be investigated as a hate crime. Thus, again, we lose out on the opportunity to examine the motivations. Additionally, even where police aggressively pursue the investigation, it is very likely that no suspect will be identified. Hate crimes are often random, anonymous events. Especially in incidents of vandalism or graffiti or other property crimes, there is no direct contact between the victim and offender that would allow identification.

Beyond these investigative problems, however, lie academic limitations as well. We frequently speak to victims of hate crime, but rarely do we engage with offenders. In part, this is due to the difficulty in soliciting volunteers for interviews or surveys. Generally, offenders are not necessarily anxious to admit their wrongdoing. In the present context, a dramatic exception involves members of organized hate groups—these typically young men are often quite happy to share their perspectives on why people of color, gays, or Jews, for example, "deserve" their victimization. However, the proportion of hate crime committed by such individuals remains a very small part of the population of offenders. Consequently, very little research has delved into the explicitly expressed motivations of the "typical" hate crime offender.

The same limitations apply here in my effort to help understand the motivations of perpetrators of anti-Muslim hate crime. To date, there have been no studies that probe offenders for their motivations. Nonetheless, by examining the contexts in which they act, and often the utterances of hate offenders, we can begin to understand what moves them. In particular, the focus in this chapter is on the ways in which the many disparaging images and stereotypes of Muslims, together with imitable state actions, provide offenders with what they must perceive as ample justification for violence against the "threat of Islam."

HOW MUCH VIOLENCE?

Prior to the terrorist attacks in New York City and Washington, D.C., in 2001, Muslims were not frequent targets of racially or religiously motivated violence. They were far outstripped by violence directed toward African Americans, Latinos, and Jews. Yet that has changed since September 2001. The reaction was immediate. Within 24 hours of the attacks, as many as eight homicides were attributed to racially motivated, reactionary violence. Most major cities experienced a rash of hate crime, ranging in seriousness from verbal abuse to graffiti and vandalism to arson and murder. In 1996, for example, The Center for American-Islamic Relations (CAIR, 2006) received only 80 civil rights complaints. But since September 2001 the number of complaints has increased dramatically, with 366 complaints filed in 2001 and 2,476 logged in 2006. By September 18, 2001, the Federal Bureau of Investigation (FBI) was investigating more than 40 possible hate crimes thought to be related to the terrorist attacks; by October 3, they were investigating more than 90; the number had leapt to 145 by October 11. The Muslim Public Affairs Council of Southern California reported 800 cases nationwide by mid-October, and the American-Arab Anti-Discrimination Committee (ADC) had recorded over 1,100 such offenses by mid-November.

Among the incidents reported to law enforcement agencies and organizations like the ADC are the following illustrative examples:

- Washington, D.C.—By the day after the terrorist attacks, the Washington-based Arab American Institute had received dozens of phone calls with messages that "they would pay for this," and that "they should go home." Several other Muslim and Arab centers had received death threats by mail, by e-mail, and from passers-by.
- Somerset, Massachusetts—Three teens lobbed a firebomb onto the roof of a convenience store owned by an American citizen originally from India. One of the teens allegedly told police that they "wanted to get back at the Arabs for what they did in New York."
- Everett, Massachusetts—Softballs were thrown through the window of a cafe owned by a Greek American. They were inscribed with slogans such as "God Bless America" and "Freedom for all."

- Encino, California—Fire destroyed an Afghan and Persian restaurant that had received phone calls and messages with anti-Afghan statements, as well as a threat to burn the restaurant down.
- Washington, D.C.—By September 18, CAIR had received more than 400 reports of hate crimes (compared to the FBI's investigation of 40).
- San Francisco, California—A corner store owned by an Iraqi was vandalized three nights in a row, with messages such as "Arab, go home." In addition, garbage was dumped at the front door, and eggs were thrown at the windows.
- Bronx, New York—The Bronx Muslim Center has received several threatening calls, one of which included the statement that "You better watch your back, Muslim."
- Montgomery County, Texas—A store owned by a man originally from India sustained an estimated $3,500 in damages and $16,000 in lost business after being pelted with a barrage of gunfire. In a similar incident, another Indian-owned convenience store was hit by 14 bullets.
- Potomac, New York—Ongoing harassment of children at the Muslim Community School has included passersby shouting slurs and insults and throwing rocks. One 13-year-old student, whose screen name was Arabgirl, received the threatening e-mail message that "America's going to wipe your country off the face of the earth."
- San Diego, California—A Sikh woman was driving to work when two men riding a motorcycle burst into her car at a stoplight and threatened to slash her throat. One of the men shouted, "This is what you get for what you done to us."

Two interesting trends emerge from these examples. The first has to do with perpetrator motivation and perception. Such is the level of ignorance and insularity of Western hate mongers that the victims of discrimination and violence have been anyone who looked like they may be from somewhere in the Middle East, or may be Muslims—dark-skinned, bearded men who wear turbans or *kufis*, or women who wear *hijab*. Addressing a public hearing by the Los Angeles County Commission on Human Relations (1991), then assistant director of UCLA's Von Grunebaum Center for Near Eastern Studies, Medhi Bozorgmehr, observed that "Arab nationalism, Arab–Israeli wars, and anti-Arab discrimination in the U.S. have all contributed to the emergence of an all-encompassing Arab identity despite a diverse background" (p. 9). As early as 1978, Edward Said himself tacitly recognized this conflation in Western "orientalist" ideology between Arab and Muslim:

Since World War II, after each of the Arab–Israeli wars, the Arab Muslim has become a figure in American popular culture, even as in the academic world, in the policy planner's world, and in the world of business very serious attention is being paid to the Arab. (Said, 1978, pp. 284–285)

There is deep-seated and widespread ignorance in the West of the diversity of religious faiths in the Arab lands and their diaspora; it is commonly assumed that all Arabs are Muslim. Westerners moreover often fail to distinguish Arabs from other ethnic groups originating in the Middle East, and assume that all Middle Easterners are Arabs. Furthermore, the vagaries of phenotype as a marker of supposed "race" can mean that "Middle Eastern appearance," for instance, may be ascribed to some South Americans, southern Europeans, South Asians, or even Australian Aborigines.

As a result of these factors, a number of the victims of anti-Muslim vilification have not been Arab or Afghani or Muslim but Sikhs, or second- and third-generation Americans of Indian descent; Lebanese Christians have been mistaken for Muslims, and even Greeks have been taken for Arabs. The director of the Sikh organization Khalistan Affairs Center estimated that by September 29, 2001, more than 200 bias incidents against Sikhs had been reported. To the perpetrators, it mattered not who these victims really were; rather, the significant factor was who they were thought to be. The Mesa, Arizona, shooting of a Sikh store owner was no less tragic for having been a case of mistaken identity. It was no less motivated by hostility toward Muslims, as was evident in the words of the killer, who had in fact fired shots at two others presumed to be Middle Eastern. When arrested, he uttered such telling phrases as "I am a patriot!" and "I'm an American. Arrest me and let those terrorists run wild!" (*Arizona Daily Sun*, 2001). Parallel examples from Canada abound. Sikhs in Canada are also mistaken for Muslims and accordingly attacked for their perceived identities. In one case, a Hindu temple was apparently confused with a mosque and was targeted by arson (Kilgour, Millar, & O'Neill, 2002). In Australia, attacks on Sikhs were also reported in the wake of 9/11, and churches bearing Arabic script and even a Russian Orthodox church were vandalized (Poynting, 2002). Very recently an apparently Sikh man was pursued and racially abused by two men in a Melbourne street screaming, "fucking Arabs . . . Aussie pride . . . we have to kill them all," according to a Jewish and an Asian-background man who intervened. Ironically, the latter was afterward assaulted with baseball bats by the same perpetrators, who called him a "fucking Jew" (Oakes, 2007).

MOTIVE FORCES: ANTI-MUSLIM IMAGING

The other outstanding pattern typical of so many acts of anti-Muslim violence is the invocation of negative images and stereotypes associated with Muslims. The slogans that accompany the violence noted above reveal a strong sense of the illegitimacy of Arab residence in the United States along with a similarly strong desire for revenge. Thus, while the current wave of anti-Muslim violence clearly was motivated by anger and outrage at the 9/11 terrorist attacks, it is also informed by a broader history and culture that supports anti-Muslim, anti-Arab, and anti–Middle East sentiments. Muslims and Arabs in general have a long, if largely unknown, history of defamation, violence, and nonviolent discrimination in the United States. Moreover, the past and current patterns are nested in an array of cultural and political practices that enable the hostility to fester, and violence to ensue.

Foremost among the motivating forces shaping anti-Muslim violence are ideologies and images that mark the Other, and the boundaries between self and Other, in such a way as to normalize the corresponding inequities. It is within the cultural realm that we find the justifications for these inequities, and for ethnoviolence. For it is this body of discourse that articulates the relations of superiority/inferiority, thereby establishing a hospitable environment for openly racist activity. In line with an essentialist understanding of racial classification, the overriding ideology is that of inscribed traits, wherein "the stereotypes confine them to a nature which is often attached in some way to their bodies, and which thus cannot easily be denied" (Young, 1990, p. 59). The "New Racism" (Barker, 1981) tends to see such characteristics less in biological and more in cultural terms, but nevertheless conceives the boundaries between cultures as relatively fixed and immutable, resulting effectively in a similar essentialism.

Stereotypes that distinguish the racialized Other from white subjects are thus grounded in what are held to be the identifying features of racial minorities. They help to distance white from not white. Here "white" may be a metaphor for Western- or non-"Third-World-looking," rather than a matter of skin pigmentation or other such phenotype (Hage, 1998). The latter is to be feared, ridiculed, and loathed for their differences as recognized in the popular psyche. Almost invariably, the stereotypes are loaded with disparaging associations, suggesting inferiority, irresponsibility, immorality, and nonhumanness, for example. Consequently, they provide both motive and rationale for injurious verbal and physical assaults on minority groups. Acting upon these interpretations allows dominant-group members to recreate whiteness as superiority, while punishing the Other for their presumed traits and behaviors. The active construction of whiteness, then, exploits stereotypes to justify violence.

Where the popular image of the Other is constructed in negative terms—as it frequently is—group members may be victimized on the basis of those perceptions. Hate crime is thus "bolstered by belief systems which (attempt to) legitimate such violence" so as to "limit the rights and privileges of individuals/groups and to maintain the superiority of one group" (Sheffield, 1995, pp. 438–439). Members of subordinate groups are potential victims *because of* their subordinate status. They are already deemed inferior, deviant, and therefore deserving of whatever hostility and persecution comes their way. In sum, they are "damned if they do, and damned if they don't." If they perform their identities on the basis of what is expected of them, they are vulnerable. If they perform in ways that challenge those expectations, they are equally vulnerable.

Such negative constructions of Islam undoubtedly provide motivation for the victimization of Muslims in most Western nations. In fact, many commentators have suggested that Arabs generally and Muslims specifically may represent the last "legitimate" subjects of slanderous imagery and stereotypes (Abraham, 1994; Said, 1997; Stockton, 1994; Suleiman, 1999). For example, Moore (1995) observes that

> Crude caricatures of Muslims appear abundantly in the production and organization of popular culture. Events and situations, whether fictional or real, are presented to us within a framework of symbols, concepts, and images through which we mediate our understanding about reality . . . The news and entertainment media both generate stereotypes and rely on our familiarity with them in order to formulate the world in their terms and communicate ideas in an efficient, i.e., timely, fashion. (p. 16)

As Moore (1995) suggests, the media are especially complicit in the dissemination of anti-Muslim imagery. The widespread perpetuation of such caricatures—by the media and by public figures—fuels sentiments of suspicion and mistrust by shaping public perceptions in less than favorable ways. There are few, if any, positive images of Arabs, Muslims, or Middle Easterners generally. Rather they are portrayed collectively as wholly evil and warlike. Based on his observations of cartoons and other public media, Stockton (1994) has identified eight "assigned image themes" that consistently appear in depictions of Arabs: sexual depravity (e.g., harems and belly dancers), creature analogies (e.g., vermin, camels), physiological and psychological traits (e.g., unappealing physical characteristics, fanaticism, vengeance), savage leaders (e.g., warmongers), deceit (in business and politics), secret power (e.g., use of oil wealth to manipulate others, especially the West), hatred of Israel, and terrorism.

In a 2002 nationwide survey of some 300 Canadian Muslims of South Asian, Arab, African and European background, Council on American Islamic Relations–Canada (CAIR-CAN) found that 55 percent of respondents thought the Canadian media were more biased since 9/11. The report remarked on "A startling similarity between media myths on Islam and Muslims and the hate-text of many documented anti-Muslim incidents" (Khan, Saloojee, & Al-Shalchi, 2004). Disparaging and inflammatory coverage of Islam, tending to emphasize extremist "tendencies," is endemic. Writing of Canada, for example, Ismael and Measor (2003) observe that, after 9/11,

> The blend of the xenophobic fears of the "other," and that of terrorism, provided media consumers in Canada with a clear path to the conclusion that

Islam was a faith in which acts of unspeakable violence were acceptable and that terrorism was endemic to Muslim and Arab culture. This framed Arab and Muslim societies and individuals as somehow fundamentally different from the average Canadian. By refusing to represent the diversity of Islam as a faith, the obfuscation of its tenets, and through their lack of coverage of the articulated ideas of Muslims the world over endorsing peace and supportive of human rights, the media conducted reductive exercises of the highest order. (p. 103)

Such treatments did not begin in September 2001, they point out, but the "war on terror" marked an intensification of existing Islamophobia in the media. It is also important to keep in mind that the patterns of anti-Muslim sentiment and activity that have characterized Canada, the United States, Australia, and other nations have a historical grounding. In the Western world, Anti-Muslim sentiment is not new. Rather, it is often latent, over-shadowed by what are the typically more evident schisms among whites and blacks, Asians, and Aboriginal peoples, for example. Nonetheless, there exists a history of colonialist deprecation that provides the foundation for the current rash of anti-Muslim threats and intimidation: Western preoc-cupation with things Islamic is episodic, to say the least; it seems to take moments of extreme gravity—the Arab–Israeli wars, the Palestinian Inti-fadas, the 1979 revolution in Iran and the ensuing hostage crisis, the Gulf War of 1991, the horrendous terrorist attacks on the World Trade Center and the Pentagon—to awaken its dormant interest. Little wonder, then, that Islam has been at the receiving end of so much stereotyping—depicted as intolerant, reactionary, fanatical, and, when resisted, violent. Such caricature notions of Islam rarely are far from the surface (Malley, 2001). As Malley contends, it is not uncommon for reactionary incidents to follow triggering events. In particular, the 30-year trend toward typifying Arabs as "evil" or as "terrorists" has yielded a similarly long history of backlash violence, of which the months following the September attacks are the most recent in a lengthy series of retaliatory violence directed toward U.S. citizens and resi-dents of Middle Eastern descent. Abraham (1994) concurs: "The pattern of jingoistic violence . . . had become fairly predictable. Events occurring in the Middle East, particularly violence against U.S. citizens, often trigger jingo-istic violence against Arabs and others who could conceivably be confused with them, such as Muslims, Iranians, or Palestinians" (p. 194). Abraham characterizes such "jingoistic racism" as a dangerous hybrid of "knee-jerk patriotism and homegrown white racism toward non-European, non-Christian dark skinned peoples . . . spawned by political ignorance, false pa-triotism, and hyper ethnocentrism" (p. 193).

This is an apt description of the current backlash violence against Mus-lims. Not since the Gulf War, and perhaps not even then, have we seen such frenzied patriotism in the West, from the run on American flags in retail stores, to the replacement of "Take Me Out to the Ballgame" with "God Bless America" or "America the Beautiful" during major-league baseball games' seventh-inning stretches. In Australia, which has never had such an extensive tradition of displaying the national flag, there has been a burgeoning of flag-waving and jingoism. The "Aussie! Aussie! Aussie!" chants during the Islamophobic and anti-Arab (they were both) mob riots at Cronulla Beach in 2005 (Poynting, 2006) were accompanied by mass wearing of the flag—and often little more—as apparel, and people were bullied into kissing the flag at the "Big Day Out" pop concert in 2006, or assaulted if they refused.

A series of recent historic events that include the 9/11 attacks by Islamic revolutionaries, the ensuing U.S. invasions of two predominately Muslim countries (Afghanistan and Iraq) and President George W. Bush's vilification of two other Muslim countries (Iran and Syria) as "evil," have reinforced this tendency to vilify Muslims. For example, when survey respondents were asked, "When you hear the word Muslim, what comes to mind?" 32 percent used negative terms, many of which alluded to images of war, guns, and violence. In addition, a stunning one-fourth of the respondents believed that Muslims teach their children to hate (CAIR, 2006).

The result has been a significant increase in blatant and often violent forms of religious persecution and discrimination of not only Muslims, but also of those associated with them, as well as those who appear to be Muslim but who are not. Beneath these complaints lie three types of unfounded or erroneous assumptions of guilt by association.

Assumed Terrorists

As she opened her beauty salon, Zohreh Assemi was viciously assaulted and robbed, her establishment was vandalized, and she was left with a towel stuffed in her mouth. Like many Iranian Americans, she came to the United States to escape Ayatollah Khomeini's terrorist regime. In recounting her experience to a *Newsday* reporter, she claimed the anti-Muslim slurs painted on her salon's mirrors hurt more than the physical abuse. Having been a victim of terrorism, she explained, "the worst thing they can do is call me is a terrorist" (Maloney, 2007).

Assemi's story, while extreme, illustrates a disturbing pattern of hostility justified by an erroneous suspicion that those who openly practice Islam must be terrorists, friends or family of terrorists, or sympathetic to the cause of Islamic terrorism. For example, while in transit from a religious conference, six imams were deplaned, handcuffed, and questioned by law enforcement because their observance of evening prayers was deemed suspicious by a U.S. Airways passenger. When asked to account for the mistaken identity, a U.S. Airways spokesperson stated, "We're sorry the imams had a difficult time, but we do think the crews have to make these calls and in this case they made the right one" (Miller, 2006).

Assumed Un-American

Even when Muslims are not assumed to be terrorists, hostility toward them has been justified by the assumption that the practice of Islam is simply un-American. Thirty-two percent of participants in a 2006 *Newsweek* poll believed that fellow Muslim citizens are less loyal to the United States (Ghazali, 2007). When Keith Ellison, the first Muslim American elected to Congress, chose to take his oath on the Koran rather than the Bible, high-profile blogger Dennis Prager argued he should not be allowed to do so "not because of any American hostility to the Koran, but because the act undermines American civilization . . . If you are incapable of serving your country on that book, you shouldn't serve in Congress" (Prager, 2006). Apparently, Prager's distrust of Muslim loyalty is more mainstream than extreme, as a shocking 44 percent of participants in a Cornell University national opinion survey believed the curtailment of the civil liberties of Muslims a necessity for national security (Friedlander, 2004).

Mistaken Identities

As noted earlier, widespread ignorance about Islam and Muslims undergirds much of the misplaced suspicion that lie behind Islamophobia. Like Dennis Prager, more than two-thirds of Christian Americans are unaware that Muslims worship the god of Abraham (CAIR, 2005). According to the same report, even fewer Americans appreciate ethnic and denominational diversity of the Islamic World. Despite the facts that the majority of Muslims in America are South Asian in origin, and not all Arab-Americans are Muslim, too often Americans assume that if you are Arabic, you must be Muslim and if you are Muslim, you must be either a terrorist or an un-American sympathizer.

As a result, merely speaking Arabic in public can provoke unfounded suspicion. An American Airlines flight from San Diego to Chicago was forced to return to its gate and all passengers deplaned because a passenger defined six men speaking Arabic as suspicious. They were neither Muslims nor terrorists, but were in fact U.S. military subcontractors on their way to train Marines. In requesting an apology from the airline, their attorney explained, "You can't just assume that everyone who speaks Arabic has a bomb strapped to [his] chest" (Colson, 2007).

Similarly, slightly more than half (52%) of the civil rights complaints made to CAIR in 2006 regarded mistreatment based upon mistaken identity.

According to the Sikh Coalition (http://www.sikhcoalition.org), simply because they wear turbans, the American Sikh community has suffered a significant spike in anti-Muslim hate crimes since 9/11. Two days after the 9/11 attacks, Balbir Singh Sodhi was murdered in drive-by retaliatory shooting, and more recently, Iqbal Singh was stabbed while standing on a street corner because his assailant wanted to "kill a Taliban."

PERMISSION TO HATE

Hate-motivated vilification and violence can flourish only in an enabling environment. In Western nations like Australia and Canada, such an environment has historically been conditioned by the activity—and inactivity—of the state. State practices, policy, and rhetoric have often provided the formal framework within which hate crime—as an informal mechanism of control—emerges. Practices within the state, at an individual and institutional level, which stigmatize, demonize, or marginalize traditionally oppressed groups legitimate the mistreatment of these same groups on the streets.

The role of the state in legitimating hate crime is linked to its role in the politics of identity-making and the construction of difference. Omi and Winant (1994) make the argument that the state is increasingly the preeminent site of racial conflict. The state is implicated in constructing popular notions of identity in racialized terms. Ascendancy—or domination—"which is embedded in religious doctrine and practice, mass media content, wage structures, the design of housing, welfare/taxation policies and so forth" (Connell, 1987, p. 184) applies as much to the construction of hierarchies of race and ethnicity as it does to class. West and Fenstermaker (1995) remind us that race, along with class and gender, acts as a "mechanism for producing social inequality" (p. 9). Of course, segregationist laws are the strongest historical example of this racial ordering. But the weakening of Affirmative Action legislation—on the grounds that "quotas" are unjust—is a more contemporary expression of the "proper" place of minorities. The state not only holds us accountable to race, but plays a critical role in shaping what it means to "do" race. Thus, the state serves to both define and maintain what it is to "do difference."

To facilitate this enterprise, the state can call upon existing public sentiment around race and gender. The political rhetoric of hate does not fall on deaf ears. Degradation of the Other is on fertile ground in a culture with a history of—indeed origins in—a worldview that saw nonwhites as heathen savages, for example. The United States, Australia, and Canada share a legacy of centuries of persecution of minorities, whether they be Aboriginal peoples, immigrants, or homosexuals. Such a history normalizes mistreatment of those who do not appropriately conform to the preconceived hierarchies. That leaves us with a culture reflected in bitter letters to the editor, opinion polls that seem to tap deep divisions and resentments, and ultimately, hate-motivated violence.

Political discourse reaffirms and legitimates the negative evaluations of difference that give rise to hate crime. The state is a contested site, wherein the "deliberate use of hate by rhetors is an overt attempt to dominate the opposition by rhetorical—if not physical—force" (Whillock & Slayden, 1995, p. xiii). Muslims in many Western nations, especially post-9/11, have been subject to the stigmatizing effects of state action intended to control and contain the terrorist threat by which all Muslims become suspect. Since the attacks, political and public figures have intensified their "crusade" against Muslims.

Political expressions of hate and bigotry are to be located at any number of different sites. Press releases and related sound bites, judicial decisions, parliamentary debates, commission hearings, and certainly single-issue and electoral political campaigns are laden with images and language—both implicit and explicit—representative of the dominant ideologies of race. The demonization of minority groups is reinforced by the racialized discourse of other politicians, judges, political lobbyists, and more. Interestingly, *failure* to engage in public discourse can also leave groups vulnerable. Silence, as well as speech, can effectively render victimized groups impotent, excluding them from protections afforded others. Both acts of commission and omission raise questions about the particular groups' legitimacy and place in society; in some cases, they explicitly define their "outsider" status. For example, consider Canadian Prime Minister Jean Chretien's failure to condemn the hate-motivated violence perpetrated against Canadian Muslims in the aftermath of 9/11. No public calls for peace and understanding were forthcoming; no strengthening reforms to hate crime legislation were ever considered (in contrast to rabid action on antiterrorist legislation); nor were increased police or prosecutorial vigilance on the public agenda. Rightly, Muslim organizations—as well as respondents surveyed by such organizations— were critical of Chretien's lack of intervention. Such inaction suggests sympathy with the perpetrators rather than the victims of hate crime. It lends legitimacy to the reactionary violence, rather than condemning it as a means of protecting Muslims.

Even more powerful in providing justifications for anti-Muslim violence is the explicit exploitation of public images and related fears by political leaders. To the extent that this is so, there emerges a climate that bestows "permission to hate." In the case of Muslims, successive administrations, along with numerous congressional figures and political aspirants, have manipulated those images, such that "its impact has no doubt left a deep if subtle mark on the political consciousness of Americans, contributing to the public's tolerance of anti-Arab racism" (Abraham, 1994, p. 195). Examples of such cultural imaging abound. Prior to the post-9/11 Bush administration,

the Reagan administration probably did the most damage to the public identity of Arabs and Middle Easterners. Reagan's "war on terrorism" provided
a context for the escalation of anti-Arab rhetoric. A former Reagan cabinet
adviser wrote in his memoirs about the extensive use of anti-Arab jokes and
slurs in White House conversations about Middle East issues. Reagan's Secretary of Labor, Raymond Donovan, held a fund-raiser that featured men
dressed as Arab sheiks handing out fake money—a reference to what Stockton (1994) characterizes as the myth of "secret power."

Politicians of every stripe have engaged in Arab-baiting. Henry Kissinger
once stated publicly that you "can't really believe anything an Arab says"
(cited in Suleiman, 1999, p. 2). While still vice president, Dan Quayle vilified
Islam with his claim that the "three most dangerous movements of the twentieth century were Nazism, Communism, and Islamic fundamentalism" (cited
in Los Angeles County Commission on Human Relations, 1991, p. 15). More
recently, former Secretary of Education William Bennett publicly expressed
his view that "there is no moral equality between Israel and the Palestinians.
One is a nation of violence and terrorism, and the other is one of democracy
and peace" (cited in ADC, 2001, p. 71).

The September 11 terrorist attacks have, not surprisingly, resurrected a
barrage of hateful rhetoric. Since the attacks, political and public figures have
intensified their "crusade" against Middle Easterners. Perhaps the most disturbing pattern has been President Bush's simplistic references to "evildoers," and his invocation of the theme of an evil empire, a theme that Stockton
(1994) refers to as the "war of darkness against light." A newspaper article
observed that Bush typically refers to terrorists or their misdeeds as "evil" a
few times per public appearance, occasionally more:

> He hit two on the "evil" scale in his radio address last Saturday, a light
> day. "Our enemies are evil," he told troops last week at Fort Campbell, KY,
> where he also noted, "Good triumphs over evil." Asked recently why the
> threat of terrorism was keeping the White House closed to public tours
> during the holiday season, he said, "Evil knows no holiday", and "Evil
> doesn't welcome Thanksgiving or Christmas." (*Arizona Republic*, 2001,
> p. A14)

Moreover, Bush has re-created Reagan's "cowboy" rhetoric. Again and
again, he has vowed to "hunt down" the "evildoers." Most memorable, perhaps, is his statement, right out of his Texas roots, that those evildoers were
"wanted, dead or alive."

Moreover, deeds speak louder than words, and as I will demonstrate
below, the actions of the state have also served to stigmatize and marginalize
Muslims, thereby enhancing their vulnerability to violence. Indeed, unlike
many other religious minorities in the United States, the primary complaint

among persecuted Muslims is not necessarily hate crimes, or even workplace discrimination, but rather abuse of authority by government officials.
A majority of Muslim Americans believe the USA Patriot Act encourages
surveillance and detention for purposes of intimidation rather than for crime
investigation and intelligence gathering (CAIR, 2007). Imam Malik Maja-
hid claims a quarter (25%) of Muslim American households have, in fact,
been visited by the FBI and 35% of the Council on American Islamic Relations civil rights complaints regard unexplained detention and deportation
(CAIR, 2007).

One of the consequences of the demonization of Muslims on the part of
politicians and policy makers is that it finds its way into policies and practices
that further marginalize the group. There is a lengthy history of discriminatory law and practice within the state that has limited, if not outright violated, the rights of racial and ethnic minority groups—Arabs and Muslims
among them. This is especially the case with respect to the activities of law
enforcement and security agencies. In the aftermath of 9/11, patterns of surveillance and harassment of Muslims have reached their zenith. A 2001 CAIR
report lists a number of reports filed with them in which federal agents from
the Federal Bureau of Investigation,, Immigration and Naturalization Service, Internal Revenue Service, and even the Secret Service "approached" or
"contacted" Arabs and Muslims, often with no explanation for the contact.
A few examples:

- An FBI agent contacted one man, saying he wanted to talk to the man
  about someone else but would not explain what was at issue.
- A founder of an Islamic organization reported that an FBI agent wanted
  to talk about another organization and another individual but would not
  explain why.
- An Algerian imam (prayer leader) was approached by the Secret Service,
  who said that they had received a letter about him, but that there was
  no problem and there would be no additional contact. They would not
  explain what was in the letter, who sent it, or why it instigated contact.
- A man claimed that FBI agents followed him, made surprise visits to his
  house, and asked his neighbors about his "terrorist activities."
- A community leader was asked to meet with FBI agents with no explanation.
- Two FBI agents came unannounced to an immigrant man's house, asked
  him about his residency status, and asked for personal photographs,
  again with no explanation.

Indeed, nothing in history compares to the surveillance and detainment of
Muslims in response to the attacks of 9/11. Not hundreds, but thousands of
Middle Eastern people—mostly men—have been detained by federal author-
ities. Many times those people are under surveillance and at risk of detention.

Moreover, the problem has been facilitated by an array of new antiterrorism statutes. An ADC (2002) fact sheet highlights the key civil rights threats posed by the Patriot Act:

- The act provides the government with sweeping new powers to detain noncitizens indefinitely with little or no process at the discretion of the Attorney General.
- The law also permits the government to conduct searches, seizures, and surveillance with reduced standards of cause and levels of judicial review, although these elements will expire in four years unless reapproved by Congress.
- The law contains elements that could be construed as embodying guilt by association, in effect criminalizing many kinds of otherwise lawful contacts with groups that engage in any form of politically motivated violence, sabotage, or vandalism.

These provisions of the USA Patriot Act raise serious concerns regarding civil rights and liberties, especially as regards due process, and undermine the separation of powers and system of checks and balances between the branches of the federal government.

Equally disturbing are the activities of local law enforcement agents. They have followed the lead of federal agencies in their increased use of racial profiling and harassment of "suspicious" individuals. Hundreds of such reports have come in to ADC and CAIR, ranging from unjustified highway stops, to police harassment, to failure to take seriously complaints of civilian harassment. By November 2001, the ADC had logged hundreds of such complaints; by January 2002, CAIR had recorded over 200 cases of police profiling or harassment, and nearly the same number of cases of airport profiling. Among the incidents reported are the following illustrative examples:

- Westbury, New York—Police stormed the house of a Muslim man with their guns drawn and dragged him out of bed. He was taken outside and interrogated, while other officers searched his home. He was not shown a search warrant and was not charged with any crime.
- Fairfax, Virginia—A Muslim man took his pregnant wife to the hospital because of severe bleeding. She was made to wait while others were seen ahead of her. When the husband complained, the hospital staff called the Fairfax police. The officer made him stand outside while his wife was taken in to be treated. The man was told he would be arrested if he didn't leave.
- Rhode Island—State police and federal agents pulled two Sikhs and an elderly Muslim man off of an Amtrak train, without provocation. One—a telecommunications specialist originally from India—was detained and questioned for six hours until it was determined that he was not a "terrorist." However, he was charged with a misdemeanor for possession of a weapon—a six-inch ceremonial knife.

• Longview, Texas—A Muslim man who had been awaiting his labor certi-
fication before the law was changed was picked up by officers who arrested
him and forced him to sign a paper calling for his deportation. He was told
that he had 30 seconds to sign it or he would be held in jail for a year.

Islamic leaders are justifiably concerned that such actions fuel the backlash. As noted at the beginning of this section, state practices provide a
context and a framework for the broader demonization and marginaliza-
tion of minority groups. Through its rhetoric and policies, the state absorbs
and reflects back onto the public hostile and negative perceptions of the
Other—in this case, Muslims. Public expressions of racism by state actors
are constituted of and by public sentiments of intolerance, dislike, or suspicion of particular groups. Thus, the state seems to reaffirm the legitimacy
of such beliefs, while at the same time giving them public voice. Political
rhetoric simultaneously evokes and exploits fears of this erosion of identity boundaries (i.e., backlash) at least, and the threats posed by the Other
at most. In so doing, state actors play on cultural symbols that differentiate "Us" from "Them": good from evil, the "savage" from the "civilized."
Political discourse thus reaffirms and legitimates negative evaluations of
difference, in that it is central to the "enactment, expression, legitimation
and acquisition" of bigotry of all types (van Dijk, 1995, p. 2), including hate-
motivated violence.

The biases embedded in the state create an environment hostile to Arabs
and Muslims in the United States. Discriminatory policies by government
agencies reinforce anti-Arab sentiment. Moreover, they have a trickle-down
effect, by which "official use of profiling (for example) sends a message to
the larger community that a person who fits a certain physical or religious
description is suspect, if not guilty until proven innocent" (CAIR, 2002, p. 7).
Consequently, political manipulation of public perceptions and its attendant
discriminatory practices bestows permission for other forms of discrimination, including anti-Muslim violence.

CONCLUSION

As noted at the outset, the observations made in this chapter provide a
starting point for more concentrated examinations of the motives of the perpetrators of anti-Muslim violence. In the absence of dedicated studies of these
offenders, we must derive their motives from the contexts in which they act,
and the statements they might make before, during, and after their assaults.
And indeed many such offenders have been quoted at length in newspapers,
in organization reports, and in human rights commissions. A number of common threads emerge. First and foremost, Muslims are perceived to be terrorists, regardless of who they may be as individuals. Third, and closely related

to the first, all Muslims are thought to be the same. There is no willingness to acknowledge the ethnic, cultural, or even racial differences that characterize either the Muslim communities or Middle Eastern communities. Any one who remotely resembles a "Muslim"—whatever that "look" may be—is vulnerable to attack. Finally, Muslims are perceived to be "out of place," that is, illegitimate residents of this country. Like people of color, Muslims are assumed to be inassimilable, and in fact, un-American.

These trends should come as no surprise given the long-term tendency of the media to provide fodder for perpetrators' paranoid delusions. Many of the same images implied by offenders' statements draw from the widely distributed media caricatures that portray Muslims as terrorists, or inherently warlike. Movies, newscasts, and newspaper accounts frequently focus on negative messages about Islam, rather than making any effort to inform the public about the "true" nature of the faith, its diversity, or its strengths. This is exacerbated by media reporting on government words and deeds that also paint Muslims as "evildoers," to quote G. W. Bush.

I have argued throughout that there is a connection between the demonization, and victimization of Muslims. Stereotypes of the "fanatical terrorist," for example, have consistently served to enable violence against Muslims. These stereotypes disempower those who are different, since their difference is assumed to be immutable and deviant. Consequently, the key to empowerment is to eliminate the discriminatory and/or privileging effects of difference.

If we are to intervene in hate crime against Muslims, an important first step must be countering the negative portrayals of Muslims. The Council on Arab-American Relations and The Canadian Islamic Congress, for example, closely monitor media treatment of Islam. Yet their findings of media and political bias rarely if ever appear in the mainstream media. Such organizations clearly have a role to play in developing positive relationships with media outlets so that they are in a position to lobby for inclusion of their findings. This would prove valuable in drawing attention to the nature, extent, and impact of the problem of media stereotyping.

REFERENCES

Abraham, N. (1994). Anti-Arab racism and violence in the United States. In E. McCarus (Ed.), *The development of Arab-American identity* (pp. 155–214). Ann Arbor: The University of Michigan Press.

American-Arab Antidiscrimination Committee. (1996). *1995 report on anti-Arab racism.* Washington, DC: Author.

American-Arab Antidiscrimination Committee. (2001). *ADC fact sheet: The condition of Arab Americans post 9/11.* Washington, DC: Author.

American-Arab Antidiscrimination Committee. (2002). *Lawyers for Arab-American Secret Service officer present facts of airline discrimination.* Retrieved November 12, 2007, from www.adc.org/press/2002/03january2002.htm

Arizona Daily Sun. (2001, September 18). Sikh killing labeled hate crime, p. A4.

Arizona Republic. (2001, December 1). President believes that "evil" is precise, p. A14.

Barker, M. (1981). *The new racism: conservatives and the ideology of the tribe.* London: Junction Books.

Canadian Council on American-Islamic Relations. (2005). *Presumption of guilt: A national survey on security visitations of Canadian Muslims,* Retrieved May 21, 2006, from http://www.caircan.ca/downloads/POG-08062005.pdf

Canadian Council on American-Islamic Relations. (2002). *Canadian Muslims one year after 9/11.* Ottawa, Ontario, Canada: Author.

Colson, N. (2007, September 21). *Socialist Worker Online.* http://www.socialistworker.org/2007–2/645/645_03_Racist.shtml

Connell, R. (1987). *Gender and power.* Stanford, CT: Stanford University Press.

Council on American-Islamic Relations. (2006). *American public opinion about Islam and Muslims,* Retrieved May 16, 2006, from www.cair.com

Council on American-Islamic Relations. (2007). *The presumption of guilt: The status of Muslim civil rights in the United States.* Retrieved October 9, 2007, fromwww.cair.com.

Friedlander, B. (2004). Fear factor: 44 percent of Americans queried in Cornell national poll favor curtailing some liberties for Muslim Americans. *Cornell News,* December 17, Retrieved July 20, 2007 from, http://www.news.cornell.edu/releases/Dec04/Muslim.Poll.bpf.html

Ghazali, A. S. (2007, September 13). American Muslims six years after 9/11. Retrieved September 23, 2007, from http://www.khabrein.info

Hage, G. (1998). *White nation: Fantasies of white supremacy in a multicultural society.* Sydney, Australia: Pluto Press.

Ismael, T. Y., & Measor, J. (2003). Racism and the North American media following 11 September: The Canadian setting. *Arab Studies Quarterly, 25*(1/2), 101–136.

Khan, S., Saloojee, R., & Al-Shalchi, H. (2004). *Today's media: Covering Islam and Canadian Muslims.* Ottawa, Ontario, Canada: Council on American Islamic Relations-Canada

Kilgour, D., Millar, S., & O'Neill, J. (2002). Strength under siege: Canadian civil society post-September 11th. In K. Kassam, G. Melnyk, & L. Perras (Eds.), *Canada and September 11th: Impact and responses* (pp. 151–161). Calgary, Alberta, Canada: Detselig Enterprises.

Los Angeles County Commission on Human Relations. (1991). *Violence and intimidation: Rising bigotry toward Arabs and Muslims.* Los Angeles: Author.

Omi, M., & Winant, H. (1994). *Racial formation in the United States,* New York: Routledge.

Malley, R. (2001). Faith and terror. Retrieved May 20, 2006, from www.cairnet.org/nr/10–11e.asp

Maloney, J. (2007, September 17). Muslim woman victim of hate crime. *Newsday.com,* Retrieved October 25, 2007, from http://www.newsday.com/news/local/crime/ny-libias

Miller, L. (2006, November 28). At national airport, prayers against profiling. *Washingtonpost.com.* Retrieved October 11, 2007, from http://www.washingtonpost.com/wp-dyn/content/article/2006/11/27/AR2006112701184_pf.html

Moore, K. (1995). *Al-Mughtarib-un: American law and the transformation of Muslim life in the United States.* Albany NY: SUNY Press.

Oakes, L. (2001, November 3). A sly-dog race card. *Bulletin*, p.18.

Poynting, S. (2002, July). Bin Laden in the Suburbs: Attacks on Arab and Muslim Australians before and after 11 September. *Current Issues in Criminal Justice, 14* (1), pp. 43–64.

Poynting, S. (2006). What caused the Cronulla Riot? *Race and Class*, 48(1), 85–92.

Prager, D. (2006, November 28). America, not Keith Ellison, decides what book a Congressman takes his oath on. *Townhall.com*. Retrieved October 11, 2007, from http://townhall.com/Common/Print.aspx)

Said, E. (1997). *Covering Islam: How the media and the experts determine how we see the rest of the world.* New York: Vintage.

Said, E. (1978). *Orientalism.* New York: Pantheon Books.

Sheffield, C. (1995). Hate violence. In P. Rothenberg (Ed.), *Race, class and gender in the United States* (3rd ed.; pp. 432–441). New York: St. Martin's.

Sikh Coalition. *New York City Bills*, Retrieved July 20, 2007, from http://www.sikhcoalition.org/NewYorkCity_Bills.asp

Stockton, R. (1994). Ethnic archetypes and the Arab image. In E. McCarus (Ed.), *The development of Arab-American identity* (pp. 119–153). Ann Arbor: The University of Michigan Press.

Suleiman, M. (1999). Islam, Muslims and Arabs in America: The other of the other of the other . . . *Journal of Muslim Minority Affairs*, 19(1), 33–48.

van Dijk, T. (1995). Elite discourse and the reproduction of racism. In R. K. Whillock & D. Slayden (Eds.), *Hate speech* (pp. 1–27). Thousand Oaks CA: Sage.

West, C. & Fenstermaker, S. (1995). Doing difference. *Gender and Society*, 9(1): 8–37.

Whillock, R. & Slayden, D. (1995). Introduction. In R. K. Whillock and D. S. (Eds.), *Hate Speech* (pp. ix–xvi). Thousand Oaks CA: Sage.

Young, I. M. (1990). *Justice and the politics of difference.* Princeton, NJ: Princeton University Press.

CHAPTER 12

INTERVIEW WITH A HATE OFFENDER

Randy Blazak

On May 24, 2003, a group of racist skinheads vandalized the Shaarie Torah Jewish cemetery in Portland, Oregon, with swastikas and anti-Semitic phrases. After an investigation by local police and the Federal Bureau of Investigation (FBI), two young men were arrested and charged with conspiracy to deprive individuals of their civil rights. In 2005, one of those skinheads, a young man named Sean, pleaded guilty to the bias-motivated desecration and faced a maximum sentence of 10 years in prison. Assistant Attorney General for the Civil Rights Division, R. Alexander Acosta, commented on the case, saying, "That acts such as these occur at all is offensive, that such ignorance exists in modern America is despicable" (Department of Justice, 2005). Sean's judge was Ancer Haggerty, the African American magistrate who presided over the 1990 civil trial that held Tom and John Metzger liable for the brutal murder of Mulugeta Seraw by Portland skinheads. Judge Haggerty sentenced Sean to one year in SeaTac Federal Prison.

I met Sean in 2005, before he was sentenced to prison. We had several conversations at his parents' house about his beliefs and the local skinhead scene. We corresponded while he was in a federal prison in Washington state, where I visited with him. He was released in 2007, after a year in prison. Sean and I continued to correspond, and I invited him to speak at a hate crime conference and in my hate crimes class to discuss his racist worldview.

In February 2008, Sean agreed to be interviewed about his life and the hate crime he was convicted of. I arrived at his small apartment with a case of beer and a digital recorder. He was with his two small sons while his wife worked at her service-sector job. He's had a hard time finding work since his release from prison. His Nazi tattoos might be a factor in that. When I arrived, I was struck by the large swastika flag hanging on his living room wall. While he made Raman noodles for one of his sons, I perused the DVDs on the shelf; they included films as diverse as *Fight Club* and *Children of Men.*

Sean had asked me to bring a CD by Rancid, a punk rock band that uses black music forms like ska and reggae. After I arrived, he voluntarily took down the Nazi flag out of consideration. I wondered what his neighbors thought, as the flag was clearly visible through the sliding glass door. I informed him that the interview was about his views and experience, not about the criminal activity of any of his peers; however, he could speak off the record or ask me to turn off the recorder at any time. I offered to allow him to change or delete any of his comments after the interview was transcribed (which he did).

For the next two hours, the conversation covered a number of topics, most linked to excessive alcohol consumption and the problem of antiracist skinheads known as SHARPs (Skinheads Against Racial Prejudice). Occasionally, his rambunctious sons interrupted us. Sean was a doting father while opening another beer and attempting to keep the train of thought. We occasionally went off the record when discussing specific members of the local skinhead scene or the intersection of his crime with the 2003 murder of a homeless vet by skinheads in Tacoma, Washington.

> R: When did you first start developing a racist ideology?
>
> When it really kicked in was when I went to [a local community college] at 18. It wasn't like I met other skinheads goose-stepping down the school-yard or nothing. I just saw a lot of the hypocrisy. You just heard a lot the of same questions over and over again. Why can't we have a white student union, blah, blah, blah. Why is it not cool to say "White and proud," when you have a Queer Day? Black student unions, Hispanic student unions and those guys, the Hispanics, they're pretty racist on their union thing.
>
> R: So it was being in that diverse environment?
>
> I just didn't care for it. It was like every pride had its place except for white pride.
>
> R: But you never thought of it before that? You had to have some ideas about it before that point.
>
> That was it, really. There was nothing for the white youth. For a hetero-sexual white dude that doesn't do drugs there's really nothing out there.
>
> R: How did you become a skinhead? When was the first time you met another skinhead? What was the process?
>
> Uh, I don't know . . . If I knew what I knew now, not that I regret ever becoming a skinhead, it's just that everyone thinks skinheads are going to make a huge difference, you know, we can solve all our problems with whatever solution we want and all we end up doing is getting tattoos where we can't get a better job or becoming felons.

I personally first met racists on the Internet, which is a funny story, but not one for a book.

R: What's the story?

No, it's nothing illegal. I actually met a couple racial people when I was at this chick's house. She was like 6-3 or 6-4. Total Amazon chic. I ended up going to her house and she was talking to two guys on the Internet and they asked, "Is he a skinhead?" And she said, "Yes." And at the time I was just a wannabe. I didn't know nothing about actually loving your own people or trying to better your race. I just knew I was pissed off and young. And that's how I met them, which was over the Internet. And then, like a week later, we met up.

R: Was it, I like these guys' style, or I like what they're doing? Did you have long hair at the time?

I already had a shaved head.

R: So you were already dressing in that style?

Yeah, it had a little to do with beliefs but I didn't really understand it all. I just liked the style, the boots, the shaved head. I never cradled my laces or nothing. I just wore whatever I wanted. Here's a picture of me when I was 13. (Sean shows me a picture of himself with a friend, both dressed in a punk style).

R: Man, I totally wouldn't recognize you. You're a little punker.

Yeah, I'm in shape and everything. I wore whatever. I wore ripped-up jeans, neon green socks. (Laughs) I just didn't care.

R: Was this skinhead that you met connected to a larger group?

No, not at the time. It's funny how he got involved. He and his buddies got pissed off at pretty much the same things. We were cool with enjoying other people's cultures and studying other people's cultures, but I think first you should embrace your own. Not necessarily keep traditions, because that's just not going to happen nowadays, but just don't piss on your ancestry because it's cool to sag your pants. I mean in the '90s, man, I thought it was cool as hell to wear flannel and Doc Martens and dye your hair. Now it's cool to sag and wear bling bling. I mean, what's the next thing? Pretty much you take a style or a culture and corrupt it. It's pretty sick.

R: Yeah, but youth culture pretty much always does that. I don't know what the style will be like in five years . . .

Emo! Emo is big now. I went to a festival. It was a Christian festival, which was really nice because I could go there and not worry about any problems. I brought my son there and it was like four days of camping and it was real nice. No drunkards . . . well I'm sure there was beer there and drugs but no one was out in the open about it. Kids there. It was a nice safe environment. I went to the first one they ever put on. It was in '95 and it was funny because some of the kids I went with are part of [the SHARPS] now. Go figure.

R: So this festival, was it a mainstream Christian festival?

It's not mainstream at all. For Christians I guess there are some main-stream bands. But it's mostly hardcore [punk bands]. When we first went there, no one showered. It was five days of no showers, staying up all night, eating pork and beans. And I went this year and I've never seen the line for the showers so long. Emo guys were in there with their curling irons. It was like, "Whoa."

R: So when you met this person, did you start hanging out with more skin-heads?

It was just a small group. Maybe six.

R: Did the skinheads you hung out with support violence, either on a small scale, like bashing people, or a big scale, like Rahowa (a term referring to Racial Holy War)?

No we weren't progressed that much. We were just a bunch of pissed-off kids. In theory we never had to look for fights. When we hung out it St. Johns, we'd turn around the corner and we'd be jumped, you know?

R: So you guys were the targets of the violence?

Oh, yeah! I'd walk around Northeast Portland (an area with many black residents) by myself and I never got much grief. They would laugh at me because there's one skinhead walking around. What an idiot, you know? So I got kind of fortunate with that.

R: Did the skinheads or any other racialist group help you to better under-stand the world?

It's kind of sad to see the movies that are trying to stop hate. They'd just piss us off more, like *American History X, Romper Stomper.* I mean, they show a lot of the shit that happens, the guy dies or he goes to prison. They show all these shit skins, like the skin that raped the guy. They are pecker-woods, the prison skins. They're garbage. Any race, it doesn't matter what you are. They're pieces of shit, plain and simple.

But in the same token, no matter how bad they make it seem, they glam-orize it. I'm sorry but guys and testosterone . . . drinking beer, having a hot chick on your arm and kicking the shit out of someone. That's going to appeal to someone. Especially if you've been beat up by the black kids in the neighborhood.

The only group I've really hung out with was like a big family. They were really big on not selling yourself short.

R: But what about the overall philosophy?

Overall philosophy? I think the older people actually have quite a bit. They don't really teach hate. Some do. Some definitely do, but a lot of them, they teach . . . they talk to you about staying in school, they're tying to help kids better themselves now. Instead of saying, go out and smash someone, or go out and pick a fight, or go out and spend all your money on beer, they're like save up for a car so you can get a better job. Don't get tattoos on your hands. If you're going to get racial tats, make sure they can be covered with a normal T-shirt. All sorts of stuff.

Things have changed a lot over the years, from gangs to more like an organization.

R: Yeah, it seems less confrontational now. I'm just trying to get how you started to see the world when you started hanging out with these folks. I mean, was it just the fact that they were confrontational that was cool? Did you guys talk about the "Zionist Occupational Government" and stuff like that?

Oh, yeah. You know, shit like that got brought up all the time. There's a lot of truth to it and there's a lot of fallacy to it. You can find a Jew that owns 150 TV stations, but does he oversee every single one of them? No, no he doesn't. So, in theory, does he have the power? Yes. Be he doesn't control everything that's on every station. He can't. It's just not possible to run that much stuff.

So, a lot of people get sucked in by the big conspiracy theory, that there's a big Jew behind every corner. There's a lot of grey area and a lot of people leave when they don't see Jews always running stuff. The want shit to be black and white. You can only be fueled by hate for so long. And then it dies.

R: Say that again . . . You can only be fueled by hate?

You can only be fueled by hate for so long. It's like a car. You can be driving as long as you want, to your heart's content and then . . .

R: That's a great quote. I might quote you on that.

You need to be driven by love, like the love of your people.

R: But, at the time, when you're really getting into it, you know, when you're basically just putting the fuel in, are those ideas about conspiracy theories and ideas about saving the white race, is that what pulls you into it? Obviously everyone has a choice, you can go over here or over there. There had to be some appeal to it that pulled you into it.

Well, the violence aspect to it, which I think you're trying to get to, is this. You get pissed off. What are you pissed off about? The gangbangers going around beating people up, the SHARPs beating people up saying, "Why be proud?" Everything that instigates people to reevaluate their life gets pissed off by violence. When push comes to shove, you push back. And that's why I think predominantly of all the racist crimes, hate crimes are predominately 18 to 25.

R: Why? Because those are the folks who feel they are being pushed?

Yeah, they haven't grown up enough or seen enough to know that you are going to do a lot more by getting an education, raising your kids, by staying off drugs, to go to college, you know. OK, you want to take the power back. Cool. You can go out and kill someone and then what? You're locked up for the rest of your life. Or B, you can get out and you have a shitload of fines to pay. Or you can stay out, raise two kids, and let the other guy go to prison. It's like The Order. Rest in Peace David Lane. They killed Allen Berg. I mean, I understand why. That's cool and all but they could've done a lot more by educating people.

If people want to kill people, I mean it's in our nature to kill. Some people can control it, some people can't.

R: That's interesting that you say that. Do you think that maybe there are some black criminals that are the same? You say it's in our nature to kill and some people can control it and some people can't. You hear a lot of rhetoric from white supremacists about black crime. Isn't it kind of the same thing?

The white-supremacist rhetoric of blacks' nature to kill . . . I think that's because of the black community. There's not much in the black community. There's not much of a middle-class black community. You either have the well-off or you have the, you know, lower class, from what I've noticed.

R: It's true that in the '70s it started to expand, but in the '80s the black middle class started to contract. A lot of that had to do with Ronald Reagan, but that's a whole other thing.

The white man keeping him down (said mockingly), right?

R: Well, he cancelled a lot of the programs that were moving people out of the ghettos, you know, like *The Jeffersons*. The reason I bring it up is because of this rhetoric about black violence but you talk about The Order and people, "it's in their nature to kill." To me that sounds like what people who are racist say about blacks: "Well, they just can't control themselves."

Well, they've embraced violence as a lifestyle.

R: Who? Black or white?

(Pauses). Both. I mean it's never gonna stop. If you feel like you are going to be attacked you are going to attack back. I don't know a lot of skinheads anywhere else but in Portland they are trying to steer away from petty fights. Getting drunk and going out and starting something. In fact, they're starting to have people be designated drivers, which is just crazy different.

R: It's a long way away from what it used to be, for sure.

But I mean, it's a vicious cycle. You got kids that grow up with violence and that's what they're gonna do is violence. All you see publicized are the rap stars talking about smacking their bitch or killing someone. Do you want your neighborhood to look like that?

Plus, in terms of the cycle, you've got all these gangbangers and rappers glorifying drugs and money and you've got a lot of black kids growing up in the lower class hearing it and the appeal has gotta be insane.

R: How did you become Christian Identity? What role did Aryan Nations play?

I've got good friends who are Aryan Nations. I could go off on Aryan Nations for a while. I was raised Christian, so it just kind of came natural.

R: But there's certainly a difference between being Christian and Christian Identity. (Sean laughs in agreement.) How did you find out about it?

There was a guy in Washington that was affiliated with America's Promise Ministries. I tried to get stuff from them, Aryan Nations, Church of Jesus Christ Christian, Virginia Israelites, and couple of other places while I was in prison and they denied it. And I brought it to their attention that we just won a huge court case. You can look it up. I had everything.

[A black prison official] comes up to me and starts speaking German, and I'm like, "We're in America, dude," and he's like, "Oh, you're one of them." And I'm like, "Ah, jeez. What's up?" And he says, "Well, I'm in charge of all the white-supremacist groups that come through here." Big black dude, married to a white girl. And I was like, "Ah, fuck."

They'd read the letters I would write to you. But they'd also do some of the screening of letters and they'd see yours come in. I had one black guard come in and say, "Except for the word 'nigger' every once in a while, the letters between you and Dr. Blazak are quite interesting to read."

R: So what's the Christian Identity connection? It sounds like you were reading a lot of stuff.

Yeah, I read a lot. *One Blood*, do you know that? (He pulls *One Blood: The Biblical Answer to Racism* off the bookshelf.) That's actually antiracist. Of course, I read *The Racist Mind*, the one you sent me.

Actually, I've even got the Aryan Nations flag here.

R: So you're reading all this stuff including about Christian Identity. Why did you choose it? Did it just fit better?

Yeah, it just fit better. I can't believe in a pagan god, you know? I just don't believe in evolution. No matter what, I can't believe in something coming out of nothing. It doesn't happen. I've seen scientific shows going both ways and they go back and forth, back and forth. I'm pretty sure that even the big bang theory has been gotten rid of by evolutionists. I mean, you can't blame them. You can't take an apple and take a hammer to it and have five apples. You can have some tasty applesauce though.

R: Well, it's all theoretical, but the nice thing about theory is you've got at least some evidence for it. So it just fit for you?

Yeah. But if I am wrong, if I *am* wrong, I think evolution does have a bigger basis for white supremacy.

R: OK, then let me ask your opinion on the idea that Jesus Christ was a Jew and preached peace and "love thy enemy" and all that good hippie stuff. The reason I ask is because there are lots of Christians in the antiracist community. When I explain Christian Identity to my students they look at me like, "How can anybody believe that?"

I don't know. It's hard to explain how I feel about it. It may sound like a cop-out, but it's one of those things that you understand but you can't really explain it. It's like "love thy neighbor as thyself," the way we view our neighbor is our kinsman. "Turn the other cheek," if your brother offends you, you can't attack him. You should forgive your brothers.

In Genesis, the original translation says that Satan beguiled Eve. That's where Cain came from and he was the genetic seed line to the modern Jews.

A lot of people are staying away from (the term) "white supremacist." The big thing now is "white survivalists." People just want to keep it going. In theory, well, there is no theory about it, whites, Caucasians, only make up 9 percent of the world's population. A lot of racists are starting to wear the "9 percent" patch.

R: What is your opinion of racist Odinists? There seems to be two camps between the Christian Identity people and the Odinist folks.

One of The Order members actually said once we get rid of the nonwhites we'll off the pagans next. Whoa! The Odinists, well . . . (pauses) They're my friends. The Christian Identity people are more laid-back. For the Odinists, the biggest thing is warriors and stuff. Not that God was a pussy or nothing. There's a whole lot of wars in The Bible. He killed the shit out of people. But a "pacifist Odinist" doesn't make sense to me. Their whole thing is dying on the battlefield and going to Valhalla.

But, to tell you the truth, the Christian and Odinist thing doesn't really come up that much. They believe that Odin was millions of years before Christ. There's some Christian Identity that believe that when The Bible says God created the Earth in six days and on the seventh he rested that the original translation it says "six eras," which could be any amount of time. So some believe that there were six eras. So Adam was created as the first man who could blush (this is the CI belief that only whites can blush because God gave them a sense of morality), although I remember you saying that you had a Jewish girlfriend and that you made her blush quite a bit. (laughs) But all different beliefs come together for the common goal.

R: Can you sum up what skinheads and racialists want? Or what are the main problems in the world?

I'm just one person. This is just my opinion. This is going to sound weird. I think diversity and lack of diversity is what's wrong with the world. People celebrate diversity, which is a good thing. But some, depending on where you're at, there are some cultures and diversities that are shoved down people's throats. Like here (in Portland) we want to celebrate diversity but we don't want white racialists here. In China, they want diversity but they don't want females born. Everywhere they want to celebrate diversity but they want to pick and choose what kind of diversity they have. We're not included in that diversity. It seems like communism. It's diversity on their terms.

I mean, here if we want to celebrate diversity, yeah there's gonna be violence and people won't get along, but I should be able to walk down the street as much as you.

R: So it's the idea that diversity is fake?

Yeah, it is. I mean, you, Randy, could throw a diversity party and if I came with beer, you'd be like, "Cool." But a lot of people wouldn't consider me part of diversity. It's a closed door policy.

R: So if that's the problem, what the solution from a racialist perspective? You're still a part of it, so there must be some feeling that you are accomplishing something.

There's lots of solutions. There's ones that are feasible, and . . . (laughs). First of all we have to stop the cycle. I think the best way to accomplish the goals of white supremacists, priders, skinheads, whatever you want to call us, is just education.

R: Like what? Give me an example kind of education you mean. Because your idea of education and my idea of education are two different things. Or maybe not.

We should learn from our past mistakes. Take Rome, a great white nation. It wasn't until the last hundred years that they started race-mixing and tolerating homosexuality, which brought the downfall.

R: Is that what you mean by education?

I think the reason why you see all these white kids trying to be black is that they don't know their own culture. They're trying to find somewhere they can fit in. The black culture nowadays, well I don't think it really is even the African culture at all. Fuck, if they went back to their original roots they'd get the shit kicked out of them or they wouldn't know what to do. I just think we should educate people.

R: About European culture?

If you're European.

R: I just wonder what you mean when you say, "your own culture," because a lot of us white people are a mix, you know? Like I'm Czech, and English, and probably a lot of other stuff too that I don't know about.

Yeah, but those are all from the same European root.

R: But they are dramatically different cultures.

Well, there's no really easy solution. Hell, we go to war to find peace. The way I look at it is that there are three races: Mongoloid, Negroid, and Caucasoid. If you only have X amount of food, you are going to feed your family first.

R: I want to talk a little bit about the night in question in the cemetery. So how did that happen? What was the sequence of events?

What really happened or what I said happened?

R: I'm interested in the truth. This is after the fact so you can say whatever you want, but I'm interested in the process that led up to this federal
offense.

Oh, jeez, OK (laughs), the infamous night. OK, so I was working at [his
metal fabrication job] and I was helping a guy move. I had spray paint
in my car because I deal with the paint shop, too. So the paint was old,
like eight months old. It was ridiculous. There was no plan. No nothing.
I couldn't even find the place. If [the judge] had said at that time, "Here's
keys, you have three hours, with no help, to find [the cemetery] and I'll
drop all charges," I'd have been like, "It ain't happening." I have no clue
where it is.

So we were drinking and we were drinking, holy shit we were drinking. Then we drank some more. Obviously we were on the side roads. I
know that much because we didn't want to get a DUI. So, we pass the
thing and we were like, "What the fuck?" Because it took us by surprise,
you know?

R: Yeah, it's a very dramatic-looking place. It looks like something from
Europe 60 years ago.

It's a beautiful-looking place, don't get me wrong. One of the youngsters . . .
One of the guys that actually testified against me in the Grand Jury, he was
like, "Let's fuck that place up."

And I'm like, "No we're not. No way. It's stupid, dude." So somehow we
hit a dead end and had to go by it again.

R: And how many people are in the car?

Let's just say that I was the only one that went to prison.

So we drive by a second time and (one of the crew) who bench-presses like
275 was like, "Dude, there's a Jewish star on the gate." I had lead pipe because
I work in the metal shop. He's like, "Dude, I can pry that thing off." I'm like,
"Whatever man. If you want to do it that bad, do it. I don't give a shit. You're
whining, you're moaning." There's another youngster in there, his "brother"
and he says, "Hey, there's spray paint in the car." And I'm like, "Yeah, sure."

So they got it and me and [another skin] hung back and kind of laughed
a couple times. But we were like, "What the fuck? Hand it to us." And we
had a little bit of fun. We all took part in it.

(This part of the discussion relates how there was heat from the FBI
on the Portland skinheads at this time because of the recent murder in
Tacoma by skinheads.)

But yeah, that night was a fluke accident. I'll never do it again. Never
did it before.

R: When it was happening, did you know about hate crime laws and civil
rights laws? I mean did you know that if you got caught for it, it wasn't just
going to go down just as a vandalism?

Um, well yeah! You know that shit when you are sober and thinking about
it! I mean when it happens you don't consciously understand it. That's why

the hate crimes laws don't prevent shit. I mean they do if you think about it beforehand but most times it's just a bunch of guys out drinking and it gets out of hand.

R: You could make that case about crime in general. Most people aren't in the most rational frame of mind. So what was it like when you were first arrested?

I thought I'd do like two weekends in jail. And the feds picked it up and I was facing eleven years in jail. All I could think was my kids would be teenagers when I got out.

R: Let me ask you about that. When you found out that you were going to prison, knowing who you were and what you were going in for, did you have any concerns? What was going through your mind right before you went in?

My kids. I'd miss the shit out of my kids.

R: Were you worried that there would be a large minority population that you would have to deal with?

Oh yeah, I knew there would be. It's like they took smoking out of the prisons, which even some of the guards wish they wouldn't have because it cause so much grief. Quitting smoking didn't bother me or nothin'. I just missed my kids.

You have to remember that in prison it's very primal. Everyone sticks to their own. The blacks want to have as much to do with me as I want to have to do with them. Blacks look at whites as either a Klan member or a punk.

R: But prisons have big minority populations and you're all tatted up.

They did a good job of segregating us. SeaTac is a fucked-up prison, anyway. No, in fact I got most of my shit from white guys.

R: Did you have any problem with minority inmates?

Not really. I mean, there was a couple of times. I mean, shit happens. Shit gets kicked off. They put me in a medium/low (security) unit. I don't know why they didn't just shove me off to Sheridan (the Oregon federal prison). The DA did not want me in my own backyard.

R: Did you meet any other racialists in prison?

There was one full-fledged skinhead, but me and him didn't like each other. He was a tweaker. That was one thing I got a lot of grief from a couple of the white guys in there, the Peckerwoods (prison skinheads) were like, "This is prison." And I'm like, "I'm only doing a fucking year." They wanted me to act like it was prison and I'm only there for a year; I'm not going to institutionalize myself. I don't want to have to reprogram myself. It was hard enough when I got out. It was weird.

But towards the end . . . Once you're sentenced you are not supposed to be housed with pretrial people. That's like a big no-no. And towards my last three months they threw me in a pretrial unit. I got thrown in a max unit. That was actually kinda cool in one way because yes there was a lot of crazy people in there but they didn't want to fuck up too much because they haven't been sentenced.

But it sucks because they took out all the paperwork (that identifies an inmate's offense), the feds. Because there were too many rapists and child molesters, and snitches. I have to do my time and I gotta pay the consequences for what I did. I think they should too. I still think snitches should have to do day-for-day. All that is is telling the kids that you can go out, have all the fun in the world, but if you tell on someone, there's no consequences.

R: Did your experience in prison reinforce your ideology, or did it undermine it like the *American History X* story?

Well, it reinforces it in one way. All the stereotypes about blacks and Mexicans are in there. It's not a stereotype; it's a fact. And Jewish child molesters. You hear about the Zionist Occupational Government. This guy was got copped out, this child pornographer, because he heard that I was going to beat him up. Which is weird because he had like 200 pictures of kids and he got less time than I did, but he probably sold someone else out.

R: So they kicked him out?

They kicked *me* out. I got put in lockdown. I got pictures of my kids in the bathtub in my photo album in prison. I'm like, "I don't want that guy here."

The warden was trying to be multicultural. He celed up the Norteños with the Suereños. That was fucking stupid.

R: What's the hardest thing about being on parole?

Not drinking. Remembering to do my monthly reports. I am so horrible with that.

That's the problem with hate crime enhancements, or any enhancements. It doesn't matter how much time you have to do. If you ain't gonna learn a lesson, you ain't gonna learn a lesson. If you do too much time, you get institutionalized and you don't even care and if you don't do enough time, you're like "Oh, I fucked the system." There has to be a certain balance.

So I did enough time, but yeah, I had a fuckin' blast in there. I mean I made the most of it. But by the same token, originally they wanted me to do 40 to 50 months. I would have been no good to no one after that, you know? I don't agree with weed at all but you've got people that get busted for a petty amount of weed and get like five years. And by the time they get out, they've already got a record, they need money, and they've learned how to make every kind of meth out there.

R: Well, you know that you and I are pretty much on the same page with how screwed up the sentencing guidelines are. Let me ask you these last questions. What do you think the future of the racialist movement is in this country? Or here.

The thing is, the more tools they have to recruit people . . . You can recruit 300 people, in a year there will be 200 people and 10 years you are going to have the hard-core few. By that time they either, A, in prison, they're lifers, or B, they've calmed the fuck down. They're raising a family. So it's going to be fifty-fifty.

There was one cat in California who was handing out literature on the sidewalk. He wasn't being rude or yelling, "White power!" And there was a Jewish shop owner near him who felt that his civil rights were being violated. Now here's this kid who was trying to take a nonviolent approach that's going to do five years in San Quentin. What do you think he's gonna be like when he gets out?

There was another guy in Pennsylvania who said his rights were violated because he saw a guy with a swastika tattoo. Now that guy's in prison.

R: Really? That seems a little weird.

So if you try to snuff out racism, or racialism, or white pride, all you're going to do is piss off a bunch of kids who don't know any better, don't want to study anything, don't want to better their race, just pissed off and they're going to start stabbing people and killing people. And a couple years later, they're gonna be like, "Wow, I went about it in the wrong way. I've still got another 40 years left on my sentence." So you are going to have some that are going to take the violence route and some that don't.

R: So you think the way that it's going it's going to push people to the extremes? The reason I ask is because you talk about how the movement is more family-oriented now. It's older. It's not a bunch of 18-year-olds. It's people, like you, with families. But it also sounds like that you think, because of the clampdown, there's going to be more people pushed to the extremes.

A lot of the older guys who have been through it know where it gets you. But in the same token, with all these laws, I don't really want to be around anyone new. They go off and do something stupid, I could get another conspiracy charge. I'm seen walking down the street with them, and we walk past a bunch of black people or SHARPs and someone yells, "Fuck you!" and my buddy gets beat and I jump in and the next thing, I'm back in prison forever.

So a lot of older guys like me don't want to go through it. There's a new wave of motherfuckers coming in. [A local skinhead group] gets like 20 e-mails a week from kids and they're like, "I don't need this shit." If they seem decent, they get a [group] patch. Six months later they stab a guy and [the group leader] is in jail.

So a lot of these guys are promoting things like education, good jobs, let's buy land, let's get together. They really don't want anything to do with the youngsters.

R: Do you think your life is better because you are a racialist, or do you think your life would be different if you had taken a different path?

I don't know. I'm still young. But I feel good about myself. I have no regrets.

R: Did you ever reflect on that while you were in prison?

Being a racialist has helped me in certain aspects. I like to have fun. I really do. Being a racialist teaches you not to sell yourself short. Take responsibility for yourself, have a clear mind, such as not take drugs. Personally, I like to live life to the fullest.

R: Yeah, but certainly there are racialists who take drugs.

I think it's benefited my life in a couple of ways. I want to live my life as an example. I've done a lot of maturing because of it. But it's hard to say because I didn't go the other way. I don't think it's affected me too negatively. I'm still big on respect. Even when I was a fresh-cut, totally ready to have a good time and fuckin' bleed on the streets and have people bleed, when a black person said "Hi" and I'd say "Hi" back. I'd say "excuse me" if I bumped into someone no matter what. That was one of the big things. If we are supposed to be better we should lead by example. I was raised by my parents to be respectable, and that means respectful to everyone. That was an example I thought I should set. It's kind of a hard question.

R: OK, here's the last question. You've got these two great boys here. Really cute and energetic. Do you think their lives will be better if they follow the same path that you have?

Well, that's their decision. I hope they keep the same morals as me.

R: But do you think that (being racist) might limit their options? We live in a diverse world that's getting more diverse. Do you think that might create problems for them? Not just saying, "White power," but having that way of looking at the world. I know, these are heavy questions!

I think being white will hinder them with all the programs for minorities.

I'm real big on respect and I'm teaching them that. They're not going to be raised on the 14 Words, by example they will be, but I'm not going to introduce them to anything, like, "Hey, read *this* book." I want them to read unbiased materials, too, so they can know the other side. I want them to make their own minds up. I don't know.

R: Do you think it has an impact on them, having a swastika flag on the wall in their living room? Do you think that when they go to school and learn about Hitler they'll have a different view than the other kids?

No, when they get a little bit older I won't have it up, you know. I'm sure when they learn about it they'll be like, "Hey, my daddy's got that tattoo." Not that you're going to like this but one of the pictures in *The Racist Mind* (a book I sent him while he was in prison), I got it blown up and a guy tattooed it on my back. (He shows me the swastika tattoo.)

R: Hey, I'm glad I could help out (said ironically). I've assigned that book to my students many times, but you are the first person that took it that way.

Kind of original, huh? (laughs) Yeah, I'm not planning on forcing it on them. I take them to the skinhead get-togethers, but there's not really any Nazi paraphernalia. You hardly ever see boots and braces and flight jackets anymore. Most of the guys nowadays wear Slayer T-shirts and Converse. It's probably it's a BBQ, that's it. If you came to one, you might not even notice the difference.

R: Well, my BBQ might be a little more diverse.

We have diverse gathering at our skinhead events. All kinds of people!

One of the things that pissed me off was a comment that I read in *The Oregonian*. At Oregon State University a black woman was saying how sad she was that there were whites who actually wanted a white student union. She was sad that people could be so racist and ignorant as to want a white student union. But they have a black student union. You've got a 16-year-old that's going to read that and get pissed off. They're going to go to one little (racist) Web site and be like "Fuck this! Fuck that!" and go out and try to make a difference. And they're gonna go to prison and learn all of the hate aspects and none of the love aspects.

So I understand where you guys are trying to come from with the diversity and stopping the blind hate. But a lot of the local people who get attacked, not physically, verbally are the people who are trying to keep shit together at the seams.

R: In their own lives?

In the movement. The documentaries and the media just portray the hate as this mongrel thing. They show swastikas and think there are human sacrifices and shit.

R: Well, for a lot of people that swastika represents what we went to war against, to defend democracy. Do you see yourself as part of something that is antidemocratic?

Well, if you look at the movement nowadays, it's not really Hitler-oriented. I mean Hitler, I understand where he was coming from. After World War I he was pissed and the government told the Jews to get out. And I'm gonna leave it at that because that's a whole 'nother conversation. It's like Abraham Lincoln. He wasn't racist. He didn't believe in slavery. But after it was over he said, "Hey, I'm shipping you all back. Sending you back to your homeland." That's it. To be with your own.

A few weeks after our conversation, Sean had been dwelling on the issues we talked about and left the following message on my cell phone.

Yeah, I'm sitting here drinking a beer thinking about our conversation and how I got involved in this shit. Well, what I told you was true, and wow, it kind of dawned on me that it goes a little deeper than that. And

I never really realized it, but when I was a younger teenager I had a couple of friends who were full geeks and they got picked on all the time. And predominately since I grew up in a black neighborhood, um, maybe it's a good thing or a bad thing, but I didn't like seeing people get picked on. I was like, if you were a bully I wanted to kick your ass. If you were no one or weren't popular then I was your friend, you know?

Anyway, we get to fight for the people or the average white person getting shafted because of Affirmative Action, which I know you don't believe it. But growing up, you get fuckin' picked on. A heterosexual white person gets hell growing up. So I got sick of being a white boy and seeing all these other people get beat up and picked on. And the black people, black people are the cool thing nowadays or gay is cool or Jewish people. And Mexicans, they're flying in like fucking rats. So I guess it sort of dawned on me. I saw oppression and wanted to fight it.

SUMMARY

Sean's story reinforces a number of themes common among hate criminals as well as members of the larger white-supremacist counterculture. The most obvious is the utility of misinformation and contradictions. Sean's views on subjects like Affirmative Action, the scarcity of white people, and even Roman history are not rooted in any factual reality, only a perception that reinforces a racist belief system. The contradictions of views about minority crime compared to white crime are also typical. Minority criminality is viewed as evidence of their savagery, while white criminality is a form of self-defense (and any other white criminality is ignored or blamed on alcohol consumption).

There are some other themes present in this conversation. Sean's crime reflects the banality of anti-Semitism, discussed by Paul Iganski in chapter 8 of this volume. While Sean would certainly qualify as a "hate monger" (the Nazi flag in his living room has since been replaced by an Aryan Nations flag), the desecration of the Shaarie Torah Cemetery was not an act of planned terrorism against the Jewish community. Like most hate crimes, it was a crime of opportunity. The act was committed by a group of drunken young males who saw an opportunity to act on their anti-Semitic beliefs. As pointed out in chapter 7 of this volume by Fisher and Salfati, these crimes do not easily fit within simple typologies. In 2003, according to the FBI, 12 percent of the 7,489 reported hate crimes were anti-Jewish, and 35 percent of reported hate crimes were vandalism or property destruction (FBI, 2004). Sean's crime was one of those.

Sean's comments also illustrate a theme of "ethnic envy" (Blazak, 2008). His comments about "black student unions" and "European culture" reflect a desire by young whites to have the same opportunities to express ethnicity that minorities have. This desire, of course, is absent knowledge about the history of oppression that necessitated black student unions in the first place. Sean's comment that "a heterosexual white person gets hell growing up" seems laughable compared to the incredible obstacles that nonheterosexual, nonwhite persons face every day. However, without a clear understanding of heternormativity and white privilege, it is an honest expression felt by many majority group members.

Perhaps most instructively, Sean's story offers a glimpse into the question, "What happens when racist skinheads grow up?" Clearly, the ideology does not resonate as strongly with him as it did in his youth. He struggled to clarify his beliefs, regularly saying, "It's hard to explain." His prison term behind him, he is focused on his family and staying out of trouble. The world of white supremacy provides a second family, although he knows there are those who would turn against him or lead him back into prison. His tattoos will stigmatize him (including the one he got in prison modeled on an image from a book I sent him to help him leave racism). Without the economic opportunities to lift him out of the role of "house husband," the appeal of the macho world of skinheads will persist.

REFERENCES

Blazak, R. (2008). Ethnic envy: How teens construct whiteness in globalized America. In D. C. Brotherton & M. Flynn (Eds.), *Globalizing the streets* (pp. 169–184) New York: Columbia University Press.

Department of Justice. (2005). Oregon man pleads guilty to desecrating Jewish cemetery [press release]. Washington, DC: Department of Justice, January 13, 2005. Retrieved August 8, 2007, from http://www.usdoj.gov/opa/pr/2005/January/05_crt_015.htm

Federal Bureau of Investigation. (2004, November). *Hate crime statistics, 2003*. Washington, DC: Author.

ABOUT THE EDITOR
AND CONTRIBUTORS

Randy Blazak is an associate professor of sociology at Portland State University, where he is the director of the Hate Crime Research Network (www.hatecrime.net). He earned his Ph.D. from Emory University in 1995 after completing a long-term ethnographic study of racist skinheads. His research has been published in journals and books, including chapters in *Home Grown Hate: Gender and Organized Racism* (2004) and *Hate and Bias Crimes: A Reader* (2003). He is the chair of the Coalition Against Hate Crimes in Oregon and is writing a textbook on juvenile delinquency. He is currently researching the development of a program for paroled hate group members and the role of Serbian nationalism in the skinhead movement.

Kathleen M. Blee is a Distinguished Professor of Sociology at the University of Pittsburgh. She has written extensively about organized racism and hate crimes in the U.S., including *Women of the Klan: Racism and Gender in the 1920s* (1991) and *Inside Organized Racism: Women in the Hate Movement* (2002).

Tammy L. Castle is an assistant professor at James Madison University. She has conducted research projects and published in the areas of serial murder, sexual behavior in prisons, sex advertising online, media and crime, and the work environment of correctional officers. Her research has been published in the *American Journal of Criminal Justice, The Prison Journal, International Journal of Offender Therapy and Comparative Criminology*, and the *International Journal of Cultural Studies*. Her current research interests center on female involvement in hate crimes and hate groups, and she recently completed an examination of female-targeted propaganda on the Web sites of various hate groups.

Steven M. Chermak is associate professor of the School of Criminal Justice at Michigan State University. His research interests include examining media coverage of crime, terrorism, and right-wing extremism, and evaluating strategic approaches to violence reduction. He is a lead investigator for the National Consortium for the Study of Terrorism and Responses to Terrorism (START), a Center of Excellence of the U.S. Department of Homeland Security, on a project that examines far-right involvement in criminal incidents. Professor Chermak is the author of *Victims in the News: Crime and the American News Media* (Westview Press, 1995), in which he examines how the news production process affects the ways in which crime, victims, and criminal justice are presented to the public. His second book, *Searching for a Demon: The Media Construction of the Militia Movement* (Northeastern University Press, 2002), explores media coverage of the militia movement following the Oklahoma City bombing. He has recently published articles in *Justice Quarterly, Journal of Criminal Justice,* and *Criminal Justice and Behavior.*

Abby L. Ferber is a professor of sociology, director of women's studies, and director of the Matrix Center for the Advancement of Social Equity and Inclusion at the University of Colorado at Colorado Springs. She is the author of *White Man Falling: Race, Gender and White Supremacy* (1998); coauthor of the American Sociological Associations' *Hate Crime in America: What Do We Know?* (2000) and *Making a Difference: University Students of Color Speak Out* (2002); coeditor, with Michael Kimmel, of *Privilege: A Reader* (2003); and editor of *Home-Grown Hate: Gender and Organized Racism* (2004). She has co-edited two new volumes, *The New Basics: Sex, Gender and Sexuality* (2008) and *The Matrix Reader: Examining the Dynamics of Privilege and Oppression* (2008), both designed for classroom use.

Christopher Fisher is an adjunct professor at John Jay College of Criminal Justice and the assistant commissioner for strategic planning at the New York City Department of Juvenile Justice (DJJ). His research has focused on hate crime, homicide, offender profiling, forensic psychology, and policy evaluation. The current research was conducted in an academic capacity, and the author's opinions, statements, and conclusions should not be considered an endorsement by the DJJ for any policy, program, or service.

Joshua D. Freilich is the deputy executive officer of the criminal justice Ph.D. program and an associate professor in the Sociology Department at

John Jay College, the City University of New York. Dr. Freilich's research interests include far-right extremism, domestic terrorism, and criminological theory. He is a lead investigator for the National Consortium for the Study of Terrorism and Responses to Terrorism (START), a Center of Excellence of the U.S. Department of Homeland Security (DHS). He is currently the principal investigator on a project with Dr. Steven Chermak (Michigan State University) to create the first-of-its-kind national database on the perpetrators, victims, event, and group characteristics of all known crimes committed by supporters of the domestic far right since 1990. Incidents are identified and data are collected from open sources. This research has been funded by both DHS and START. Dr. Freilich's research has been published in *Justice Quarterly, Law and Human Behavior, Criminal Justice and Behavior, Journal of Criminal Justice, Behavioral Sciences and the Law,* and the *Journal of Contemporary Criminal Justice.*

Colin K. Gilmore is a doctoral student at Vanderbilt University in Nashville. He completed a master's thesis in 2007 at Portland State University that focused on the role of music in the contemporary white-supremacist movement. This volume contains his first publication, which is based on his research in this area. Since completing his thesis, he has spent time working in a residential treatment facility for emotionally and behaviorally disturbed adolescents.

Jeffrey Gruenewald is a Ph.D. student at the School of Criminal Justice, Michigan State University, and predoctoral fellow for the National Consortium for the Study of Terrorism and Responses to Terrorism (START). His research interests include bias crimes, domestic terrorism, homicide, restorative justice, and the relationship between race, crime, and media. He has coauthored articles appearing in peer-reviewed journals such as *Justice Quarterly, Policing,* and *Journal of Criminal Justice and Popular Culture,* and has authored and coauthored book chapters related to the topic of domestic terrorism. His current research focus is on studying the nature of far-right-wing extremist homicide incidents and participants, and how they compare to other bias-motivated and nonideological homicides.

Paul Iganski is a lecturer in criminology in the Department of Applied Social Science at Lancaster University, England, and formerly Civil Society Fellow at the Institute for Jewish Policy Research, London. He is editor of *The Hate Debate* (2002); coeditor, with Barry Kosmin, of *A New Antisemitism? Debating Judeophobia in 21st Century Britain* (2003); and coauthor, with Vicky Kielinger and Susan Paterson, of *Hate Crimes Against London's Jews* (2005). His most recent book is *Hate Crime and the City* (2008). He served as an expert witness providing written and oral evidence to the 2005–2006 UK All-Party Parliamentary Inquiry Into Antisemitism.

Michael Kimmel is professor of sociology at SUNY Stony Brook and editor of the journal *Men and Masculinities*. He is the author or editor of more than 20 books about men and masculinity, including *Manhood in America: A Cultural History* (1996), *The History of Men* (2005), and "'White Men Are This Nation': Right-Wing Militias and the Restoration of Rural American Masculinity" with Abby Ferber in *Home-Grown Hate: Gender and Organized Racism* (2003). Kimmel is a spokesperson of The National Organization For Men Against Sexism (NOMAS).

Barbara Perry is professor of criminology, justice and policy studies at the University of Ontario Institute of Technology. She has written extensively in the area of hate crime, including two books on the topic: *In the Name of Hate: Understanding Hate Crime* and *Hate and Bias Crime: A Reader*. She has just completed a book manuscript for the University of Arizona Press entitled *The Silent Victims: Native American Victims of Hate Crime*, based on interviews with Native Americans, and one on policing Native American communities for Lexington Press. Dr. Perry continues to work in the area of hate crime and has begun to make contributions to the limited scholarship on hate crime in Canada. Here, she is particularly interested in anti-Muslim violence and hate crime against Aboriginal people.

C. Gabrielle Salfati is an associate professor at John Jay College of Criminal Justice. Her main areas of expertise are homicide and sexual offenses, in particular with reference to offender profiling, classifications of violent crime, linking serial crime, and cross-cultural comparisons. She is currently working on a number of interrelated projects dealing with various facets of violent crime and deviance. In particular, this work is now being developed within an international framework through collaboration with major research centers and law enforcement agencies internationally.

Pete Simi is an assistant professor in the School of Criminology & Criminal Justice at the University of Nebraska, Omaha. His research interests include extremist groups, street gangs, violence, and juvenile delinquency. He has published a series of articles that examine racial extremist groups in the United States and has a book manuscript, *American Swastika: the Hidden Spaces of Racial Extremists* (2008).

INDEX

Affirmative Action, 47, 75, 180, 204

African Americans: vs. Christian Identity, 42; in gangs, 17; vs. KKK, 41; lynching of, 63, 103, 164; nationalist groups of, 16, 37; vs. white-power lyrics, 63; vs. white supremacists, 46, 79, 160. *See also* Arklof, Jackie

Allen, Kenneth "German," 164

Anger issues: vs. activism, 73; in anti-Muslim violence, 174; with skinheads, 154, 163; in white-power music, 57, 58

Anti-Defamation League (ADL), 25, 51, 87, 167, 168

Anti-Discrimination Committee (ADC), 172–73

Anti-Muslim violence: Arab hate crimes, 105, 139; degree of, 172–74; motives for, 174–80; permission to hate, 180–85

Anti-Semitism: banalization of, 148; by Christian Identity, 27, 42, 46; contemporary, 137–38; as "every day" crime, 144–48; extremism as, 138–41; police data on, 141–44; by racist groups, 44, 45–47, 152; by skinheads, 189, 193; spatial hate, 45–47

Antiracist skinheads. *See* Skinheads Against Racial Prejudice

Arab hate crimes, 105, 139

Arab–Israeli wars, 143, 173, 177

Arklof, Jackie: alienation of, 152–54; EXIT organization, 155–56; Swedish Nazism, 154–55

Arson crimes, 26, 89, 93, 99, 172, 174

Aryan Brotherhood, 24–25, 28–29, 162

Aryan Nations: anti-Semitism by, 45–47; Christian Identity, 195–96; crimes by supporters, 14; and Hispanic gangs, 17; as study group, 9

Aryan Prisoners of War (POWs), 26, 31, 32, 37

Ásatrú. *See* Odinism

Assault crimes. *See* Harassment/assault

Bias-motivated homicide, 10, 105, 115, 121–27

Blazak, Randy, 23–40, 77, 189–205

Blee, Kathleen M., 41–50

British National Party (BNP), 143, 159

Bureau of Justice Statistics (BJS), 86

Byrd, James (murders), 2, 29

CAIR. *See* Council on American-Islamic Relations
Castle, Tammy L., 85–101
Chermak, Steven M., 1–21
Chretien, Jean, 181
Christian Identity: vs. African Americans, 42; anti-Semitism, 27, 42, 46; Aryan Nations, 195–96; Odinists, 34, 196; The Order, 26–27, 29
Christianity, 30, 34–35, 37, 195
Civil rights issues: Affirmative Action, 47, 75, 180, 204; Anti-Defamation League, 25, 51, 87, 167, 168; anti-Muslim, 179–80; attacks against white males, 75; CAIR complaints, 172, 179, 183; Odinism, 23–26; in recording industry, 53; USA Patriot Act, 184. *See also* Southern Poverty Law Center
Community Security Trust (CST), 140, 141
Compton, Samuel (murder), 157, 166
Constructionist theory, 5, 72
Cooper v. Pate, 24
Council on American-Islamic Relations (CAIR), 172, 179, 183
Council on American-Islamic Relations–Canada (CAIR-CAN), 184
Crazy Fuckin Skins/Confederate Front Skins (CFS), 165
Crime-scene characteristics, 108–9, 112–13, 119–20
Crime studies, 10
Cross burnings: by KKK, 14, 26–27, 89; statistics, 93, 98; by white supremacists, 16
Cruz v. Beto, 24
Cultural context, gender crimes, 73–75
Cutter v. Wilkinson, 24

Data collection: on anti-Semitism, 141–44; hate crime trends, 105–6; limitations of, 130–32; on offenders, 103–6, 121–27; research questions, 9, 12, 31–37; skinhead violence trends, 167; Smallest Space Analysis, 109, 113–14, 121, 122–23, 129–30; terrorism, 15. *See also* Federal Bureau of Investigation
Defensive-type hate crime, 111, 118, 126–27, 128–29

Degenerative violence, 161
Discrimination: against Anti-Discrimination Committee, 172–73; in bias-motivated crimes, 70; Southern Poverty Law Center aid, 87; stereotypes, 74, 79, 174–76, 186, 200; by U.S. government, 185; by white supremacists, 78–79; against whites, 76. *See also* Anti-Muslim violence; Anti-Semitism; Racism/racial violence
Duke, David, 78

Eastside White Pride (EWP), 165
"Ethnic envy," 204
European Kindred, 26, 38
European Monitoring Centre on Racism and Xenophobia (EUMC), 138–40
EXIT organization, 155–56

Far-right extremism: definition, 2–5; existing literature on, 5–13; vs. hate crimes, 13–17; publication outlets, 8; vs. religious racism, 28–29
Federal Bureau of Investigation (FBI): Hate Crimes Statistics Act, 70, 85–86, 103–4, 122; National Incidence Based Reporting System, 86, 87, 88, 92; terrorist investigations, 172; underreporting to, 69; Uniform Crime Reporting, 85–86, 88, 92, 103, 122
Feminism, 30, 70, 76–79, 154
Ferber, Abby L., 69–83
Ferri, Enrico, 106–7
Fisher, Christopher, 103–35
Franklin, Karen, 77, 78
Freilich, Joshua D., 1–21

Gang violence: far-right extremism, 9; Odinists, 38; The Order, 27, 29; in prisons, 17, 24, 162; by racists, 25–29; rape, 74; in schools, 58; by skinheads, 14, 33, 158, 159–63, 166–67
Gardell, Mattis, 27
Gender crimes: cultural context, 73–75; and hate crimes, 69–71; masculine privilege, 77–80; perpetrator privilege, 71–73; political/social context, 75–77. *See also* Women's issues

Gilmore, Colin K., 51–68
Global Aryanism, 47
Global racism, 42–45
Gods of the Blood: The Pagan Revival and White Separatism (Gardell), 27
Gruenewald, Jeffrey, 1–21

Hammerskin Nation (HSN), 42, 162
Harassment/assault: anti-Semitic, 144–46; by police, 184; in schools, 103, 173; sexual, 74; statistics, 90, 93, 95–100; verbal, 165. *See also* Victims/ victimization
Hate crime statistics, 69, 85–87, 88–92
Hate Crimes Research Network (HCRN), 31
Hate Crimes Statistics Act (HCSA), 70, 85–86, 103–4, 122
Heterosexuality, 66
Hispanic gangs, 17
Homicide crimes: bias-motivated, 10, 105, 115, 121–27; defensive-type, 111, 118, 126–27, 128–29; empirical model of, 113–18; retaliation-related hate crime, 118, 125–26, 127–30; statistics on, 6, 94, 97–98; studies on, 107–9; by terrorists, 3; thrill-type, 111, 115–17, 123–25, 127, 129–30

Iganski, Paul, 137–50
Intelligence crimes, 94
Intelligence Project (SPLC), 88–89
Internet racism: EUMC, 139; Odinism, 25, 26; online groups, 42–44, 191; white supremacists, 71
Intimidation crimes, 94, 95
Islam, 35–36, 37
Islamic terrorism, 6
Islamophobia, 179
Israeli-Palestinian conflict, 143, 147, 148

Jenness, Valerie, 69–70, 74
Jews. *See* Anti-Semitism
John Birch Society, 16

Kemp, Richard, 27, 38
Kimmel, Michael, 151–56
Ku Klux Klan (KKK): cross burnings, 14, 26–27, 89; and prison gangs, 162;
as racist group, 9, 41–42, 48; and skinheads, 160; white-power music of, 53

Lane, David, 27, 38, 194
Leafleting crimes, 94, 97
Literature, far-right extremists, 5–13
Local racism, 42–45
Lombroso, Cesare, 106–7
Lynchings, 63, 103, 164

Masculine privilege, gender crimes, 77–80
Mathews, Robert, 64
Matthew Shepard Act, 70
McDevitt, Levin, and Bennett offender typology, 110–14, 129–30, 132
McVeigh, Timothy, 2, 3, 29, 80
Media issues: accuracy, 11, 56, 58; anti-Muslim imagery, 176; multiculturalism, 62; terrorism, 4
Messerschmidt, James, 29–30, 80
Metropolitan Police Service (MPS), 141, 143–44, 147
Million Man March (men's movement), 76
Mission-motivated hate crime, 117, 126, 128–29, 160
Multiculturalism, 57, 58, 62
Multidimensional Scaling Analysis (MSA), 109
Multiple-authored far-right publications, 7
Muslims, 105, 138–41, 142, 148. *See also* Anti-Muslim violence

Nation of Islam (NOI), 37
National Alliance, 42, 54
National Consortium for the Studies of Terrorism and Responses to Terrorism (START), 15
National Crime Victimization Survey (NCVS), 86, 88
National Focal Points (NFP), 139–40
National Incident Based Reporting System (NIBRS), 86, 87, 88, 92
National Socialist Movement, 42
Native Americans, 96, 163
Nazi Lowriders (NLR), 162
Nazi party (Nazism), 154–55, 159

Neo-Nazi skinheads: Arkoff as, 151; new
    recruits, 41–42, 51; as terrorists, 1;
    white-power music by, 52–54. *See also*
    Skinhead violence
NIBRS. *See* National Incident Based
    Reporting System
Nonsystematic interviews with far-right
    extremists, 11–12

Odinism: vs. Christian Identity, 34,
    196; in prisons, 24–26, 28, 36; racist
    groups, 26–28; as racist religion,
    23–26; research on, 31–37; and
    right-wing hate groups, 28–29;
    theoretical perspective, 29–31; views on,
    33–34
Offenders: data and trends on, 103–6,
    121–27; far-right vs. hate crime,
    10, 13–17; of homicide crimes,
    113–18; interview with, 189–204;
    male vs. female, 87–88, 92, 97–100;
    methodology, 118–21; privileges,
    71–73; typology/profiling, 106–13,
    127–29, 132; vs. victim interactions,
    73, 146–47. *See also* Victims/
    victimization
Oklahoma City bombing, 2, 28, 80
The Order (racist gang), 27, 29
Organization for Security and
    Cooperation in Europe (OSCE),
    137, 140
"Others" distinction, 175

Pacific Northwest racism, 43
Pakistani immigrants, 159
Pan-Aryanism, 44, 45
Perpetrators. *See* Offenders
Perry, Barbara, 171–88
Police data on anti-Semitism, 141–44
Political context, gender crimes, 75–77
Prison gangs, 17, 24, 162
Prison Odinism, 24–26, 28, 36
Profiling offenders, 106–13, 127–29,
    132
Promise Keepers (men's movement), 76
Public Enemy Number One (PEN1), 162,
    167
Publication outlets, far-right
    extremism, 8

Racial Holy War (RAHOWA), 28, 30, 192
Racism and Xenophobia Network
    (RAXEN), 138–39
Racism/racial violence: anti-Semitism,
    44, 45–47, 152; education of, 197;
    gangs, 25–29; by KKK, 9, 41–42, 48;
    local vs. global, 42–45; lynchings,
    63, 103, 164; male vs. female,
    91–92; against Native Americans,
    96, 163; Odinism, 23–28; religious,
    31–37; vs. SHARPs, 190, 201; social
    homogeneity, 47–48; stereotypes, 74,
    79, 174–76, 186, 200; in white-power
    lyrics, 63. *See also* African Americans;
    Discrimination; Internet racism
Racist Skinhead Project (ADL), 167
Rahowa (white-power band), 63
Rape crimes, 74
Religious issues: Arab hate crimes, 105,
    139; Christianity, 30, 34–35, 37, 195;
    Muslims, 105, 138–41, 142, 148;
    Racial Holy War, 28, 30, 192; racism
    as, 31–37. *See also* Anti-Muslim
    violence; Anti-Semitism; Odinism
Religious Land Use and Institutionalized
    Person Act (RLUIPA), 24
Reporting/nonreporting: by Anti-
    Defamation League, 25; of assault
    victims, 78; by National Incidence
    Based Reporting System, 86, 87,
    88, 92; by police agencies, 15, 26;
    underreporting, 69; by Uniform Crime
    Reporting, 85–86, 88, 92, 103, 122.
    See also Data collection; Federal
    Bureau of Investigation
Research questions, 9, 12, 31–37
Resistance Magazine (white-supremacist
    journal), 59
Retaliation-related hate crime, 118,
    125–26, 127–30

Salfati, C. Gabrielle, 103–35
School gangs, 58
September 11, 2001, 6, 28, 105, 172, 182
Sexual assault, 74
SHARPs. *See* Skinheads Against Racial
    Prejudice
Shepard, Matthew (murders), 2, 70
Simi, Pete, 157–70

Single-authored far-right publications, 7

Skinhead violence: characteristics, 160–61, 162–65; gangs, 14, 33, 158, 159–63, 166–67; against Jews, 193; management/territory, 165–66; methodology, 158–59; organizational factors, 161–62; vs. SHARPs, 190; trends, 167; in U.K., 159; in U.S., 159–60. *See also* Neo-Nazi skinheads

Skinheads Against Racial Prejudice (SHARPs), 190, 201

Skrewdriver (white-power band), 53–54, 56, 60, 61, 63, 64

Smallest Space Analysis (SSA), 109, 113–14, 121, 122–23, 129–30

Social context, gender crimes, 75–77

Social homogeneity, 47–48

Southern Poverty Law Center (SPLC): female offenders, 87; hate crime statistics, 69; Intelligence Project, 88–89; Odinism statistics, 25; white-power music monitoring, 51

SSA. *See* Smallest Space Analysis

Stereotypes, 74, 79, 174–76, 186, 200

Swedish Nazism, 154–55

Targeted violence, 63, 65, 76

Tax-refusal movement, 16

Terrorism: assumption of, 178–79; defining, 3–4; "fanatical," 186; September 11, 2001, 6, 28, 105, 172, 182; by skinheads, 1; statistics on, 15

Thrill-related hate crimes, 111, 115–17, 123–25, 127, 129–30

Typology of offenders, 106–13, 127–29, 132

Uniform Crime Reporting (UCR), 85–86, 88, 92, 103, 122

United Kingdom (U.K.) skinheads, 159

United Nations (UN), 138

United States v. Trainer, 24

USA Patriot Act, 183, 184

Vandalism crimes, 91, 94–98

Verbal harassment, 165

Victims/victimization: assault reports, 78; of heterosexuals, 66; masculine privilege, 77–80; vs. offender interactions, 73, 146–47; religious, 24, 33. *See also* Gender crimes; Harassment/assault; Homicide crimes

Violence: arson crimes, 26, 89, 93, 99, 172, 174; degenerative, 161; leafleting crimes, 94, 97; targeted, 63, 65, 76; vandalism crimes, 91, 94–98; in white-power music, 62–65; by white supremacists, 80; against women, 74. *See also* Anti-Muslim violence; Homicide crimes; Skinhead violence

Violence Against Women Act, 70

Vogt, Kimberly A., 76–77

White Aryan Resistance (WAR), 14, 160, 166

White-power music: concerts, 55–56; history, 53–55; lyrics, 59–62; recruitment tactics in, 58–59; view of, 55–58; violence in, 62–65

White supremacy movement: cross burnings, 16; online presence, 71; violence by, 80; women's roles, 78–79. *See also* Odinism; White-power music

Women's issues: feminism, 30, 70, 76–79, 154; hate crime statistics, 85–87, 88–92; violence against, 74; violence by, 87–88, 94–97; white-power lyrics, 64–65; white supremacist roles, 78–79

World Church of the Creator, 14

Xenophobia, 44–45

Zionist Occupation Government (ZOG), 45, 62